SLAPSTICK!

TONY STAVEACRE

SLAPSTICK!
THE ILLUSTRATED STORY
OF KNOCKABOUT COMEDY

ANGUS
& ROBERTSON
PUBLISHERS

FOR GAIL
WHO LIKES A GOOD LAUGH

ANGUS & ROBERTSON PUBLISHERS

Unit 4, Eden Park, 31 Waterloo Road,
North Ryde, NSW, Australia 2113, and
16 Golden Square, London W1R 4BN,
United Kingdom

First published in Australia
by Angus & Robertson Publishers in 1987
First published in the United Kingdom
by Angus & Robertson UK in 1987

Copyright © Tony Staveacre 1987

ISBN 0 207 15493 7

Typeset by Graphicraft Typesetters, Ltd.
Hong Kong
Printed in Singapore

CONTENTS

ACKNOWLEDGEMENTS

THE MAGPIE author would like to express his gratitude to all those who have contributed to his protracted researches. Sadly, some are now playing the Glasgow Empire.

For ideas, interviews, inside stories, and other incidentals: thanks, Jack Melville, Tim Brooke-Taylor, Jimmy Jewel, Roy Hudd, Sandy Powell, Graeme Garden, Spike Milligan, Max Wall, Charlie Drake, Arthur Askey, Jerry Lewis, George Carl, John Cleese, Bill Oddie, Billy Russell, Victor Spinetti, Billy Dainty, Popov, Gert Frobe, Eric Sykes, Les Dawson, Ethel Revnell, Kenneth Connor, Arthur Haynes, Tommy Cooper, Fred Emney, Jimmy Nervo, Eddie Davis, Kenneth Williams, Charles Hawtrey, Jacques Tati, Nat Jackley, Chesney Allen, Michael Palin, Terry Jones, Eric Idle, Bourvil, Peter Sellers, Chris Harris, Barry Crane, Kevin Lloyd, Kerry Shales, Pierre Etaix, Dick Emery, Mel Brooks, Ken Campbell, Bob Hoskins, Chris Langham, Dave Hill, Sid Colin, Ken Dodd, Jimmy Edwards, Los Trios Ringbarkus, Norman Wisdom, Barry Took, Ted Ray, Roy Castle, Roy Kinnear, Marty Feldman, Charlie Cairoli, Ellis Ashton, Jonathan Miller, Eleanor Bron, John Bird, Wee Georgie Wood, Boleslav Polivka, Juri Pecha.

For pictures, posters, prints and other souvenirs: thanks, John Jensen, Stephen Moreton Prichard, Geoff Tookey, Jimmy Jewel, Josie Whittaker, Tim Brooke-Taylor, Raymond Mander and Joe Mitchenson, J. D. Bamforth, Linda Polan, George Carl, Michelle Snapes (BFI Stills Collection), David Drummond (The Pleasures of Past Times), Desi Maxim (Thames Television International), *Punch*, Miranda Pollock (BBC Pictorial Publicity), Bob Bright (Radio Times Hulton Picture Library), Nick Soulsby (LWT), Richard Graves (Nostalgiasongs), K. C. Robertson (The Rank Organisation), 20th Century Fox, Paramount, UIP, EMI, RKO, Warner Bros, MGM, Universal, United Artists. I have done my best to contact all the relevant copyright-holders. Apologies to any that I have failed to trace.

Extracts from *My Autobiography* by Charles Chaplin reprinted by permission of The Bodley Head.
Extracts from *Particular Pleasures* by J. B. Priestley reprinted by permission of Rainbird Publishing Group.
Extracts from *The Hastings Flyer* reprinted by permission of Spike Milligan Productions.
Extract from 'Send In the Clowns', words and music by Stephen Sondheim, © Revelation Music Publishing Co., 1973, reproduced by permission of Chappell Music Limited.

PICTURE CREDITS

Many of the photographs and illustrations in *Slapstick!* are from the author's private collection, including some rare souvenirs of the British comic tradition, which were left to him by Jack Melville. The publishers acknowledge with thanks the permission given by the following sources to reproduce photographs and illustrations on the pages listed below.

Art Institute of Chicago 83
Bamforth & Co. Ltd, Holmfirth, Yorkshire 146 (all)
BBC Copyright Photographs 6 (left), 35, 132, 160, 161, 164, 172
BBC Hulton Picture Library 25 (top), 30 (top), 33 (right), 61 (left), 65 (both), 116 (left), 130, 159, 168 (bottom), 175 (bottom), 183
Carl, George 67 (all)
Columbia Pictures 48 (bottom), 168
Dodd, Ken 176 (left)
EMI 46 (left), 168 (top)
Jewel, Jimmy 87 (top right)
London Weekend Television 40, 66 (right)
Mander and Mitcheson Theatre Collection 17, 18 (top), 22, 54–55, 57 (behind), 88, 89, 90, 106, 144 (left), 168 (right), 179
MGM 121 (all) , 128 (all)
Moreton Prichard, Stephen 64, 183 (top right)
National Film Archive 25 (bottom), 27 (top left and right), 28 (top), 29, 33 (right), 50–51, 85, 97, 99 (top), 100, 111 (all), 113
News Limited 108 (both)
Northwestern University Press (from *The Fool and his Scepter* by William Willeford) 13
Paramount Pictures 116 (right)
Rank Organisation 34, 39 (both), 117, 118, 120, 131, 148–149 (all), 162, 176
Spike Milligan Productions 49
Thames Television International 79, 86, 87 (top left), 175 (top), 178 (top)
Tookey, Geoff viii, 3 (all)
Twentieth Century Fox 171, 180 (left)
UIP 33 (left), 46–47, 53, 80–81, 91, 102, 137 (both), 138, 163
United Artists 6 (right), 51 (both), 126 (both), 153, 155, 173
Universal Pictures 114, 165, 167, 169, 182
Whittaker, Josie 73, 76 (left), 94, 95

INTRODUCTION

A PINK-AND-WHITE clapboard building, on an
island in the Thames. Like something out of *White
Horse Inn*, turrets, gables, flagpoles. Now past its
prime, with broken windows, peeling paint,
graffiti. 'That's Karno's place,' I learned from a
small, compact old man who sat most weekends
in a garden on the island, his teak motor cruiser
moored alongside. This was Jimmy Nervo, late of
Nervo and Knox, founder-member of the Crazy
Gang, now enjoying his retirement in the
company of thirty garden gnomes and a yappy
Yorkshire terrier. A full turn of the circle had
brought Jimmy back to Taggs Island, and
'Karno's place', for Nervo kicked off with Karno's
Krazy Komics way back in 'nineteen hundred and
frozen-to-death'. Karno, master showman,
invested the profits from his comedy sketches to
build a Fun Palace on the Thames. He called it the
Karsino. 'But it didn't
do him any good,'
said Jimmy, 'he was
bankrupt in 1926,
and died broke.'

Fred Karno in his heyday. A gentlemanly pose for the ruffian

I wanted to know more. The Chairman of the British Music Hall Society (motto — 'There's Not Many of Us Left') provided me with an address in Worthing and an introduction to a 91-year-old gentleman who was in at the very beginning. Jack Melville was his name, and he told me how, before the First World War, he had played opposite Charlie Chaplin at the Glasgow Empire. 'And as we stood in the wings, waiting to go on, I asked him — "Charlie," I said, "How'm I doing?" "Jack, my boy," he replied, "I'm getting quite jealous of you!" Well, of course, that was only his little joke — he knew how duff I was in comparison to him.'

Chaplin and Melville — the double-act that never made it. Chaplin went to Los Angeles in 1910 and Jack stayed behind. Chaplin made two-reel film comedies and, for the first two years at Keystone and Essanay, reworked for the silent

camera the same Karno routines that he had played with Melville. In his council flat by the sea, the old man sat chuckling in his carpet slippers, as a clattering film projector threw images of *Charlie at the Show*, *The Champion*, *Police*, and *Easy Street* onto the bedroom wall. 'Good old Charlie! — nice to see him so young-looking, eh? So light on his feet, wasn't he? A lovely mover . . . Yeah, I remember these gags . . . they're all Karno routines, I reckon. 'Cos that's where Charlie learned the business, you see, in Karno's sketches.'

The trail led from Worthing, down the coast to Eastbourne, and Sandy Powell, master ventriloquist. He joined the Karno company in 1923 to play the part of Stiffy, the goal-keeper, in Karno's sketch 'The Football Match'.

We played the Alexandra Theatre, Stoke Newington. And I was very unhappy after the

Jack Melville *(centre)* in 1970, with souvenirs of Karno and Chaplin. There's half a century between the two photos of Chaplin

MONDAY, JAN. 18th. 1915, and during the week
FULL MATINEE EVERY MONDAY AT 2-30   Phone—HOP 1460
6.30   TWICE NIGHTLY   9.0
FRED KARNO   Presents his Great Laughing Creation, entitled
THE HYDRO
JACK MEL... "Nick Sharp"
Scene 1 - The Pump Room at the Hydro, Ma... 2 - Interior of the Bath de Luxe, at the Hydro
A REAL SWIMMING BATH ... EAUTIFUL BATHING GIRLS

CHARLES CHAPLIN

Dear Jack,
    It was a pleasure to hear from
after all these years - of course I rem...
you and Lucy.   She used to play H...
wife in The Football Match...
good too !

    And I remember...
I playing Weldon's - wh...
And what a lot of wate...
bridges since then !

    If ever we...
certainly give you...
Enclosed. you will...
the one you like.

    Yours alwa...

The final performance on the stage of Karsino, March 1971: *(from left)* Roy Hudd, Ethel Revnell, Billy Powell, Leon Bronesky, Jack Melville, Jimmy Jewel

Below: Sandy Powell, a Karno protégé, revisits the Karsino in 1971

Karsino, after the bulldozers

first house, because the show hadn't gone very well — I didn't get many laughs. And I was sitting in my dressing-room, close to tears, when Fred Karno put his head round the door. He just looked at me and said, 'To think I paid Charlie Chaplin three pound ten a week.' And shut the door. Well, that was just about the end of the world for me — but that was Karno. He could be really cruel, vicious I'd say — but of course he was a genius, a genius at comedy.

An American property developer bought Taggs Island, demolished the Karsino and chopped up Karno's stage for souvenirs. Roy Hudd came along for the wake, with Roy Kinnear. Also there were Jimmy Jewel (without Ben Warriss), Billy Powell, who started as a scene painter for Karno, Tim Brooke-Taylor, Graeme Garden, and Ethel Revnell (remember Revnell and West?). Wee Georgie Wood sent a telegram.

Having bulldozed Karno's dream-palace, the American financier disappeared without leaving any forwarding address. Nowadays a flight of crumbling stone steps leads to a wasteland of nettles, and Karno's memorial is a deserted building site.

Charlie Chaplin died, fêted and knighted, in 1977. Jack Melville died only a few months earlier. And a nice letter from his widow, Doll, drew me once again to Worthing, this time to collect four battered cardboard suitcases. Inside them — the Karno inheritance: twenty-seven foolscap diaries covering the years 1902 to 1929. Each filled to bursting with Jack's spidery writing. Lists of sketches, songs, gags. A guide to the galleries of London theatres ('Daly's — seats very close, 30-minute wait; Hippodrome — far side best, not so draughty'). Accounts of other acts seen, and 'business' worth stealing ('Revolver Fight in Dark, Camberwell Empire; Sailors' Chorus, Alhambra; Madame Fralala's Balloon, Coventry Hippodrome'). Bills: from 'George Wilton, Theatrical Property Maker, Kennington — To/making one explosive frying pan . . . 12/6.'

Occasional disputes for arbitration: a letter from Hedley Claxton querying the ownership of the 'Funnel Gag'.

I want to do it in panto, and Jimmy Wheeler says he'll charge me a fee for it! Is it his, Jack? You remember the gag — comic stands on stage singing 'It ain't gonna rain no more' while people come on, first with a glass of water, then a small jug, then larger jugs, and pour them over his head. The water disappears (it goes into a pipe at the back of his collar, and runs off under the stage).

There are topical jokes, year by year. 'If only Asquith had the courage of his wife's convictions!' . . . 'The Kaiser has taken umbrage' — 'What, Umbrage Wells?' . . . 'I hear they're catching U-boats in nets; what do they do with them?' —

'Keep the big 'uns, throw the little 'uns back!' Prop lists: for the Kitchen Scene (16 lb of fresh dough, a dozen eggs, a large tarpaulin); the Wall-papering Scene (two buckets of whitewash, two buckets of water, two buckets of glue, a very large tarpaulin). Account books, wage bills, inventories. The state of the chairs in the Victoria Pavilion, Herne Bay, 1914: '216 Stacked in Shed, 102 Good Decks, 93 Canvassing Required, 44 Past Repair'.

At the end of every year, carried forward to the next, is Jack's index of 'gags' — the accumulation of comic routines and 'business' that are the fundamentals of the slapstick tradition. Handed down from one generation to the next, sometimes hijacked, endlessly recycled, they are none the worse for having been aired a hundred times before. Because, as a Victorian commentator wrote, 'the invaluable peculiarity of pantomime wit is that it weakens nothing by repeating, for a pun tells only once, but it is not so with a poke in the eye'. In Jack Melville's diary for 1911, alongside 'Jumping on Hat' and 'Matrimonial Bliss', is a sketch called 'Broken Mirror'. The premise is simple: servant has broken master's mirror and, to prevent him finding out, impersonates his reflection in the frame. A bit of detective work, and we find an account of the same piece being performed by Charles Manetti and Rhum, in the Cirque Olympique, 1848. The Hanlon-Lees (six tumbling Irish brothers) did it at Niblo's Gardens, New York, in 1860. They also claimed to have invented it. According to Lupino Lane, it was his grandfather, George Lupino, who had originated it for a Harlequinade at Drury Lane. The routine recurs in films: Max Linder's *Seven Years' Bad Luck*, the Marx Brothers' *Duck Soup*, Abbott and Costello's *The Naughty Nineties*, Woody Allen's *Sleeper*. And who really started it? The smart money's on the anonymous author of a seventeenth-century Spanish play, *The Rogueries of Pabillos*.

Treasures from the Melville archive. Star billing with Karno earned Melville the princely wage of 50 shillings a week, at a time when Chaplin was being paid 1250 dollars a week by the Essanay Company

At Last the 1948 Show — the quintessential quartet: *(from left)* John Cleese, Marty Feldman, Tim Brooke-Taylor, Graham Chapman

The Goodies: Tim Brooke-Taylor, Graeme Garden, Bill Oddie

Peter Sellers, as Clouseau, with Herbert Lom (Dreyfus) in *The Pink Panther Strikes Again*

Visual comedy, the comedy of *action*, the falling-down, not the stand-up comic. Karno gave his name to it, and his story is one of the connecting threads running through this book. Other strands are drawn from other encounters. In fifteen years of hanging around stage doors and studios, I've bumped into some of Karno's rightful heirs. There was Jerry Lewis at the Dorchester Hotel; Eric Sykes at Cinecitta; Les Dawson and The Goodies in Montreux; Fred Emney in Brighton; and Ken Dodd in Liverpool. At a south London workshop Jimmy Jewel initiated me into the mysteries of the 'haunted bedroom' — the ropes, flaps and pulleys that work the scenic magic. From the attic of a terraced house in Paddington, I witnessed the nightly comings and goings of Messrs Frost, Cleese, Chapman and Brooke-Taylor — a comic cabal that hatched *At Last the 1948 Show*, crazy comedy for the 1960s. Marty Feldman was a part of that. R.I.P. So also Sellers, Tommy Cooper, Morecambe, Charlie Cairoli, Sandy Powell . . . .

At the Bristol Old Vic in 1984, the spirit of Karno was conjured up by Chris Harris, clever man, for my first play. A video-age audience chuckling at antique stage routines, re-worked and re-vitalised: 'Funny stuff, laughter, isn't it? I was watching you, then: you caught your breath, then you let it out. It was a relief, wasn't it, almost as if you was in pain before?'

In the summer of 1985, a charabanc journeying from Prague to Bristol brought the answer to a question that had been troubling me for years. Did the *Commedia dell' Arte* really make its audience laugh? Two loose-limbed, false-nosed Czechs, Polivka and Pecha, breathing sweaty, vulgar and hugely comic life into dusty old sketches from the Italian archives, proved the point unequivocally. ''Cos it's the same in any language, isn't it? Just a noise from a hole, like other noises . . . from other holes!'

A bit of history, then, to get things rolling. Chapter 1 is a chronological catalogue of the main events over the centuries. The rise and fall of the 'Top Bananas', the shifting trends, the changing styles. Thereafter, I have attacked the subject from a series of tangents, to examine the living tradition in its different guises — the physical, the acrobatic, the shambolic, the eccentric, the salacious — the separate orders of our long-established 'ministry of mirth', in which many a noble head has been bowed. Harlequin and Pantaloon, 'The Italian Tumblers', John Rich, Grimaldi, Dan Leno, Buster Keaton, Little Tich, Harry Tate, Charlie Chaplin, Grock, Jacques Tati, Laurel and Hardy, the Crazy Gang, the Marx Bros, Max Wall, Charlie Drake, Spike Milligan, Benny Hill, John Cleese, Woody Allen, Richard Pryor.

But where are the clowns?
Quick, send in the clowns.
Don't bother — they're here.

Boleslav Polivka (Harlequin) and Jiri Pecha (Pantaloon), star clowns of the Czech 'Theatre on a String' company

CHAPTER ONE

TUMBLING
THROUGH·THE·AGES

The acrobatic, patchwork-suited Harlequin of the Italian Commedia dell' Arte

THE OCCASION is an American political convention — boaters, banners, brass bands and razzamatazz. On stage, the President's wife, Mrs Nancy Reagan, advances to take her place beside the Great Man. The television camera picks her out as she crosses in front of beaming aides, behind a knee-high covered railing. The band plays 'America the Beautiful', the crowd roars its approval, when suddenly — now you see her, now you don't! — the First Lady takes a tumble and disappears from view. The slow-motion replay confirms that this was not just a mundane trip, or stumble, but rather a beautifully executed, totally unexpected, ninety-degree 'pratfall' which, disseminated worldwide by satellite, earned Mrs Reagan the biggest laugh in the history of falling bodies.

It's a cruel business. Laughter, at root, is an instinctive, physical reflex, like sneezing or crying. It can be induced by tickling the sole of the foot, or by inhaling nitrous oxide, or by the electrical stimulation of a particular nerve. And, things that happen can stimulate laughter, as the President's wife discovered, even though the event witnessed has in itself no intended comic purpose. There's no preparation, no sense of anticipation. Simply, the unexpected misfortune of another affords us pleasure. 'Surprise, surprise!'

Freud was one of the first to analyse the curious connection between laughter and cruelty. He wrote:

> From childhood, our hostile impulses against our fellow men have been subject to the same restrictions, the same progressive repression, as our sexual urges. We have developed new ways of releasing hostility, and lifting inhibition — and laughter is the most important of these.

Hmmm. Of course Freud never played the Glasgow Empire on a wet Monday night.

W. C. Fields did. He said: 'I never saw anything funny that wasn't terrible. If it causes pain, it's funny; if it doesn't, it isn't.'

Pre-Freud, the comedy of misfortune — the deliberate exploitation of the ridiculous — has its roots in primitive ritual, religious ceremonial, professional storytelling, and court jesting. Anything for a laugh.

The Hopi Indians of the American south-west used to perform a tribal dance to the Gods of Fertility which would keep them going for several days. On Day One, while the formal dancers (*kachinas*) are parading in the village square, the *chuku wimkya* suddenly appear on a roof above. Six or more of them, covered in mud, wearing furry wigs made from animal skins, and face make-up — a black V over each eye and U-shapes under eyes and mouth. Chattering noisily, they survey the scene below; then, en masse, they make as if to step off the edge of the roof — only at the very last minute pulling back in mock terror. One finds a plank, and they take turns to slide down it — head first. On the ground, they pretend to be amazed at the dancing in progress; they try to join in, ineptly, dancing out of step, improvising rude parodies of the ceremonial chant.

In the eastern highlands of Papua New Guinea, the *gimis* stage short farces with costumes and props made from feathers, marsupial furs, leaves, flowers, berries, mosses, barks and coloured clays. An 'ugly old man with no nose', cuckolded by a handsome warrior, confronts his rival in a violent assault, which spills over into the front rows of the audience. Spirits of the dead are evoked in a comic parody of the first encounters between the *gimi* and the white man. Birds and animals are given human form and speech, just like Mother Goose and Puss in Boots.

In Greece, as early as the seventh century B.C., there were troupes of itinerant clowns and acrobats. Described by Xenophon as 'birds of passage', these primitive performers were classed as *mimi*, the Greek word which we translate as 'mime' but which originally meant 'imitation' or 'parody', rather than 'silent acting'. Xenophon describes *mimi* who could mimic the neighing of horses and the sounds of a thunderstorm. He also points to their expressive use of gesture and their acrobatic ability. But their social status was low, which gave them licence to be vulgar, rude and funny. They performed short plays or sketches that were mostly improvised, and involved a

A Gimi farce: jealous husband on the rampage

Pueblo Indian clown. From a sketch by Frank Bock

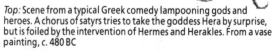

number of well-known stock characters; such as
the boasting soldier (Bucco), the villainous
servant (Dossennus), the lecherous old man
(Pappus). The Gods made occasional appearances
in these pieces, brought down to earth to be made
fun of.

The comic servant recurs in the classic Hindu
epics in the guise of Vidusaka, a bald dwarf with
teeth that stick out, and red eyes. The name
literally means 'one given to abuse'. Although
loyal to his master, Vidusaka is gluttonous,
clumsy and easily duped. In the few surviving
Sanskrit texts of these dramas, the comic element
would appear to be minimal. However, the stage
directions allow for the introduction of
improvised 'business', to build up the part, and to
get a few laughs. Vidusaka also has a partner in
crime, a ne'er-do-well called Vita who has all the
characteristics of Shakespeare's Sir Andrew
Aguecheek — the guest who outstays his welcome,
the sponger, the braggart. The scenes between
Vita and Vidusaka form the blueprint for the
comic 'double-act' — the interchange of badinage
and body blows.

In the traditional Chinese theatre, there are
two classifications of comic types: the *wen ch'ou*,
who uses words, and the *wu ch'ou*, who uses
actions. In the court theatre of Peking, the *ch'ou*
was kept firmly in his place whereas 'out of town',

Top: Scene from a typical Greek comedy lampooning gods and
heroes. A chorus of satyrs tries to take the goddess Hera by surprise,
but is foiled by the intervention of Hermes and Herakles. From a vase
painting, c. 480 BC

Bottom: Pappus, the traditional dirty old man of Greek *mimi*

encouraged by unsophisticated audiences, the
comedians would take over and play all the parts
'for laughs'. A whole range of comic stereotypes
was thus developed: the emperor (pompous, vain,
miserly), the fop with ideas above his station, the
lazy hanger-on, the 'dame', the village idiot, and
the drunken servant.

GETA SERVVS

DEMIPHO SENEX

GRATINVS ADUOCATI

DEGIO III

CRITO

Characters from Roman comedy, c. 160 BC. Demipho, the old skinflint, appeals to his friends for help in sorting out his son's amorous entanglements

In the Balinese dance-drama, the comedian is a servant/interpreter, who translates the hero's lofty speech into a language the audience will understand. At the same time, he is liable to introduce scurrilous asides about his master's meanness and sexual inadequacy. He pretends to misunderstand his orders, tells lies, creates confusion, courts disaster. Penasar is Bali's most famous comic character and is often paired with Kartala, the 'master' character, for double-edged drollery.

The Romans took their cue from the Greeks and created the *mimus*, a strolling player with shaven head and bare feet. His costume was a patchwork jacket with a hood, knee-length tights and a distinctive phallus. The *mimi* were not yet denied the use of speech; improvised dialogue was crucial to their short sketches which revolved around a number of set situations. The plots were simple, crude and often indecent, and adultery was a favourite theme.

A later Roman development of the Greek idea was the *pantomimus*. Literally an 'all-in-one' imitator, the pantomime was in fact an interpretative dancer. He was silent, behind a mask which had several facets, thus enabling him to act out all the parts in a mythological scenario, the story of which was sung by an off-stage chorus. The emperor Nero's favourite pantomime was Paris, whose 'speaking hands' were so expressive that foreign visitors could follow the plot, although not understanding a word of the sung narration.

These two different styles of performance appealed to different sections of the Roman public. The *mimi* used makeshift stages and played to common folk at fairs and festivals. The *pantomimi*, on the other hand, were highly regarded and played to posh audiences in exclusive theatres. Today, curiously, the reverse applies. Mime is up-market, Marcel Marceau, polite applause. Pantomime is village hall, custard pies and belly-laughs.

Nero patronised both genres. When the Dorian *mimi* from Sicily were in town, he would be carried, secretly, to watch them. According to Suetonius, 'from a nearby balcony the emperor would watch the brawls of the *mimi* and urge them on. When they came to blows and threw stones and broken benches at one another, he himself would throw missiles at the crowd beneath'. Audience participation: a key ingredient of comic rough-and-tumble, then and now.

In pictures of the Italian mime from the fourth century A.D., the masked player usually carries a knuckle-bone, or what looks like a small cosh, as a weapon. Through the next fifteen hundred years, it is possible to trace the wobbly line of the knockabout succession as this slapstick 'baton' is passed from one generation to the next. En route, it becomes a turtle-shell rattle, a bladder on a stick, a sockful of dried peas, a hinged wooden sword, a red-hot poker, a truncheon, a feather-duster, a 'tickling stick'. The Italian connection remains crucial. The Latin temperament — excitable, emotionally volatile, physically vigorous — provided the seedbed for the growth of 'action comedy', fast and furious. 'It is peculiar to Italy,' wrote Professor Schegel of Bonn, 'that from the earliest of times its people have displayed a native talent for a merry, amusing,though very *rude* buffoonery, in extemporary speeches and songs, with accompanying appropriate gestures.' And the yeast to this Mediterranean fermentation was an infusion of Anglo-Saxon wit, that peculiarly English sense of humour which contrives to see the funny side of anything (including one's self);

deflationary, satirical, outrageous. 'Biting the bum of the hand that feeds' — enter the jester.

Traditionally, the court fool or king's jester presents himself as a skilled, well-paid professional entertainer, in cap 'n bells, wielding a puppet reproduction of himself on a stick. However, it is clear that some of his ancestors were 'not all there', and owed their employment to genuine idiocy rather than any acquired comic skills. At the court of Pharaoh Dadkeri-Assi in Egypt (Fifth Dynasty), a pygmy was hired to play the fool. He spoke a language the courtiers could not understand, but nonetheless all were much amused by his frantic caperings. As a weapon, he appears to have carried a pair of tongs.

When Cortes conquered the Aztecs in the sixteenth century, he found 'a miserable motley band of fools, dwarfs and hunch-backed buffoons, living in the direst squalor, whose sole function was to be paraded for the entertainment of the Court of Montezuma'. A primitive 'freak show' under royal patronage.

King Edward IV of England had a jester called Scogan who enjoyed practical jokes. Owing the king large sums of money, the jester decided death was the only way out. So, he duly died, and was laid out in state. The king came to pay his last respects — and, incidentally, to forgive his

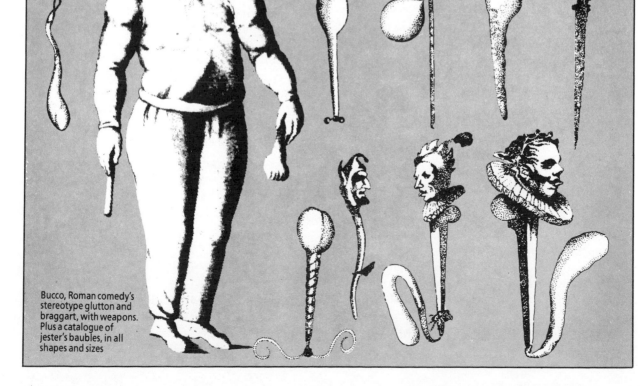

Bucco, Roman comedy's stereotype glutton and braggart, with weapons. Plus a catalogue of jester's baubles, in all shapes and sizes

Left: Tarlton, with pipe and drums; he died in the year of the Armada

Centre: French farceurs dancing, *c.* 1600

Right: 'Look out — he's behind you!' Harlequin menaces Pantaloon, who's dallying with the upstairs maid. From a Commedia dell' Arte performance, *c.* 1580

Below: Will Kempe: 'the Jest Monger'. He was an actor with Edward Alleyn's Company, before he joined Shakespeare in the Lord Chamberlain's Men

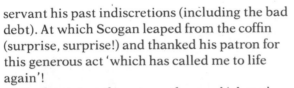

servant his past indiscretions (including the bad debt). At which Scogan leaped from the coffin (surprise, surprise!) and thanked his patron for this generous act 'which has called me to life again'!

In the sixteenth century, the word 'clown' made its first appearance in the English language. Originally 'cloyne' or 'cloine', it derives from the words 'colonus' and 'clod' which define a farmer or rustic and, by extension, a country bumpkin. Similar words are found in Icelandic — *klunne* — a 'clumsy, boorish fellow', and in Danish, *klunes* — a 'block, log or stump', or an idiot.

Richard Tarlton was the clown par excellence of the Elizabethan theatre. An illustrated manuscript of the time depicts him in a buttoned cap and country boots, playing pipe and drums simultaneously. Queen Elizabeth was a great fan of Tarlton, as was Shakespeare. It is believed that Hamlet's description of Yorick — 'a fellow of infinite jest, of most excellent fancy' — was Shakespeare's compliment to Tarlton. From 1583 until his death in 1588, Tarlton was a leading player in the Queen's Men, and played the comedy roles in the early Shakespeare plays. He was given licence to roam outside the text, add his own jokes and interject comments about the play. He was the link between the player and the

public, a conspirator with the audience, the cheer-leader, the 'warm-up' man.

After Tarlton, Will Kempe became Shakespeare's favoured clown, for whom he wrote the part of the constable, Dogberry, in *Much Ado About Nothing*. Kempe was an accomplished dancer who hit the headlines with a marathon 100-mile dance from London to Norwich. It took him a month, and made him famous, although theatrical purists bemoaned the clownish takeover. An anonymous play, *The Pilgrimage to Parnassus*, poked satirical fun at current trends (*c.* 1599):

Enter DROMO, *drawing a clown with a rope*

CLOWN: What now? Thrust a man into the commonwealth, whether he will or no? What the devil should I do here?

DROMO: Why, what an ass art thou? Dost thou not know a play cannot be without a clown? Clowns have been thrust into plays by head and shoulders ever since Kempe could make a scurvy face; and therefore reason thou shouldst be drawn in with a cart-rope.

There's a visual echo of this in Samuel Beckett's play *Waiting for Godot*, written in 1948. Beckett also pays homage to Chaplin's funny walk, the Marx Brothers' hat-juggling routine (*Duck Soup*),

the Fratellini circus family, and the tarts of the Rue Godot de Mauroy.

The puritans closed the English theatres in 1642. The clowns took refuge in the marketplace and low comedy flourished in fairs, festivals and drolls, which were short knockabout farces condensed from the funny bits of full-length plays. Merry Andrew was the generic title for the comedy lead. He appears in contemporary prints in a fancy coat, ruff, and feathered hat. His weapon is a broomstick.

Meanwhile, across the English Channel, a Continental invasion was preparing. Companies of Italian players — the *Confidenti* ('the confident'), the *Accesi* ('the inspired'), the *Gelosi* ('the zealous') — having established a foothold in France, were adapting their *commedia all' improviso* for English audiences. The English Ambassador in Paris sent word of 'a comedie of Italians that for good mirth and handling thereof deserve singular commendacion'. Notice was taken of 'the comedians of Ravenna who are not tied to any written device', and Thomas Heywood wrote of 'the Zanyes, Pantaloons, Harlakeans, in which the Italians have been excellent'. What the Italians offered was a considerably refined version of the rough and bawdy mime shows of the Roman Empire. The label *Commedia dell' Arte*

was coined to guarantee the professionalism of the comic troupes (*arte* in this context denoting the skill of the players), who were equally at home in the Municipal Theatre and fairground booth. Their short, improvised pieces used stock characters and predictable situations. Doddery old Pantaloon was always at the centre of events, trying to woo the beautiful Columbine and enlisting the support of his servants, the wily Harlequin and the clumsy, slow-witted Zany, in his romantic overtures. A simple theme, with endless variations. Today we call it 'situation comedy'.

Strolling players give a performance in the country, northern France, c. 1600. The portable stage was at least five feet high, requiring acrobatics to get on or off

Drusiano Martinelli was one of the first *Commedia* players to visit London. He stipulated in advance that a mattress and hoops should be provided at each place of performance. Biancolelli, Gherardi and Fiorilli came hot on his heels, causing one London critic to condemn the Italians' 'scurrility, unworthy of any chaste ears', and, even worse, 'their extreme forms of doltishness, fit only to lift up a loud laughter, and *nothing else*'.

In 1700 Nicholas Rowe wrote a prologue for a play called *The Ambitious Step-mother*, to be performed at Lincoln's Inn Fields Theatre, in London:

Show but a mimic ape, or French Buffoon,
You to the other house in shoals are gone,
And leave us here to tune our crowds alone.
Must Shakespeare, Fletcher and laborious
  Ben,
Be left for Scaramouche and Harlequin?

The appeal came too late. English actors and dancers were already kitting themselves out in Harlequin's patchwork suit. Joe Haines presented 'a comedy in the Italian manner' at Drury Lane Theatre. Thomas Jevon played the title role in *Harlequin, Emperor of the Moon*. William Pinkethman and William Bullock appeared as Harlequin and Pantaloon in *Harlequin, Dr Faustus*, diarist Sir Richard Steele noting:

Mr Pinkethman devours a chick with great applause; Bullock's talent lies chiefly in asparagus. Pinkethman is very dexterous at conveying himself under a table; Bullock is no less active at jumping over a stick.

In 1702 John Weaver, dancing master at Drury Lane, announced that he had devised the first entertainment on the English stage, where 'the representation and story were carried on by dancing, action and motion only, performed in grotesque characters, after the manner of the modern Italians, such as Harlequin, Scaramouche etc.'

These first English Harlequins paved the way for John Rich, the man generally acknowledged to be the founding father of the English 'pantomime'. Adapting the *Commedia* scenarios to their own particular skills, they refined crude horseplay into parody. They developed stagecraft as an art in itself, using trick scenery and elaborate machinery to create even more elaborate effects. And, in the process, they tapped a new audience for whom the 'legitimate drama' held no appeal, but who might be persuaded to pay sixpence for a glimpse of this new, magical world to which the dancing figure of Harlequin beckoned.

In 1714 John Rich inherited from his father a theatre in Lincoln's Inn Fields, in London. His first pantomimes were presented as 'after-pieces', when the more solemn business of the theatre was over. It was customary to allow admission to the theatre at reduced rates after the third act of the drama. This attracted the shopkeepers and clerks whose work prevented them from getting to the theatre in time for a six o'clock curtain. Soon, the after-pieces were being chosen to suit the tastes of this sixpenny audience, and, when pantomime had proved its popularity, the price for latecomers was increased to a shilling (full-time attendance in the pit cost half-a-crown). The next stage was to run the pantomime story between the scenes of the 'serious' drama, using Harlequin's pursuit of Columbine as a sort of 'running gag' through the acts of *Dr Faustus*, or a story from the classics. It was a strange mixture. Myths and legends, contemporary criminal records, and the old stock plays were bowdlerised by Rich, and combined with remnants of Italian sketches to create his new-fangled theatrical entertainment.

Initially, the 'pantomime' label caused confusion. The word had been used to describe formal ballets 'after the manner of the ancient pantomimes' — a remote descendant of the Roman *pantomimus*. However, Rich's 'monstrous medlies' appropriated the label and set the pattern for the English 'panto', the most durable and popular theatrical form, faithfully recycled every Christmas in four hundred and more locations. Although the figures of Harlequin and Columbine have faded from the scene, the fundamentals remain unaltered over the years: a fairy story, transformation scenes, songs and comic 'business'.

In Rich's day, intellectuals complained that the popularity of pantomime was lowering the tone of the theatre. Barton Booth, the foremost tragedian of Drury Lane, was accosted in a coffee-house by a group of worthies who berated him for meddling with 'that senseless stuff'. Booth answered frankly that 'a thin audience is a much greater indignity; it is not the business of theatre managers to be wise to empty boxes'. And pantomime was filling every kind of theatre, from the gilt and plush of Drury Lane and Covent Garden to the spit and sawdust of the East End 'penny gaffs' — the eighteenth-century equivalent of today's 'fringe' theatres, offering alternative theatre in unpretentious surroundings, admission one penny.

In 1737 the Lord Chamberlain's office reacted to the spread of 'unlicensed' theatre and an Act was passed whereby

> any person acting for hire, gain or reward, any spoken, dramatic entertainment in any place where they have not a licence from the Lord Chamberlain, shall be deemed a rogue or vagabond, and shall be sent whither they ought to be sent . . .

Transformation scene, the Haymarket Theatre, London, c. 1740. Interesting features are the proscenium door, the wide apron stage, the stage box; and benches for the patrons in the pit

But this did not prevent local magistrates issuing licences for musical performance, and so pantomime flourished as a loophole to the Act. Music, dance, mime and acrobatics were permissible on any stage but 'straight' drama was confined to the approved theatres: Drury Lane, Covent Garden and (in the summer only) the Haymarket. This legislation had the effect of encouraging the development of visual, physical comedy, just as, two hundred years later, the limitations of the silent film camera would revive the same speechless skills.

The mid-eighteenth century also saw the opening up of a new arena for comic hurly-burly, with the additional ingredient of a fast-moving, four-legged animal with a tail (useful for hanging on to). In 1768 Philip Astley, a discharged cavalry sergeant-major, staged an equestrian exhibition in an open field on the south bank of the Thames. He laid out an arena with a 60-foot diameter, where he and his wife exhibited 'activity on horseback'. There was also a conjuror, a comic sword-fight and 'tumbling — after the manner of

Left: Astley's Riding School, London, 1777. Where the public could, for sixpence, enjoy 'the greatest wonders in all the world, offered in all humility at four in the afternoon on Saturdays and Sundays only until Demand makes further performances the Vital Necessity'

Below: Astley's Amphitheatre, 'in which are combined all the splendours of Theatre and Fair, with candlelight to Illuminate both stage and arena'. Productions here included *The Roman Gladiator*, *The Chinese Enchanter*, *The Courier of St Petersburg*, and *The Vicissitudes of a Tar*

Sadler's Wells'. A clown called Fortunelly essayed some hair-raising feats of horsemanship in a routine called 'The Taylor Riding to Brentford'. The 'Taylor' is so drunk he can't mount his horse. When, with the help of a ladder, he finally arrives in the saddle, the horse refuses to move. Then it gallops off, depositing the rider on the ground. On its next circuit of the ring, horse pursues rider and bites him.

Astley's experiment led to rival schools being set up, by Charles Hughes at Richmond Gardens and by Hyam at Cromwell Gardens. Astley's pupil, John Bill Ricketts, emigrated to America and opened a riding school in Philadelphia. His 'Pantheon' was a huge, circular tent of wood, seating seven hundred. Ricketts unashamedly recycled his boss's best routines and 'The Peasant's Frolic' and 'The Taylor Riding to Brentford' became established as the classic 'business' of the horseback clown. Whose antecedents, incidentally, can be traced to the Crow Indians of North America. In each tribe there was, traditionally, a band of young 'loonies' (the *thanigratha*) licensed to play the fool and satirise the white man. Returning to camp, they would occasionally ride back-to-front, shooting arrows wildly over their shoulders. Drunkenness was another comic ploy, as was illogicality: when a stream had to be forded, the loony would roll up one trouser leg and then hop across on the other! Their comic weapon was a turtleshell rattle. In the next century, the Wild West Show became a popular variant of the three-ring circus, with 'Buffalo Bill' Cody and Pawnee Bill Lillie playing cowboys and Indians around a sawdust ring.

Philip Astley disliked the word 'circus' because of its Ancient Roman connections. His circular, grassy arena was a far cry from the elliptical Circus Maximus which could accommodate some 385,000 spectators for athletics, chariot races and gladiatorial combat. Few animals got out of there alive. So Astley billed his show 'The New British Riding School'. From the South Bank he moved indoors and opened the Royal Grove Amphitheatre, near Westminster Bridge. Here Astley combined equestrianism with theatre. After a traditional stage show, either pantomime or melodrama, the spectators in the arena ('the half-price') would be ejected, their orange peel cleared away, sawdust sprinkled in a circle, and a hoop of gas jets lowered. Then the equestrian performers would make their entrance.

New York Circus bill, 1865. The clowns merit a lowly spot

And the link between stage and ring was the ubiquitous Clown whose merry cry of 'Here we are again!' became a durable catchphrase. But this was a very different Clown from the rustic idiot of the Italian comedies. Gone are the loose shirt, the flat hat and the mask. This Clown makes a flamboyant entrance in blue and white striped breeches, fancy red waistcoat, striped stockings, frills and tassels. His face is white, the cheeks marked with broad red triangles which, together with his poll of red hair, give him the wild look of an Indian savage on the warpath. This eye-catching costume is carefully designed to do just that, to ensure that every eye in the house follows his every move, for

> whether he was robbing a pie-man, riding a giant cart-horse, imitating a sweep, wielding a red-hot poker, beating a watchman, sneezing, snuffing, courting, or nursing a child, the most saturnine looker-on acknowledged Clown's sway; and neither the wise, the proud, the fair, the young, nor the old were ashamed to laugh till the tears coursed down their cheeks . . . .

In 1806 Astley saw a French clown, Baptiste Dubois, in the Easter pantomime at Covent Garden Theatre. Impressed, he invited Dubois to forsake the stage for the ring; and Dubois became Astley's resident Clown. His tour de force was 'Frolics of My Granny', a perilous tightrope dance, with a dummy old woman perched on his shoulders. To fill the vacancy at Covent Garden, manager Thomas Dibdin recruited Joseph Grimaldi, the son of an Italian dancing master and a cockney laundress. For the next seventeen years Grimaldi held sway at Covent Garden, 'the Garrick of Clowns, the Jupiter of practical joke, the Michael Angelo of buffoonery who, if he was grim-all-day, was sure to make folks laugh all night'. His Christian name of Joe, or 'Joey', was assimilated into the language as a synonym for clown.

After Grimaldi came Tom Matthews, then Jefferini — a very tall Clown who came a cropper in a human pyramid and thereafter adopted a very real grimace of suffering as part of his act. He was succeeded by Flexmore. Meanwhile, Wattie Hildyard enjoyed considerable success at Astley's, until a bequest from an aunt promised him an income of £3 per week 'on condition that you remove yourself *entirely* from the circus ring'. Wattie did the decent thing and retired.

Another Continental invasion took place in the 1860s, when circus families from Europe were booked for London pantomimes: the Hulines, the Leclercs, the Lauris. Acrobatic skills were beginning to replace comic ingenuity. George Augustus Sala, who wrote pantomimes for Covent Garden, complained that

> modern Clowns are desperately *dull*: many are mere contortionists or acrobats, who have no admissable claim to be called Clown at all, and endeavour to compensate for their normal dreariness by tying up their limbs in knots or exhibiting dancing dogs, or educated pigs.

Changes were also taking place in the structure of pantomime. The traditional opening scene, which was formerly a 'curtain-raiser' to the Harlequinade, now became a complete story, in several acts, relegating Clown and his accomplices to a short after-piece, just before the final curtain.

American clowns and horses, 1872. John Durang was the first native American clown. After him came Joe Pentland, Pete Conklin, Dan Rice and Tony Pastor, who became a vaudeville impresario

Grimaldi: *(left)* playing The Drunken Watchman

A rowdy audience in the 'gods' on Boxing Night. Fred Barnard, 1869
Right: An early music-hall, established next door to the Rodney Inn

Instead of a magical transformation in which the fairytale characters of the opening were turned into Clown, Pantaloon, Harlequin and Columbine, two sets of performers were now employed, the cast for the fairytale now being considered the 'stars' of the show, while the Harlequinade players were often only dancers from the chorus. In *Chambers' Journal* of 1864, Clown is berated for allowing the Grimaldi tradition to fall into abeyance:

> Do you ever reflect upon the painful fact that English Boys are now growing up wholly ignorant of the nature and efficacy of the Buttered Slide? But how should they do otherwise when pantomime after pantomime ignores its existence. Again, the Spill and Pelt; to what has that degenerated? We no longer have the organised mob — greengrocers, fishwomen, bakers, police — running in Indian file across the stage, for you and Pantaloon to Spill and Pelt, and bring every scene to a conclusion amid a protracted eruption of vegetables, crockery and fish. Melancholy changes for the worse, these; but they almost vanish in comparison with the next cause of complaint to be preferred against you. What

has become of the red-hot poker? On behalf of the entire community, I repeat, with becoming warmth of expression, WHAT HAS BECOME OF THE RED-HOT POKER?

The new generation of English funny men was beginning to look beyond the stage and the ring, for an alternative platform and a new audience. A rough and boozy lot, but nonetheless enthusiastic. In 1844 Thomas Rouse extended his public house, the Eagle Tavern, in the City of London, by building a 'Grecian Saloon' on the southern end. The Eagle promised 'dancing, singing, music and other delightful amusements'. Other publicans soon followed suit, seizing this opportunity for building up trade, and the 'music-hall' was born. Often no more than an upstairs room set aside for entertainment, the more ambitious extended their premises and took over the neighbouring buildings. So, Weston's Music-Hall was constructed out of a school, the South London from a chapel, the London Pavilion from a stable-yard. Admission was by a Refreshment Ticket, half of which was given back in liquid form. A forceful and boisterous style of performance was encouraged for this spit and sawdust arena with its noisy, uninhibited audience.

In 1875 there were three hundred music-halls across the country and a crop of new stars emerged. Mostly singers, for the licensing

regulations still limited the halls to music, dancing and acrobatics. The 'Lion Comique' was the label given to the swaggering, 'heavy swell' type of singer, like George 'Champagne Charlie' Leybourne, the Great Vance, Harry Liston, Sam Cowell and W. G. Ross. In 1878 a law was passed requiring music-halls to qualify for a Certificate of Suitability, for which they had to meet the standards of the Metropolitan Board of Works. If they failed to pass muster, the magistrates would not issue a licence. Consequently, a number of smaller halls were forced to close down. At the same time the sale of drinks in music-halls was restricted to the bars at the back of the stalls, which had replaced the tables and chairs of the original 'song and supper' rooms. This paved the way for the evolution of the variety theatre — a purpose-built theatre offering better facilities and a larger, more sober audience for music-hall performers who wanted to move up-market.

In the United States a similar development saw the emergence of two distinct genres of popular theatre — burlesque, and vaudeville. Burlesque was a broad sex-and-comedy cocktail, owing something to the early Graeco-Roman mime shows. The 'burleycue' promised leggy chorus girls, acrobats, magicians, 'freak' entertainers, rude comedians, and singers. Occasionally, a real 'burlesque' was presented in

The Harlequin tradition, carried into the twentieth century by Gertrude Kaye, queen of Lancashire musical comedy

the form of a comic parody of a serious play. Michael Bennett Leavitt is usually credited as being the founding father of burlesque, American-style, in the 1860s. The audience, in the early days, was predominantly male. Liquor flowed freely and audience participation flourished. A tentative performance would provoke cries of 'get the hook!', and an ignominious exit, neck-first. Some survived and went on to better things: Al Jolson, W. C. Fields, Fannie Brice, Sophie Tucker, Mae West, Jack Benny...

Vaudeville means, literally, 'voices of the city'. Either that or something else. Tony Pastor invented it as a respectable alternative to burlesque. In 1881 he staged a variety show at the 14th Street Music Hall, New York, which, he claimed, would be 'clean as a hound's tooth'. His plan was to double ticket sales at a stroke by playing to mixed audiences. His show was more elaborate, better dressed, professionally produced. Comedy was given more time, and space; lavish set-pieces developed, using scenery, props, and stagecraft. From Pastor's classy showcase came Jimmy Durante, the Marx Brothers, George Burns, Abbott and Costello, the Three Stooges, Olsen and Johnson, Clark and McCullough, the Three Keatons; and English music-hall sent ambassadors across the Atlantic to play to their American cousins. Jolly John Nash led the way in 1874. Little Tich joined Pastor's touring vaudeville troupe in 1887 and played across the United States for three years. In 1897 Dan Leno was booked into Hammerstein's Music Hall in New York. Boastfully billed as 'The Funniest Man on Earth', Leno disappointed. 'The jokes and humour of the English Music-hall are, as a rule, so terribly out of date that the importation of them to our country is apt to be a failure', sneered the *New York Times*. American performers fared better in London. The Three Keatons (with seven-year-old Buster as 'The Human Mop') played at the Palace Theatre, W. C. Fields juggled at the Alhambra, and Eddie Cantor capered at the London Pavilion.

Music-hall flourished in Australia, where serious theatre had a rough ride in the nineteenth century. When *Hamlet* was put on in Sydney in the 1850s, the ghost was greeted with a shout: 'Well, I'm blowed! Holy Moses, does your mother know you're out?' and Ophelia's mad scene was interrupted by a sailor who roared 'Come on — give us "Black-eyed Susan", old gal!'

In 1890 Harry Rickards, a Lion Comique from London, fled to Australia to escape from his creditors. Rickards established a circuit of music-halls and brought his friends from England to top the bill. He also encouraged Australian talent. Albert Whelan had been scratching a living in the Coolgardie goldfields as the violin-playing half of a comic duo, Whelan and Wilson. Whelan went solo, smartened up the act and became a polished man-about-town, singing 'The Old Top Hat' and 'The Butterfly and the Bee'. Florrie Forde made her debut at the Polytechnic, Sydney, in 1893, singing 'He Kissed Me When He Left Me and Told Me To Be Brave'. She joined Harry Rickards' company and was billed as 'The Australian Marie Lloyd'. Florrie Forde and Albert Whelan went to England at the turn of the century, and stayed.

Away from the Australian cities, Tent Shows brought music-hall programmes to rural audiences: chorus girls, acrobats, comics, in a theatre under canvas, with portable seats, stage and scenery. Thorley's and McKay's were tops in this field. In winter, all the companies travelled north, following the sun. It was not unusual for three or four shows to be camped outside Darwin

Dan Leno, in one of his character sketches — the Railway Guard

at Christmas. Strangely, the Tent Shows remained distinct from the circus. Only the clowns were able to make the leap from stage to ring, or vice versa: Max Reddy, Ike Delavala, Dinks and Onkus, Jim Gerald. . . .

Robert Radford launched the first Australian circus in 1847 in Launceston, Tasmania, where he put up a building based on Astley's Amphitheatre. May Firth, a distinguished horsewoman, led the first, and most famous, tenting circus; it toured from Sydney in 1878 and went round the world in 1893.

The Fratellini in their dressing-room: (from left) François, Paul, Albert

But America dominated the international circus traffic, in Big Tops that expanded to match the scale of the billing: 'Macarte and Bell's Grand American Circus', 'Hernandez and Stone's Great American Circus' and 'Barnum and Bailey's Greatest Show on Earth'. Irishman Edwin 'Poodles' Hanneford, a refugee from Hanneford's Riding Family, was the comic star with Barnum and Bailey. Poodles excelled on, and coming off, horses. In full-length raccoon coat, he would dive onto a galloping horse, ride backwards, swing under its belly. He could step off the back of a galloping horse, in such a way that he would appear to be momentarily suspended in mid-air, like the cartoon cat who charges over the precipice, and *hovers*, before plummeting earthwards.

Equestrianism was also the focus of the first Russian circus, with Cossack horsemen adapting their martial skills to the sawdust arena. Akim Nikitin was the resident clown at the Nikitiny Circus. The Durov Brothers, Vladimir and Anatoly, used a whole menagerie of animals in elaborate set-pieces — the 'Pied Piper', the 'School for Animals' (which included a sea lion, pig, elephant, pelican, monkey, calf and jackass among the pupils), and a parody of *The Merry Widow* (with the pig, Chuska, in the title role).

The Durovs visited Paris in 1894 and played on stage at the Folies Bergère. Across town, an

Buster Keaton: a chip off the old block

Englishman and a Cuban, Footit and Chocolat, were developing an aggressively physical double-act in the Hippodrome du Champ de Mars. And an acrobat from Switzerland, who called himself Grock, also headed for Paris to form a partnership with a white-face clown called Brick. At the Cirque Medrano, the Three Fratellini Brothers became the darlings of the Paris intellectuals. Clowning was celebrated as 'art', formally approved by Cocteau and the Comédie Française. The Fratellini presented the three classic clown types, models for future generations: the superior white-face clown; the pretentious, tail-coated,

A music-hall bill bursting with famous names

son, named after his father.

In 1897 in Paris, Louis Lumière invited his friends to a screening of a film called *L'Arroseur Arrosé* (The Hoser Hosed), which is usually credited as being the first film comedy. In the United States, meanwhile, the pioneering Edison concentrated on filming spectacular events: a fire, a prize-fight, a (staged) train crash.

In 1905 a comedian called Max Linder was appearing in the Paris Varieties. One night a note was left for him at the stage door:

> Sir, I have observed you. In your eyes lies a fortune. Come and act in front of my cameras, and I will help to make it.
>
> CHARLES PATHÉ

So Linder went to work for Pathé, for the less than princely sum of thirty francs a day. The films were turned out at the amazing rate of six per week — short situation comedies, with Max the victim of circumstance, the frustrated lover, the failed sportsman. In all, Pathé released more than a hundred 'Max' films, and spawned a host of imitators. Andre Deed appeared in films as the acrobatic Boireau. Ferdinand Guillaume created the screen idiot, Polidor. In England, short films featuring the comic adventures of Bertie Bungles were shown as part of a music-hall programme. One of the first English film studios, Cricks and Martin, used cinematic tricks to good effect in a series of films featuring the unfortunate Scroggins.

In the United States, the director D. W. Griffith was one of the pioneers of film comedy. *The Curtain Pole* was a neat and well-constructed story in which a drunken fop tries to carry a curtain pole from shop to home and causes predictable mayhem en route. The part of the fop was played by an actor called Mack Sennett.

In 1909, an overweight English actor called John Bunny travelled to Los Angeles and talked his way into silent films. In five years Bunny made more than a hundred and fifty short subjects, usually in collaboration with the actress Flora Finch. Bunny established himself as the first funny fat man of the silver screen, before his sudden death in 1915.

In 1907, Charlie Chaplin joined Fred Karno's Speechless Comedians to appear at the Coliseum Theatre in a pantomime sketch called 'The Football Match'. He stayed with the company and played in most of Karno's knockabout repertoire: — 'G.P.O.', 'Jail Birds', 'The Bailiffs' and 'London Suburbia'. In 1909 Chaplin went with a Karno troupe to Paris to present 'Mumming Birds' at the

middle-class middle-man; and the 'Auguste' — the put-upon, bewildered, bedraggled tramp.

In 1887, an English acrobat called Fred Westcott threw up his job with Manley's travelling circus, and walked to London hoping to break into music-hall. At the Metropolitan Music-Hall, in the Edgware Road, he learned that an act called the Three Carnoes had failed to show up for their spot. Enlisting the help of two friends, Westcott stepped into the breach and the three impostors presented an impromptu performance of simple acrobatics and knockabout clowning. After a moderately successful week, the opportunist Westcott decided to hang on to the name that had changed his luck. The 'C' became a 'K', and Fred Karno became a music-hall comedian, at first on his own but subsequently with a troupe of 'Speechless Comedians', recycling for the stage the classic clown routines of circus — 'The Swiss Lovers', 'The Bear and the Sentinel', 'Gregory's Blunder'.

In 1889 Thomas Edison invented the Kinetoscope. That same year in Walworth, south London, Hannah, the wife of an Irish music-hall singer, Charles Chaplin, gave birth to a second

John Bunny: one of the first British actors wooed to Hollywood

Max Linder: one of the first European film stars

Cigale Theatre. During his six weeks in Paris, Chaplin spent many afternoons in the cinema watching Max Linder comedies: *The Collegian's First Outing*, *The Skater's Debut* and *Max Pedicure* . . . .

In Chaplin's absence, Karno recruited an 'eccentric dancer' from Ulverston, Lancashire, to play the title role in his new sketch 'Jimmy the Fearless'. This was Stanley Jefferson, son of the comedian Arthur Jefferson, subsequently better known as Stan Laurel.

In 1910, Chaplin crossed the Atlantic to play Hammerstein's Music-Hall, New York, in Karno's satirical sketch 'The Wow-Wows'. Karno's physical comedy found a more receptive audience than had Dan Leno. From New York, the company embarked on a twenty-week tour out west, on the Sullivan and Considine circuit. 'Cheap vaudeville — three shows a day', according to Chaplin's own account. He adds, prophetically, 'the further west we went, the more I liked it'.

In 1912 Fred Karno bought an island on the Thames, and spent £70,000 to build a 'Fun Palace' which he called the Karsino. With four companies on the road, and one in the United States, Karno refused to acknowledge the new celluloid medium as a threat to live theatre, and continued to recruit comedians from music-hall and pantomime: Will Hay, Jack Gallagher, Billy Danvers, Jimmy Nervo, Fred Emney, Sandy Powell, Jack Melville . . . .

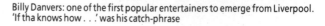

Billy Danvers: one of the first popular entertainers to emerge from Liverpool. 'If tha knows how . . .' was his catch-phrase

In the United States, 1912 saw the establishment of the Keystone studios. Producer Mack Sennett invented the Keystone Kops and launched a series of high-speed 'chase' films — man and machine in perpetual motion. Critic James Agee wrote:

Words can hardly suggest how energetically they collide and bounce apart, meeting in full gallop around the corner of a house; how hard and how often they fall on their backsides; or with what fantastically adroit clumsiness they get themselves fouled up in folding ladders, garden hoses, tethered animals, and each others' headlong cross-purposes.

In 1913, Karno once again sent a troupe to the United States. Chaplin, now the No. 1 comedian, played the drunken swell in *A Night in an English Music-hall* at the Empress Theatre, Chicago. Mack Sennett was in the audience. Six weeks later, Chaplin reported for work at the Keystone Studios.

From left: Buster Keaton, Sybil Seely and Fatty Arbuckle. Keaton said of Arbuckle: 'the longer I worked with him, the more I liked him. He was that rarity, a truly jolly fat man'

Two years later Stan Jefferson handed in *his* notice to Karno and headed for Los Angeles. Changing his name to Laurel, he joined the Hal Roach Studios, where American actor Harold Lloyd was beginning to explore the comic potential of high buildings with narrow ledges. And Buster Keaton, having outgrown The Human Mop, teamed up with Roscoe 'Fatty' Arbuckle, to create the first movie double-act.

The year 1914 brought the first Charlie Chaplin films to screens in America and Europe, with sensational results. No longer would film be seen as a novelty item, low down on the music-hall, or vaudeville, bill. Now 'moving pictures' were top-of-the-bill, and the first Bioscopes, and Biographs, offering all-film programmes, were beginning to

compete for audiences. Chaplin's success prompted further migrations to Los Angeles — from Australia came Snub Pollard and Billie Bevan; from France Max Linder; from England Lupino Lane.

In his first year at the Keystone Studios Chaplin made thirty-five short films. By the end of the year, Sennett was making as many as six prints of each, so great was the demand from distributors in America and Europe. The arrival of a new Charlie Chaplin film produced queues at the box office; indeed one cinema in New York (the Crystal) was given over exclusively to the showing of Chaplin films — a policy that paid dividends for more than a decade.

Despite the new medium's success, Karno continued to wave the flag for live theatre, while on the Western Front a new 'Fred Karno's Army' was dug in for the duration. Recruiting took its toll of male comedians, prompting Karno to devise a new sketch, 'All Women', starring Betty Balfour and the twin sisters Beattie and Babs.

The 1920s saw a half-hearted attempt to bolster up the British film industry, with a Government-sponsored campaign to 'Show a British Picture'. A middle-aged character actress, Sydney Fairbrother, was launched in a series of comedies featuring the eccentric 'Mrs May'. But against the combined talents of Chaplin, Keaton, Langdon, Lloyd and Laurel, Mrs May stood no chance. In 1926 — a sign of the times? — Karno went bankrupt. Increasing competition from the movies had the effect of creating a 'star system' in

Left: Chaplin, as a rather dapper version of the Tramp

Right: Harold Lloyd in *Safety Last* (1923). Thirteen storeys up, for real — and no back projection

From top: Jacques Tati; George Robey; Harry Tate and son: Golfing

the theatre, where only a well-established name on the marquee could guarantee a full house. In London, Little Tich was very big; other 'bankable' stars were Harry Tate, the Swiss clown Grock, and the Prime Minister of Mirth, George Robey. A lanky mime from Paris, Jacques Tati, was beginning to make a name for himself at the London Palladium.

In America, the 'Riff-raff's Caruso', Jimmy Durante, was Vaudeville's Top Banana. Jack Benny, once the serious violin-playing half of a duo billed as Salisbury and Benny — from Grand Opera to Ragtime, went solo and started playing for laughs. Bob Hope, having outgrown *Hurley's Jolly Follies*, teamed up with Lloyd Durbin as Two Diamonds in the Rough.

In 1927, the first 'talking pictures' were released. Initial audience reaction was unenthusiastic. The *New York Times* ran a poll to find the most popular films of 1928 — and the top ten were all silent. It seemed that the silent film, with orchestral or piano accompaniment, was the established art form and the 'talkies' were a commercial novelty, to be exploited by the vaudeville patter merchants — double-acts like Smith and Dale, or Van and Schenk, doing their quick-fire cross-talk.

The comedians who most successfully made the transition from silence to sound were those who made no concessions to the new medium. In the Hal Roach Studio a new partnership was being formed between Stan Laurel, ex-Karnoite, and an overweight tenor from a travelling minstrel show — Oliver Hardy. This potent combination took to the microphone in 1929 with a minimum of fuss. What had worked in silence remained effective with sound because the sound was added naturally, to reinforce the 'sight gag' with convincing sound effects. No superfluous dialogue, no jokes; a perfectly timed look, a snort, or a whimper, said it all.

Sound was the undoing of Harry Langdon and Buster Keaton. Both failed to come to terms with the microphone and lost touch with their audience. Chaplin fought a determined rearguard action; his *Modern Times* was one of the last silent films to be made in Hollywood and was released some seven years after the innovation of synchronised sound. In his own account he said:

The whole of Hollywood had deserted silent pictures, and I was the only one left. I had been lucky so far, but to continue with a feeling that the art of pantomime was obsolete was a discouraging thought. Besides, it was not easy to contrive silent action for an hour and forty minutes, translating wit into action, and creating visual jokes every twenty feet of film, for seven or eight thousand feet. And if I did make a talking picture, I felt sure that when I opened my mouth, I would become like any other comedian. These were the melancholy problems that confronted me.

But there were other changes in the air, which were to have far-reaching effects on comedy, for stage and screen. The advent of broadcasting, and later the phonograph, raised the ghastly spectre of home entertainment, and theatre managers faced the awful prospect of their customers forsaking the bright lights, and opting for the comfort and convenience of hearthside amusement. The British Broadcasting Company began transmitting in 1922. Will Hay was probably the first radio comic to raise a laugh from an unseen audience, in the guise of Professor Broadcaster. The first comedy shows were cast in the style of seaside pierrot shows, with singers, monologuists, a 'light' comedian and a 'low' comedian. The Elite Concert Party, The Impossibles and The Moonstones were the first troupes to take to the air.

By 1927 there were 2,178,259 radio sets in England and the concert-party format was replaced by Non-stop Variety. Max Miller, Tommy Handley, Jeanne de Casalis were the new radio stars. And a young man called Arthur Marshall made an impression as Nurse Dugdale. The first radio situation comedy introduced a double-act called Clapham and Dwyer and a mythical cow called Cissie. Their catchphrase 'I say, I say, I say' had an ominous ring to it — at least to those 'speechless comedians' who relied more on physical skills than a well-filled joke book. Many a funny face disappeared without trace. Sam Barton, Bob Lloyd, Tommy Jover, George Hersch . . . where are you now?

In Australia in the 1920s, Stiffy and Mo were top of the bill on the Tivoli circuit. Alf Warren had labelled himself 'The Australian Charlie Chaplin' and was reproducing Chaplin's film routines on the Variety stage. His sons were also making a name for themselves as The Warren Brothers — Acrobatic Clowns. At the Opera House in Wellington, Joe Lawman, with the baby face of Harry Langdon, the baggy suit of Chaplin and the floppy hat of Keaton, announced himself as 'Australia's Funniest Comedian'. The Wellington audience remained unconvinced.

In the United States, Jack Benny was one of the first comedians to broadcast on the newly established Columbia Broadcasting System. His

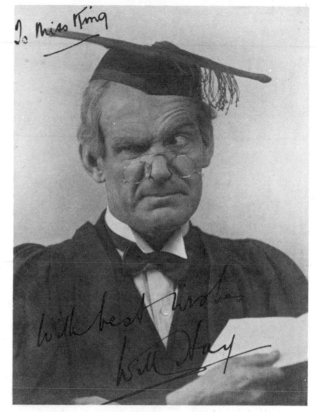

Will Hay, in the guise of Dr Muffin, headmaster of Narkover School

opening words were 'This is Jack Benny speaking. Now there will be a brief pause for everyone to say "Who cares?"'. This self-effacing debut launched a radio career that ran for twenty-five good years, with gravel-voiced Eddie Anderson playing Rochester, Benny's long-suffering butler.

In 1932 Fred Karno attempted a comeback with a show economically titled *Laffs*, at the London Palladium. This brought together three double-acts from the Variety Theatre — Nervo and Knox, Naughton and Gold, Caryll and Mundy. Plus an eccentric juggler, Eddie Gray. The show was a more sophisticated version of Karno's classic 'Mumming Birds' — 'the show within a show', where members of the audience apparently try to get in on the act. *Laffs* extended the comedians' licence to disrupt, interrupt, subvert. It was as if a gang of loonies had taken over the theatre and replaced an orderly programme with comic mayhem. So successful was *Laffs* that the same team were booked for Crazy Week at the Palladium later that year. A pair of 'singing comedians', Bud Flanagan and Chesney Allen, were enlisted to make up the numbers. In 1933 Crazy Week grew to Crazy Month, which established the troupe as the Crazy Gang, for life.

Jack Benny playing to type in *The Meanest Man in the World* (1943). Eddie Anderson (Rochester) on the right

Across the Atlantic, a parallel explosion of comic eccentricity had been sparked by the twosome of Ole Olsen and Chic Johnson. Billing themselves as Comic Nuts, Kings of Cacophony, Unconventionality and Conviviality, they hit Broadway with a show called *Atrocities of 1932*. Using similarly unpredictable devices as the Crazy Gang, Olsen and Johnson put all their comic eggs into one basket, which they called *Hellzapoppin*. A 'screamlined revue designed for laughing', it ran for a record-breaking 1404 performances on Broadway and then became a classic film.

The 1930s also saw three brothers running riot through a series of Broadway musicals, to the despair of writers, directors and fellow-performers. The Marx Brothers took their own route through a script, and plot and storyline became a springboard for their soaring comic ingenuity. The shows became films — *Animal Crackers*, *Horse Feathers*, *Duck Soup* — models of 'crazy' comedy, riotous and chaotic.

'The day war broke out' became comedian Robb Wilton's catchphrase on 3 September 1939. It lasted him for the duration. In the first weeks of the war, variety theatres across Britain were closed down. Although they were to reopen ten weeks later, the threat of German bombers was another factor in the decline of live theatre. Behind the blackout curtains wartime Britain took comfort in the reassuring silliness of radio comedy. *ITMA (It's That Man Again)* cast Tommy Handley as the Minister of Twerps and surrounded him with familiar British comic types — Mrs Mopp, Colonel Chinstrap, Ally Oop (the cheery salesman), Claud and Cecil (the polite 'broker's men'). Radio also invented an R.A.F. station staffed exclusively by incompetents, and promoted Richard Murdoch to Squadron Leader, at *Much Binding in the Marsh*.

In the real war, a number of budding comic talents were beginning to flower in the unlikely setting of barrack-room, billet and battlefield. The R.A.F. claimed Peter Sellers, Tony Hancock, Max Wall and Jimmy Edwards. Ernie Wise was in the Navy ('a deck-hand on a submarine', according to Eric Morecambe). Tommy Cooper was in the Horse Guards. Norman Wisdom was in the 10th Hussars. Harry Secombe, Spike Milligan and Frankie Howerd were in the Royal Artillery. Benny Hill was a driver in R.E.M.E. The new generation of Fred Karno's Army was in training — but the Rules of Engagement were changing.

Left: Sid Caesar in *It's a Mad Mad Mad Mad World* (1963)
Right: Danny Kaye at the Palladium, 1947

Black humour, self-mockery, the pricking of pomposity, two fingers to authority — these elements were to give a sharper edge to postwar comedy, honed in the school of hard knocks. Karno himself didn't survive the war. He died quietly in 1942. His estate was valued at £42 7s 6d.

In 1942 American burlesque was killed off, by statute. Few bemoaned its passing. Leavitt's broad but tasteful entertainment had degenerated into a squalid and boozy strip show. A self-respecting comedian wouldn't be seen dead in it. In contrast, London's never-closing striptease theatre, the Windmill, was to prove a useful launching pad for Messrs Hancock, Edwards and Bentine, demobbed and determined.

In the postwar years television (which had been discreetly shelved for the duration) was dusted off and reappraised. The first comic to take advantage of the new medium was the American, Sid Caesar. In 1949 he presented the *Admiral Broadway Revue* which was followed in 1950 by *Your Show of Shows*, which ran for four years on NBC. Caesar's collaborators on the series included all the founder-members of the New York Jewish school of comedy — Danny Kaye, Carl Reiner, Mel Brooks, Woody Allen. All had served their comic apprenticeship in the 'Borscht and Bible' belt of Jewish holiday resorts in the Catskill Mountains, where the 'toomler', like the Butlin's holiday camps' red-coat, acted as all-purpose cheer-leader, sports organiser, entertainer. The script conferences for Caesar's show were, by all accounts, wildly and noisily inventive. The demands of a weekly ninety-minute live show put the writers and performers under immense pressure, but also offered scope for experimentation. As Carl Reiner later recalled, 'We were too young to know it's impossible!'

Psychological humour flourished here ('Dr Siegfried von Sedative's Advice to Insomniacs'); there were parodies of movies ('Dark Noon', 'A Trolleycar Named Desire'); illogical interviews, and Yiddish interpretations of the classics. In 1973, extracts from the series were put together in a film to be shown in cinemas. New York critics rated this vintage compilation as the best comedy of the year. For Brooks and Allen, of course, it was only the beginning.

Your Show of Shows saw the number of television sets in America rise from 1,000,000 in 1949 to 10,000,000 in 1951. In Britain there were 14,000 sets in 1947 and 1,500,000 by 1951.

Richard Murdoch and Arthur Askey on the roof of BBC Broadcasting House (Bandwagon)

The first British television comedy was less adventurous than the American trail-blazer. *Turn It Up*, starring Jewel and Warriss, was little more than a variety show with an audience, observed by the television cameras. It would be some years before there emerged a new and original strain of televisual comedy, owing little to the broad traditions of music-hall and variety. Meanwhile, the 'patter merchants' were quick to get a foot in the door of the new medium: Arthur Askey, Frankie Howerd, Ted Ray and Benny Hill were among the first clutch of TV stars. And Bob Monkhouse wasn't far behind, with one of the first television situation comedies — *Fast and Loose*.

The spread of television coincided, in 1951, with a new departure in radio comedy, which was to have a major influence on the next generation of comedians. Launched on the BBC Light Programme as *Crazy People*, Messrs Sellers, Milligan, Secombe and Bentine threw off the shackles of traditional radio comedy to create their own surreal world of subversive, irreverent insanity. Rechristened the Goons, they introduced a gallery of idiosyncratic idiots — Seagoon, Bluebottle, Moriarty, Henry and Minny — whose weekly adventures became required

listening for the newly defined 'young generation'. At schools and colleges across the nation Friday evening broadcasts by the Goons became the most important item on the timetable. At Radley, Peter Cook became mysteriously unwell every Friday at tea-time, thus guaranteeing himself a bed alongside the sanatorium wireless. At Clifton College, in Bristol, John Cleese tuned in and took note. At Gordonstoun, some years later, the heir to the throne of England developed his own impersonation of the luckless Bluebottle: 'Ooh – my nut – ooh – I have been hitted on my bonce – oh, I have been nutted – ooooh! (clutches lump on crust)'.

His mother, the newly crowned Queen, faced an evening of more traditional fare at her first Royal Variety Performance in November 1952. Among the 'old guard' represented were the Crazy Gang (minus Chesney Allen), Jewel and Warriss, and Arthur Askey. New faces included Jimmy Edwards, Terry-Thomas, Tony Hancock, and, from Australia, the acrobatic trio of Warren, Latona and Sparks. The Grand Old Man of music-hall, George Robey, made a short appearance, to good effect: two years later he was knighted.

Royal patronage could ensure a full house at the London Palladium: but in normal times, especially for the less well-placed theatres, the prospect was bleak. Apart from their summer seaside shows and Christmas pantomimes, the huge Empires, Hippodromes and Palaces were now struggling to put 'bums on seats'. Desperate measures were being employed — striptease, all-in wrestling, Bingo — to woo customers away from the flickering pictures and crackling sound of their domestic rivals. For the cinema, the statistics were equally appalling. From 1945 to 1955 the number of weekly attendances in the United Kingdom dropped from 30.5 million to 22 million. In the United States, a figure of 90 million for 1945 was almost halved, to 46 million, by 1955.

Although the blame for this decline is usually laid at television's door, there is a counter-argument which points to a falling-off in the quality of films released in the 1950s. For film comedy these were sterile years, with Abbott and Costello outpointing Martin and Lewis at the box office, while Lucille Ball, Red Skelton, Ma and Pa Kettle, and Francis the Talking Mule filled the second rank. In Britain, Norman Wisdom was working the later Chaplin formula of 'two parts comedy, eight parts sentimentality', Arthur Askey sparkled briefly, Sandy Powell projected Yorkshire innocence, while Frank Randle and

George Formby capitalised on Lancashire innuendo.

The film industry was too busy defending its own to pay much heed to an audience survey, published in America in the 1950s, which concentrated on certain Rocky Mountain states where television was not available, but nevertheless, cinema attendances were in decline. The researchers found that film-makers had been putting their audiences to sleep! Films had become too predictable, too easy to follow. The viewers' imagination was not tested, people and events were too clearly labelled, scene followed scene chronologically, and within each scene every movement would be accounted for. No elisions, no ambiguities, no loose ends. In a word, films had become boring. A new, youthful postwar audience had emerged, questioning, impatient, intolerant. The old gags fell on deaf ears; there were new veins of Goon-inspired comedy to tap. The end of food rationing, *Rock Around the Clock*, the invasion of Suez, the launch of commercial television and *Look Back in Anger* set the context for the new era, and the seed-beds were the old-established universities of Oxford and Cambridge.

The remarkable feature of this New Wave of comedy was that it was spearheaded by a group of well-born, well-educated young men and women, few of whom had any connections with, or ambitions towards, the world of theatre, music-hall, showbiz. But for a series of accidents, they would have gone on to become doctors, lawyers, academics, even — perish the thought — chartered accountants. In the event, they put their heads together and devoted their considerable intellectual energies towards the creation of a new style of comedy for the 1960s — abrasive, irreverent, cynical, unconventional, outrageous . . . .

The Goons: Spike Milligan, Harry Secombe, Peter Sellers. Still at it, 1958

Jimmy Edwards (Cambridge Footlights, RAF, the Windmill Theatre)

Peter Cook (Cambridge Footlights, Broadway, The Establishment Club)

In Cambridge, the Footlights Club had, since 1883, provided a platform for undergraduate humour. 'Smoking concerts', before an all-male audience, were traditionally used to try out comic songs and monologues. Song-and-dance man Jack Hulbert made his debut there in the 1920s; after the war, Jimmy Edwards and Richard Murdoch starred in the showcase Footlights revue. In 1954, a show called *Out of the Blue* was successfully transferred from Cambridge to the West End of London, and a gangly young man called Jonathan Miller was acclaimed as 'the new Danny Kaye'. In 1959, the Footlights Club opened its doors to women, which let in the talented Eleanor Bron. According to John Bird, that year also saw 'the first Footlights revue to be booed on its opening night'. However, Peter Cook made his mark, especially in the guise of the moronic, mackintoshed E. L. Wisty, dispensing monotonous platitudes from a park bench. A new generation of schoolboys had a new funny voice to try out on their chums.

Cook wrote sketches for the West End revues *Share My Lettuce* and *Pieces of Eight* (to which Harold Pinter was another contributor). But the traditional 'intimate revue', light and frothy, had had its day. The year 1960 was the watershed, when Cook, cheerily biting the hand that had fed him, collaborated with three friends, Dudley Moore, Alan Bennett and Jonathan Miller, on a show for the Edinburgh Festival. *Beyond the Fringe* was a revue with a difference. No showy

musical numbers, no scenery or costumes, no easy targets. Instead, four young men in dark suits presenting comedy with an edge — political, satirical, indignant. Among their victims were the British Prime Minister, Harold Macmillan, grotesquely lampooned by Cook; the 'gung-ho' British film; Shakespeare; the Church; 'posh' music; and capital punishment. In the *Daily Express* Bernard Levin wrote:

> The satire is real, barbed, deeply planted and aimed at things and people that need it. But the final target . . . is the audience. It is they who are thoroughly, healingly, beneficially, beautifully, and properly shaken up in the process.

Beyond the Fringe ran for six years in London and a year in New York. No concessions were made for the American audiences. According to Peter Cook, 'it became an immensely *chic* show, and its very Englishness gave it built-in snob merit'.

America, meanwhile, had its own New Wave, emanating from the West Coast. Mort Sahl blazed the trail at the 'hungry i' nightclub in San Francisco. *Time* magazine labelled Sahl the first of the 'Sicknicks', and complained:

> they joke about father and Freud; about mother and masochism; about sister and sadism. They delightedly tell of airline pilots throwing out passengers to lighten the load, of a graduate school for dope addicts. They

Mort Sahl (University of Southern California, the hungry i, the White House)

The Establishment Club spawned the magazine *Private Eye*, a television series (*That Was the Week That Was*), and a satirical cottage industry that cheerily and blithely ridiculed every sacred cow within reach — royalty, judges, Conservative ministers, upper-class accents, privilege, Britain's pretensions still to be a great nuclear power, and, above all, the decrepitude of the father-figure Prime Minister, Harold Macmillan. Some dismissed the trend as student high-jinks. Others took it seriously. Journalist Christopher Booker wrote in the *Spectator*:

> The 'upper-class charade' was only the most blatant symbol of a decay that was beginning to affect the whole of English society. The satirical comedians were the first expression in society of a darker longing for sensation, chaos, collapse — without even the dream of dynamism to provide hope of a remedy.

In April 1963, Lenny Bruce flew to London for a return engagement at the Establishment Club. On the orders of the Home Secretary, Henry Brooke, he was turned back at Heathrow Airport. From another continent, Barry Humphries flounced in to overwhelm British audiences with the glittery gush of Dame Edna Everage, housewife-superstar:

> A lot of my countrymen say rude things about you — they do — just because you have the lowest standard of living in the world, and I don't think that's fair. I think that's mean and horrid, and I think they're awful. Because I know England will rise again — it will! It will! Say to the level of Sicily, or Ethiopia . . .

Dame Edna Everage (Moonee Ponds Ladies College, Melbourne Revue, Housewife Superstar)

attack motherhood, childhood, sainthood, and in a dozen night-clubs across the country — from the 'hungry i' to Manhattan's 'Den', and Chicago's 'Mr Kelly's' — audiences pay stiff prices to soak it up.

The style was conversational, improvisational, casual. The 'hip monologuists' were breaking down the mystique of the stage and provoking, teasing, or insulting their audience into reaction or participation. And King Tease was Lenny Bruce — 'America's Number One Vomic'. In the Jazz Workshop (San Francisco), the Gate of Horn (Chicago) and the Cafe au Go-go (New York), Bruce unleashed his venom on the fetishes of liberal piety, sexual hypocrisy, racism, the Bomb, organised religion, and the materialist society. He played on the very nerves of his country, making its secret obsessions his own confessed ones.

In 1962 Bruce appeared at the Establishment Club — London's first 'satirical nightclub', launched by Cook and friends under the 'Fringe' banner. Competition from Bruce sharpened the resident satirists' barbs. Cook recalls:

> Some of the things we did were as outrageous as anything that has been done subsequently. Extremely bad taste flourished at 'The Establishment'. We put on a crucifixion scene, with John Fortune as Christ and Jeremy Geidt and John Bird as the robbers objecting that (a) Jesus was higher up than they were, and (b) he was getting all the attention.

At Last the 1948 Show. Aimi MacDonald on top; Feldman, Chapman, Brooke-Taylor, Cleese, supine

In July 1963, the Footlights revue *Cambridge Circus* introduced some new faces: Bill Oddie, Tim Brooke-Taylor, Jo Kendall, and John Otto Cleese. The show was notable for the surreal silliness of many sketches and the wild-eyed rampaging of Cleese. After successful tours of Broadway and New Zealand, the cast re-formed to create a silly radio series, originally to be called *Get Off My Foot* but eventually known as *I'm Sorry I'll Read That Again*. Two funny doctors, Graham Chapman and Graeme Garden, were variously associated with the series which ran to more than a hundred programmes, from 1965 to 1973.

In 1964, the 'Establishment' team launched a new series for BBC Television, *Not So Much a Programme, More a Way of Life*. The 'Fringe' team, meanwhile, had diversified. Peter Cook and Dudley Moore were working a successful double-act; Alan Bennett was becoming a playwright; Jonathan Miller was hovering between medicine and the theatre.

In 1967 the ringmasters of 'Cambridge Circus', Cleese and Brooke-Taylor, got a foot in the door of television with a series eccentrically labelled *At Last the 1948 Show*. Doctor Graham Chapman hung up his stethoscope to join the company, which also included Marty Feldman, he of the

bulging, wayward eyes. This talented quartet made surreal mincemeat of the traditional revue sketch, with comic 'situation', characters and 'punch line'. A government inspector disintegrates during an interview. A dentist climbs into his patient's mouth to blast out a tooth, but Welsh miners in the throat object. Cops lay siege to a gangster hiding out in the skirts of an opera singer ('Come out, Bugsy, we know you're in there!'). And Cleese, in white tie and tails, with chorus and orchestra, sings the unforgettable 'I've Got a Ferret Sticking Up My Nose'.

In another corner of the woods, in the same year, two Oxford graduates, Michael Palin and Terry Jones, were getting together with a Cambridge man, Eric Idle, and an American cartoonist, Terry Gilliam, to devise a comedy programme for children. *Do Not Adjust Your Set* became something of a cult show, with dads secretly rushing home from the office to watch it. The style was anarchic and mildly fantastic. Music was supplied by the only silly rock 'n roll band in the business — The Bonzo Dog (Doo Dah) Band.

In 1969 these separate strands of Oxbridge-nurtured comedy were finally drawn together to create a definitive amalgamation. Producer Barry Took had been commissioned by the BBC to create a new 'zany' comedy series. 'Experimental', 'freewheeling', 'spontaneous', 'unpredictable' were the flavours of the month. Taking the bull by the horns, Took invited the top six 'loonies' to join him in the circular corridors of the BBC and create some comic havoc. Cleese, Chapman, Idle, Palin, Jones and Gilliam made up the team. According to Took, 'the BBC was terribly worried about these people'. The early script conferences — taking a leaf from Sid Caesar's book — were wild and woolly. The established format of television comedy and the 'structured' sketch were thrown out of the window. Conventions were overturned; illogicality ruled. The title was well chosen. *Monty Python's Flying Circus* promised thrills and spills on the high wire — 'fliers', 'twisters' and daredevil leaps. And no safety net. Monty Python was launched quietly, in off-peak viewing hours, but quickly made its mark with a youthful audience. There was satire in the mixture, but on a more surreal level than *Beyond the Fringe*. The parodies were grotesque, the style was manic.

There were four series of Monty Python between 1969 and 1974. The empire grew and expanded from television into other media. Records, books, stage shows, films for the cinema

(*The Life of Brian*, *The Meaning of Life*). And the adjective 'Pythonesque' went into the dictionary.

In 1976 there was a unique reunion at Her Majesty's Theatre in London. A charity show was organised in aid of Amnesty International, and all the leading lights of the Oxbridge Mafia, from 'Fringe' to 'Python', gathered to do their stuff. Bron, Bird, Fortune, Miller, Bennett, Moore, Humphries, Brooke-Taylor, Garden, Oddie, Chapman, Palin, Jones, Idle, Gilliam. And top-of-the-bill were Peter Cook and John Cleese, appearing together for the first time, in a noisily chaotic trial scene. Cook and Cleese — the leaders of their respective packs, the role models for their generation.

The Oxbridge Connection maintained into the 1980s. From the universities a new grouping of Rowan Atkinson, Mel Smith and Griff Rhys Jones devised a quick-fire television miscellany: *Not the Nine O'Clock News*. A witty Australian actress, Pamela Stephenson, made up the foursome. Against the trend of closing theatres and expanding video, 'The Comedy Store' in London became a springboard for 'alternative' comedy. The Punk comedians emerged from here and graduated to television as *The Young Ones* — the

unspeakable in pursuit of the unedifying. From Australia, Los Trios Ringbarkus did disgusting things with ripe bananas, and talc.

Traditional comic arenas have survived by the skin of their teeth. The Christmas pantomime still brings old talents out of hibernation to raise a childish laugh with the durable old routines — the 'Kitchen Scene', the 'Whitewash Scene', the 'Tree of Truth', the 'Busy Bee'.

The circus comes to town very rarely now. In America, Ringling Barnum has a permanent base in Florida; the Circus Vargas and Hanneford's Tented Circus still tour. In Australia, Ashton's, and Royale still follow the sun. In Britain, Robert Fossett and Gerry Cottle keep the tradition alive. Fossett's clown persona, Professor Grimble, has succeeded Charlie Cairoli as 'clown to the ring' at Blackpool Tower Circus.

From San Francisco comes the New Wave of comedy — a presentational style of performing which is as new as the theatrical avant-garde and as old as vaudeville. The movement is spearheaded by dedicated young variety artists, experimenting with modern dance and music, video techniques and martial arts. Its genesis can be traced to the late sixties, when streets and

Peter Cook in *Yellowbeard* — a film about pirates

John Cleese in *Yellowbeard* — it went down with all hands

Whoops Apocalypse. Surrounding the Quark bomb: *(from left)* President Johnnie Cyclops, Prime Minister Kevin Pork, Premier Dubienkin

campuses were filled with jugglers, mimes, guitarists and flautists. 'The streets were full of people in whiteface', says clown Bill Irwin, 'and I was one of them.' Now, they are classified as the New Vaudevillians. Top of the bill are Avner the Eccentric (sweet-tempered silent clown); the Flying Karamazov Brothers (fast-talking kamikaze jugglers); Penn and Teller (loony magicians); Bruce D. Schwatrz (with his built-in puppet theatre); and the Foolsfire Trio (dancing, juggling clowns). And Bill Irwin, inventive clown, subsidised by a 1984 MacArthur Foundation award ($36,000 a year for five years).

In Russia they take their clowning very seriously. In 1959, 500 Russian clowns were summoned to Moscow to take part in a conference on 'The Clown and the Party'. Apparently, Premier Kruschev had visited a circus earlier in the year and was not amused. The clowns performed, and received criticism. It was announced that only 17 were worthy of praise. The performers and government officials discussed various problems, including that of 'clowns who borrow jokes and whole routines without any conscience'. In his closing address, Yiri Kimitriev of the Arts Institute declared that the clowns 'must educate the people, fight for new qualities of morality, and expose the outmoded and the reactionary'. Then they all went home. Today Russia has 62 permanent circus buildings, 16 tented circuses, and a clown population of 1400.

In 1985, the Moscow State Circus toured Britain, without animals. Oleg Popov, confidently billed as the World's Most Famous Clown, led the troupe. Popov complained:

> Once you are infected, it is for life. A fine speck of sawdust enters the bloodstream. You do not take to the circus — the circus takes to you.

Meanwhile, beside the seaside, Bognor Regis played host to the first International Clown Convention. Riotous assembly was encouraged, clowns directed traffic, policemen wore red noses, and 120 dedicated idiots mounted a spirited defence of the last bastions of clowndom.

In Britain, cinemas closed at the rate of one per week in 1983. In 1984, for the first time since the 1920s, there were more theatres (707) than cinemas (690) in the U.K. The year 1985 saw the desperate launch of British Film Year (with ominous echoes of the doomed 1920 'Show a British Picture' campaign). On screen, appropriately, 'anxiety comedy' is the mood of the moment. Woody Allen, Mel Brooks, Richard Pryor, Chevy Chase and Cheech and Chong portray twentieth-century man overwhelmed by events outside his control: sex, urban violence, the Bomb. The proverbial 'last laugh' will probably emanate from the black comedy of the nuclear holocaust, as epitomised by *Whoops Apocalypse* — just the video to take with you to the lead-lined bunker. Chortle through the 'Countdown to Doomsday':

> The President is informed of nuclear attack by means of a singing telegram. Should he be asleep, a tyre lever will be rhythmically applied to his temple until signs of life appear. He will then have exactly four minutes in which to make his awesome decision. A statement to the effect of 'Holy hell shit' will not normally be considered sufficient. The order to retaliate with a counter-strike against the Soviet mainland will be transmitted down the line to the Minutemen silos in Nevada. The commander will then formally verify the order as genuine with the words 'Hey — no kidding?' After which two members of the crew will turn a series of keys and launch the missiles. The one who salivates is probably a former insurance salesman.

Laugh? I nearly died . . .

CHAPTER TWO

PHYSICAL
· ENCOUNTERS ·

JEROME K. JEROME, the Victorian writer, had ambitions to be an actor. But a starring role in a Christmas pantomime soon opened his eyes to the hazards of the profession and the niceties of the 'nap' (a slap to the face):

I pretend to go to sleep, and then the clown catches me over the head with a clapper, and then he rushes at me and hits me, and I take the nap from him, and then he takes a nap from me (it wakes you up, this sort of nap, I tell you), after which we both have a grand struggle with the cat. I fell on my head one night (lucky it wasn't another part of me), and broke a chair in the course of the struggle. I got another encore for that, but didn't take it. I suppose you could call this knockabout business.

Violence — or the parody of violence. There's a delicate distinction. The 'injury laugh' must always be carefully calculated: if a blow seems to cause real pain, there will, usually, be no laughter. Willson Disher, a noted historian of the comic arts, once observed a performance by a trick cyclist, where 'a well-intentioned rumour made it known that he had not yet recovered from a broken rib. In consequence his tumbles were watched in the silence of deep concern.'

Falls and blows are the elemental basics of knockabout comedy, and the circus ring is where the violent aspects of the art are preserved in purest form. It's no accident that the sawdust ring is marked out by a low wall, ideally suited for chasing round, tripping over, falling off.

Fred Karno was introduced to the mysteries of the 'clown entrée' when he ran away from home to join Ginetti's travelling circus, in 1882. He was sixteen. The eldest of six boys, he'd taken a lot of stick from his hard-line father, who made cabinets, and then made young Fred polish them till they gleamed. The boy vented his frustration by working out at the Nottingham gymnasium. It

was to be the making of him. In an account of his early years, Fred wrote:

I was originally one of the 'submerged', and that I am not today one of the 'won't works', I attribute to the fact that good old Dame Nature gave me an energetic disposition and a taste for athletics of any kind. I joined a gymnasium for working lads, and soon became the 'star' performer. I used to be engaged to give exhibitions at fetes and galas and similar entertainments until finally I came under the notice of Monsieur Alvene, a well-known gymnast and equilibrist . . .

Alvene gave him his chance and Fred became Leonaro. He was paid twelve shillings per week and had to provide his own pink tights. And he discovered that, after Alvene and Leonaro had done their ten minutes of juggling and tumbling, he was expected to take part in the clown routines that filled the gaps between the featured acts. Ginetti's clowns tutored him in the complexities of 'Love in a Tub', 'The Living Statue', 'The Swiss Lovers'. In the course of this, Fred had a revelation.

Chaplin in the blue corner;
City Lights (1931)

Young Karno (Leonaro) with Alvene

It came to me that Alvene and I were breaking our arses doing fancy acrobatics for a bit of polite applause, when what the customers liked best was when we were larking about and falling on our bottoms. So I thought to myself — why not cut out the clever stuff and stick with the pratting about?

So, the act was reworked, with new comedy 'business'. Instead of doing a straight 'two-man high' (Alvene on Leonaro's shoulders), Leonaro pantomimes to Alvene how he should climb onto his shoulders by clapping his knee ('One!'), hip ('Two!'), and shoulder ('Three!'). Alvene mimics Leonaro by slapping him repeatedly in the same three places. Leonaro then gets cross and blows are exchanged. At the next try, Alvene makes a running approach and drop-kicks Leonaro, who falls flat on his back.

Well, it was a start. By the time Alvene and Leonaro had expanded, by appropriation, to become the Three Karnos, the act was developing to include props and music. Something along these lines:

Fred enters from gangway with saxophone, and plays. Al enters from gangway and interrupts him, box on the ears, fall, he exits. Fred resumes playing, Tommy enters from the audience and interrupts, box on the ear, fall, he exits. Al meets Tommy on the ring, box on the ears, fall: Fred ticks Al off, box on the ears, fall. The ring-master ticks all three off, box on the ears, fall. General exit, re-entrance, concert on chairs, Al falls through chair, Tommy falls over back of chair etc., with Italian march finale when Alex and Porto enter and Al loses his trousers.

Karno's next move was to exchange the sawdust arena for the lime-lit stage of the Victorian music-hall. He had worked out that the broad and noisy comedy of the circus could, with good effect, be transferred to the proscenium stage. After all, an act that was pitched to come across through 360 degrees, against a background of trumpeting elephants, cracking whips and billowing canvas, could be explosive when presented head-on inside four walls. Like a bomb in a room . . . As well, he'd learned something about the nature of laughter. You could draw out a laugh, double it, extend it ad infinitum, if you added the element of suspense. Now, instead of simply being the observer of a ludicrous accident, the audience becomes a conspirator with the on-stage villain, who is planning to do his victim some mischief. The audience can see it coming and they enjoy the power that gives them. Like the 'Sack Gag' (sometimes known as 'Let Me Like a Soldier Fall'). Never fails.

Props: *Sack in flies, on line. Stage cloth marked where it falls. Little basket with whisky bottle and glass on trick line.*

[*FRED and AL come on*]

FRED: I'm in trouble — I've got to sing at a concert for the soldiers, and I've lost my voice, I've got a splinter in it. Could you sing for me? D'you know any soldier songs?

AL: Well, I know 'Let Me Like a Soldier Fall'. I could do that.

FRED: The very thing. Let's have a little rehearsal, to hear how it sounds.

[*AL moves to centre stage*]

FRED: No, I shouldn't stand there; come further back, it will sound better.

[*FRED leads AL to marked spot. AL strikes a pose, and sings.*]

AL: *Brave manly hearts confer my doom,*
That gentler ones may tell,
Howe'er forgot, unknown my tomb,
I like a soldier fell . . .

[*Sack falls from flies onto AL, floors him. FRED laughs merrily, exits. TOMMY comes on. AL gets up, sees TOMMY, has a brainwave. Grabs TOMMY by the arm, tells him the same story. Puts him on the spot.*]

TOMMY: Why do I have to stand here?

AL: It'll sound better there.

[*TOMMY dashes down stage*]

TOMMY: But I'd rather be down here.

[*AL pushes him back*]

AL: No, you must be back here. [*aside*] I had to, so you must!

[*Same back-and-forth biz repeated. Finally, Tommy sings.*]

TOMMY: *Tho' o'er my clay no banner wave,*
Nor trumpet requiem swell,
Enough they murmur o'er my grave,
He like a soldier fell . . .

[*Sack falls from flies, Tommy poleaxed. Does drawn-out stagger round stage. Eventually falls. Now George comes on. He's small and weedy. Al and Tommy conspire to work the trick on him.*]

AL: . . . d'you know 'Let Me Like a Soldier Fall'?

GEORGE: I know it backwards.

[*Turns his back on the audience, sings*]
Yes! Let me like a soldier fall
Upon some open plain . . .

AL: No, don't sing *there*, come back here.

[*They escort him up stage, doing funny walk. George scurries back. Chase as before. George does 'false alarm', pretending to rush back: others rush after him, but he stays where he is.*]

GEORGE: Alright, 'Let Me like a Soldier Fall' for three and a tanner.

[*Strikes a pose, sings*]
Yes! let . . .

[*Stops, clears throat. Others giggling in suspense, pointing up. George starts again.*]

GEORGE: *Yes! let me . . .*

[*Stops, coughs. Pulls up trouser legs, showing red socks. Starts again.*]

Yes! Let me like a soldier fall
Upon some open plain . . .

[*Basket descends with whisky and glass. George pours himself a glass, puts whisky back in basket. Basket is pulled up.*]

GEORGE: Good health!

[*He drinks, and exits. Al and Tommy open-mouthed. Look up, rush to the spot. With hands outstretched to receive basket, they sing together.*]

BOTH: *Yes! Let me like a soldier fall . . .*

Yes, you've guessed it! Sack comes down, floors them both. Exit on hands and knees. Laughter, and applause.

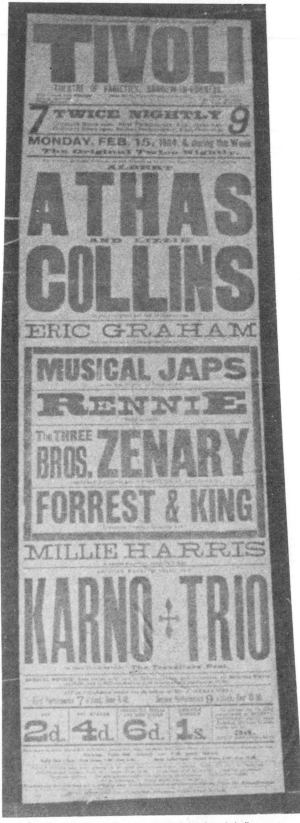

The Karno Trio, billed to appear at Stan Laurel's local music-hall

In 1902, the Three Karnos were appearing at the Palace Theatre, Hammersmith ('tip-up seats, v. comfortable' in Jack Melville's gallery guide), on a bill that included T. E. Dunville, Leslie's Leaping Dogs, and George Formby (senior). Across London, at the grander Palace Theatre in Shaftesbury Avenue ('30-minute wait, far side best'), an American act called The Three Keatons were billed to make their first London appearance, with Vesta Victoria and Prof. Ernest (the Human Orchestra). This is how one horrified critic described the Keatons.

A very abusive father, a silly, distracted mother, and a solemn child, possessed by the devil, and equipped with a suitcase handle between his shoulders so that he can be flung about the deck without tearing his clothes. Having used the child as a 'human mop', and threwn him into the scenery quite violently, the father starts making a very poor speech to the audience. The solemn son returns, with a cricket-ball tied to the end of a clothesline. He mounts a table, and swings his weapon around his head. But the rope isn't long enough. The speech continues. The solemn and still unseen son gets down, pulls the table six feet nearer, revolves the ball and at last knocks the parental hat off, and — at the next revolution, bounces the ball severely against the parental skull . . .

The solemn child was seven years old at the time. London audiences were taken aback at the ferocity of the act, and although there were some titters from the gallery, the rest of the house watched, in anxious silence, the Keatons knocking one another about.

Buster Keaton: a professional acrobat from the age of four

After the first performance, the manager of the Palace, Walter Kelly, asked Joe Keaton to tone down the rough-house. 'You're *scaring* the audience,' Kelly told him. 'They think you're really hurting the kid.' There is no doubt that the London audiences' concern was heightened by the child's obvious unhappiness. He never smiled, never gave any indication that he might be enjoying himself, and preserved a stony-faced indifference. A masterly performance from a seven-year-old. Half a century later, Buster Keaton explained the rationale behind this.

If something tickled me, and I started to grin, the old man would hiss 'Face! Face!' — that meant 'freeze the puss'! The longer I held it, why, if we got a laugh, the blank pan or the puzzled puss would double it. He kept after me, never let up, and in a few years it was automatic. Then, when I'd step on stage or in front of a camera, I *couldn't* smile . . .

The Keatons returned to America after a week, quite disillusioned with London's over-sensitive audiences. The act didn't last many more years; Buster grew too big to be thrown, and Joe became too drunk to handle him. Buster recalled that Joe

The Three Keatons: Buster, father Joe, and mother Myra

night after the show his osteopath, Mr Ying, worked remorselessly on the accumulated damage to torn ligaments, sprained muscles, wrenched bones. His fingers were raw from rope burns, his feet permanently grooved by the high wire. 'I only fell off four times,' he boasted. 'The first time I hit the stage it hurt so much I cried. I had to turn my back on the audience.'

Not so easy, in the real circus ring. When Pavel Borovikov fell off the wire at Saratov, the Russian clown Popov tried to camouflage Borovikov's exit by parodying his fall and his limping stagger. The audience laughed uproariously but Borovikov fainted once he was through the curtain and spent the next seven weeks in hospital.

In the nineteenth century, George Fréjaville described a French clown 'whose left cheek — having been too often " caressed", had become as dry as parchment, and whose left eye revealed a detached retina caused by the repeated shock of professional cuffing'. Will they never give up? In our century, in Copenhagen, the Danish clown Volkerson could still be seen, at the age of eighty, giving as good as he got. He made only one concession to his age: in falling, he would have to be lowered, ever so gently, to the ground by his fellow clowns.

was 'mad most of the time, and he'd look at you as if he didn't know you .... When I smelled whiskey across the stage, I got braced.' He got his own back the night Joe forgot to put the protective steel cap under his comic bald wig. Buster banged away with a broom-handle as usual, until Dad lay unconscious on the stage floor.

The line between the 'nap' which is pulled (which doesn't hurt) and the 'straight nap' (which does), is a very fine one, and the road to the audience's heart is littered with broken limbs and damaged organs. Lupino Lane, stalwart of British pantomime for a quarter of a century, sustained a Pott's fracture (broken shin) after a daredevil leap through the scenery. 'They told me I would never dance again,' he recalled, but, nothing daunted, he allowed himself to be matched in a straight nap routine with Will Evans, a heavyweight comedian. 'It began to be very painful,' said Lupino after the event, 'but I was foolishly too proud to admit that I couldn't take it; only after an operation on my ear did Will Evans find out that he'd been hurting me ....'

Michael Crawford, playing the part of P. T. Barnum at the London Palladium in 1981, broke box-office records, at some physical cost. Every

Michael Crawford in the title role of *Barnum*

Charlie Drake, up to his neck in it as usual; *The Cracksman* (1963)

Abbott prepares Costello for the fray; *Abbott and Costello Meet the Invisible Man* (1951)

Charlie Drake's X-ray plates must take pride of place in any catalogue of comic casualty. This bouncing ball of a man made a speciality, on British television, of being thrown, Keaton-like, through windows, bookcases, fireplaces, drainpipes. He's 5 feet 1½ inches tall. Today he says:

> I can't remember the worst bruises. But they're all in the game — you just take 'em and keep going. In a way, I prefer a broken bone. It's easy enough to carry on when you're in plaster, but it's no joke in bandages.... I broke my neck in the West country. I've broken nearly all my toes — two of them at the Palladium. Both my legs, and a thigh, too. I did my ribs all down one side, my thumb's been busted, collar-bone's gone. But I never pull my punches. You can't, can you, if you want the big laughs?

Charlie was launched on his bone-crunching career at a Butlin's holiday camp, where he was a red-coat entertainer. One of his duties was to referee the wrestling matches. More often than not, the fight ended with two heavyweights throwing the pint-sized referee into the audience. Today, all-in wrestling owes more to the circus ring than to the gymnasium, and it seems to have inherited the vociferous and boisterous audience of the music-hall, cheering their fancy and baying for blood.

The essential 'business' of the comedy wrestling or boxing match was laid down by Karno for his sketch 'The Yap Yaps'. The protagonists were Harry Weldon, a dour, ill-tempered 'heavy' with a vicious straight nap, and a new recruit to the company, Charlie Chaplin, whose elder half-brother, Syd, had been with Karno for some years. It was Syd who suggested to the 'guv'nor' that he should give Charlie a chance. At their first meeting, Karno was not impressed:

> Syd brought him along — a pale, puny, sullen-looking youngster. I must say that when I first saw him I thought he looked much too shy to do any good in the theatre.

Chaplin's encounter with Weldon is annotated in Jack Melville's notebook for 1908. To remove any doubt, Jack marked the Good Laugh Points with an asterisk.

> Charlie enters first. Cheers from crowd. Then Harry enters ring. When Charlie sees him, he falls back on his stool, tries to escape from the ring*. Second fetches him back, Chas does nancy walk round ring*. They spar up. Harry swings, Charlie ducks under his arm * and runs round ring. Harry misses Chas, hits ref*. Harry falls on hands and knees, Charlie kicks him on the bum*. Harry gets wild, goes for

Chaplin, recycling the old routine for *City Lights* (1931)

Charlie, hits him. Charlie very groggy, waltzes with Harry*. Ref stops them, sends them back to corners. Second gives Charlie oxygen. He quivers, goes mad, knocks ref and seconds out of the ring, then floors Harry*. Cheers. All sing 'For He's a Jolly Good Fellow'.

When Chaplin made his film version, *The Champion*, six years later, he added some new 'sight gags' to the Karno framework. His opponent was the villainous Mack Swain.

Before they enter the ring, Mack wipes his feet in the rosin tray — Charlie wipes his *bum*!* In the ring, Charlie bows to the audience over the top rope, somersaults*. They rush at each other, miss, knock out seconds*. Charlie walks along bottom rope as if it were a tight-rope*. They spar up. Charlie rests on Mack's right, while Mack hits him with his left. Charlie swings, misses — Mack falls as if blown down by wind*. Mack on floor, bum in air, Charlie uses it as a chair*. Mack up, rushing at Charlie, missing, bouncing off rope, Charlie also bouncing, missing. Charlie's dog comes to the rescue, bites Mack's bum*. Charlie KOs Mack.

Caption: 'To the victor belong the spoils.' Charlie kisses Edna, drinks beer.

Harold Lloyd was the next to try his hand at film fisticuffs. *The Milky Way* was one of a sequence of Lloyd comedies that followed closely on the release of Chaplin two-reelers, with a marked similarity in setting and 'business': Chaplin's *The Fireman* preceded Lloyd's *Fireman, Save My Child!*; *The Cure* inspired *Pipe the Whiskers*; and *Easy Street* was the basis of *Lonesome Luke on Tin Cat Alley*.

Buster Keaton donned the gloves for *Battling Butler* (1926), which is remarkable for the ferocity of the punches: straight nap here, no pulling.

With the coming of sound, Lou Costello went three rounds with the Invisible Man. Bud Abbott was Lou's heartless second.

LOU: Throw in the towel!

BUD: I can't — it's too dirty!

Danny Kaye lost on points, won on laughs in *The Kid from Brooklyn*. And Frank Randle, the Lancashire grotesque, added further refinements to the basic routine in *It's a Grand Life*. A nice touch was the second's handling of the water bottle ('get it well down his throat!'), while in the fight itself, Randle used such neat ploys as stamping on his opponent's feet, blowing him over, getting the ref to 'hold him still while I belt him!', and standing on his victim's hair for the count.

In the comedy of violence, how it *sounds* is all-important. A slap makes a more satisfying noise than a punch — even more so if the impact is accentuated by a stagehand providing a synchronised 'clap' from the wings. The original 'slapstick' — a sword-shaped wooden bat — was devised on the principle of creating the maximum amount of noise with the minimum injury. Its blade was split down the middle to produce a most convincing sound effect whenever it was applied to head or bottom by the knavish Harlequin, up to his tricks.

In the nineteenth century, a pinch of gunpowder was inserted in the cleft of the slapstick, with suitably explosive results. In the early cinema, the percussionist in the pit orchestra provided the aural punctuation by synchronising a crash on the drums to every on-screen impact.

Lupino Lane as Harlequin, armed with the slapstick

With the coming of sound, the actual recorded sound of fall or blow became available, but was soon rejected in favour of juicier noises selected from the sound-effects library and 'dubbed' onto the sound track, thus enhancing the visual impact of every violent encounter.

The Three Stooges were masters of this antic art. Their films are memorable for the ferocity of the trio's treatment of one another. No opportunity is missed for the slap on the head, the punch in the belly, the poke in the eye. Carefully orchestrated, their collisions sound almost musical.

LARRY, CURLY, MOE *are trying to get through a door, simultaneously.* LARRY *gets cross.* LARRY *slaps* MOE (SPLAT!).

CURLY: Here, don't do that! [LARRY *pokes Moe in the eye* (BOING!). LARRY *turns to poke* CURLY, *but* CURLY *covers his eyes, so* LARRY *slaps* CURLY's *head* (BAP!). CURLY *covers his head, uncovering his eyes, so* LARRY *pokes* CURLY *in the eye* (BOING!). CURLY *covers his eyes, so* LARRY *slaps* CURLY's *head, again* (BAP!).]

MOE: Here, don't do that! [LARRY *turns to poke* MOE, *but* MOE *covers his eyes, so* LARRY *punches* MOE *in the belly* (BOOF!). MOE *clutches belly with both hands.* LARRY *pokes* MOE *in the eye* (BOING!). MOE *covers belly with one hand, eyes with the other.* LARRY *slaps* MOE *on the head* (BAP!)]

And so on.

Slapstick in sound *only* was a logical development of this, but it took radio producers twenty-five years to wake up to the possibilities of the non-verbal joke — the 'unseen action gag'. The pioneers in this unlikely field were a quartet of ex-service performers who, in 1951, used to gather in the upstairs room of a London pub to feed one another's appetite for nostalgic non-sense: Milligan, Sellers, Bentine and Secombe. At first, the BBC called them *Crazy* People, which was fair enough. Within a year they were *The Goon Show*, with a weekly licence to disrupt the sedate BBC Home Service in unspeakably silly ways. The Goons' 'cartoon in sound' overturned the conventions of

The Three Stooges: (from left) Curly Howard, Moe Howard, Larry Fine

radio situation comedy, and created a surreal aural landscape in which anything could happen. And when it did, the noise was awful. Sound effects of horrendous complexity were devised to give a new dimension to the fall, the blow, the explosion. . . .

BLUEBOTTLE: Oh, a cocktail — good health [*Gulp*].

FX: MAMMOTH LONG RUMBLING EXPLOSION. BOOTS FALLING TO FLOOR, TEETH, ODDS AND ENDS.

BLUEBOTTLE: You rotten swine! You have nearly deaded me — look, my kneecaps have dropped four inches. Who made that cocktail?

GRAVELY: Molotov.

Meanwhile, in another corner of the forest,

BLOODNOK: He's escaping!

SEAGOON: Where?

BLOODNOK: There — stick your head out of the window.

FX: HEAD BEING STUFFED THROUGH GLASS WINDOW. BREAKING GLASS.

BLOODNOK: Bandage?

SEAGOON: No thanks.

BLOODNOK: But you're bleeding awful . . .

Three weeks later, at the head office of the South Balham Gas Board,

FX: MATCH STRIKING — QUICK WHOOSH OF SHELL — SHELL EXPLODES.

SEAGOON: Any questions?

CRUN: Yes — where are my legs?

The crash that's *heard*, but not seen, was also exploited in film by canny editors, who saw that you could extend the laugh and add an element of suspense, if the inevitable impact took place off-camera. Oliver Hardy was a past-master of this.

Falling off the roof, or through the window, or down the chimney, his long, wailing 'oooooooooooooh' would be curtailed by the awful sound of 260 pounds of Ollie hitting mud, brick or water. A moment of suspense, and then, the cut to the pathetic tableau: Ollie surfacing in the rain-barrel (iced), floored in the kitchen under the contents of every cupboard within reach, or framed in the fireplace, in the debris of the demolished chimney, a few single bricks dropping like afterthoughts onto his head. Another moment of suspense, then Ollie wonders 'Was that the last one?', looks up to check, and gets 'one more for luck' right in the eye.

Peter Sellers, as the accident-prone Inspector Clouseau, also created some memorable after-the-event tableaux. In *The Return of the Pink Panther*, the inept inspector is investigating a curious table-lamp. He tries a finger in the socket (well, he would, wouldn't he?). A blinding flash, cut to sofa on the other side of the room to see Clouseau slowly rising behind it, each individual hair standing on end, light-bulb glowing cheerfully in his hand. There's always a look of puzzlement on Clouseau's brow when fate has dealt him another drop-kick. He never sees them coming, although the audience can see them a mile off. Sellers explained:

You must remember that Clouseau thinks of himself as one of the world's best detectives. Even when he comes a cropper, he must pick himself up with that notion intact . . . I think a forgivable vanity humanizes him and makes his fortitude kind of touching. It's as if the audience is kept one fall ahead of him.

Sellers' Clouseau is the latest in a long line of comic coppers, bumbling their way through the story of knockabout. Along with the pratfall and the 'nap', the *chase* is an essential element,

Doodles from Spike Milligan's *Goon Show* script, 'The Hastings Flyer', first broadcast in 1956

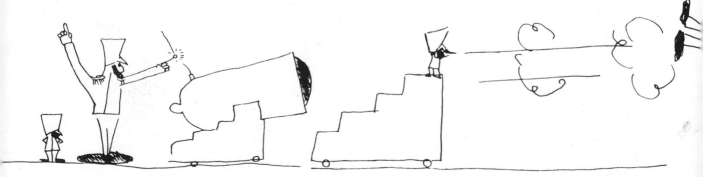

building up the momentum for a suitably bone-crunching collision in the last scene or reel. The officer of the law (or'leauw' in Clouseau's vowel-mashing drawl) observes the villain *in flagrante delicto*, and the chase is on.

As early as 1725, John Rich devised a pantomime called *Harlequin Sorcerer, with the Loves of Pluto and Proserpine*, in which the roguish Harlequin is chased by a village constable.

Trade is at a standstill; journeymen of all crafts are knocked down in the pursuit, and eased of their moveables by this most open and bare-faced ill-doer. Redress is out of the question; a shopkeeper aims at him with his broom, and smashes — his own window. The constable at last catches him; he tumbles down amidst his guards, and slips down from 'em, like an unskinned eel; every cranny is a refuge; he bolts through doors, darts through glass, climbs walls, and slips down chimneys with a celerity that sets pursuit at defiance.

When Sir Robert Peel created his first official police force in 1829, the 'Peeler', 'Raw Lobster', or 'Blue Bottle' became the villain of the piece — an object of derision, fair game for any kind of baiting, teasing or provocation. George Sala describes a pantomime scene in the 1870s in which

shopkeepers are tripped up, old ladies are pushed, young girls romped with, babies sat

upon or crammed into pillar boxes. There is a general row; the police make their appearance, and are duly bonneted and trampled upon . . . and the scene closes.

Fifty years on, the 'Blue Bottles' are still rushing to the rescue, but now the speed has quickened. A blur of helmets, flying tailcoats, waving truncheons, pelting from entrance to exit, trampling anyone or anything in their path. The Keystone Kops are passing through — but they can't stop, destined as they are to spend their celluloid lives in perpetual motion, spilling in and out of cars, running in every direction, falling in great heaps. And all this at the frantic, para-normal speed of forty-two frames per second.

Mack Sennett set this whirlwind in motion, and by 1913 he was producing one-reel and two-reel silent comedies at the rate of four per week from his studios in Edendale, a suburb of Los Angeles. A graduate of the early Biograph Studios, Sennett was a supreme technician. From epic director D. W. Griffith, he had learned how to pace a film — the skills of shooting and editing that allow a scene to build to its climax, and keep the audience sitting on the edge of their seats. Like all great showmen, Sennett had a 'nose' for popular taste. If he found something funny there was a good chance that millions of others would laugh with him. The Sennett style was a blend of lunatic fantasy, preposterous physical typcs, exaggerated costumes and make-up, frantic pace,

The Keystone Kops in full flight. Their last-reel pursuits provided the whirlwind climax to dozens of Keystone comedies, 1912 to 1920

and violent action. Many of the early films were improvisations, shot off the cuff and on the spot — a laundry, a restaurant, a park, a crossroads.

In *The Knockout*, the Kops are in pursuit of Fatty Arbuckle, who is himself in pursuit of Edgar Kennedy. Their chase takes them over the rooftops of Los Angeles: we see them silhouetted against the skyline, leaping, sliding, diving from roof to roof. Kennedy plunges down a skylight into a fashionable party. Arbuckle follows; then come the Kops, hot on their heels, driving a swathe through the high-society crowd. It's as close as Sennett came to making a social comment.

Clouseau as himself, shedding groceries

Peter Sellers disguised as Chief Inspector Clouseau disguised as Quasimodo; *The Pink Panther Strikes Again*

Fred Kitchen, the gentle giant:
never missed a performance,
1875 to 1945

In contrast to his frenzied celluloid colleague, the music-hall policeman, in the early 1900s, was characterised as a slow-moving, gormless booby. For his 'Jail Birds' sketch, Fred Karno created one such in Sergeant Lightning, who makes his first entrance with an oil lantern, and some excruciating puns.

LIGHTNING: I've had a very busy day. They sent for me to the public house, publican was knocking his wife about. I couldn't arrest him — being a publican, he was licensed to lick 'er!

Then I was called to the baker's shop. Poor girl had been electrocuted. Sat on a bun and the currant ran up her leg!

Then I had to go to the railway station. A man was eating fruit in a carriage: he was chewing the date off his ticket!

VOICE OFF: Hoy, Mister Policeman, there's a bloke here knocking his wife about — he's kicking her —

LIGHTNING: Ain't he got a hammer?

VOICE OFF: Come and help.

LIGHTNING: How big is he?

VOICE OFF: About six foot four.

LIGHTNING: Sorry — I'm off duty.

This unpromising material was turned to good advantage by the first 'star' comedian to emerge from the Karno stable — Fred Kitchen. His father was a Clown in Drury Lane pantomimes. Young Fred made his first stage appearance at the Prince's Theatre, Portsmouth, where he was carried on stage in his father's arms, in a play called *The Dumb Man of Manchester*. Thirty years later, he lumbered on-stage at the Paragon, Mile End Road, and, as Jack Melville recalled,

he was *made*. I used to go round the back of the gallery to watch him, 'cos he always made me laugh. He was a big, burly man. When he talked, he made a noise something between a whistle and a lisp. He always took his teeth out before he went on stage! He used to do a huge, exaggerated shrug of resignation when things went wrong for him. And of course they always did!

Kitchen's most distinctive features were his feet, which were huge and always encased in even larger black boots. His legs were bandy in the extreme, so that, from the stalls, Kitchen's lower half took on the perfect shape of the last letter of the Greek alphabet: Ω. When he moved, arms and upper body were as if paralysed, while legs advanced in a rocking part-shuffle, part-hop.

Other members of the Karno company were very envious of Kitchen's 'funny walk', which never failed to raise a laugh. It's even been suggested that in later years one or two of them tried to copy it. What an unkind thought.

CHAPTER THREE

BEST FOOT
· FORWARD ·

'THE EXPRESSION of a clown is mostly in his knees,' wrote the American poet E. E. Cummings — and certainly a good turn of foot puts the acrobatic comedian one jump ahead of his more articulate colleague, who has to *say* something to raise that first, elusive laugh. At the first glimpse of Kitchen's outsize boots, music-hall patrons sat back and relaxed, hilarity guaranteed. First impressions are all-important. Here's how John Rich dashed onto the stage of Drury Lane Theatre, some two hundred years before Kitchen:

In comes Harlequin, bending himself now this way, now that: bridling up like a pigeon: tipping out his toe like a dancer: then taking a fantastic skip: then standing ready at all points, and at right angles with his omnipotent lath-sword. Giddy as we think him, he is resolved to show us that his head can bear more giddiness than we fancy; and lo! beginning with it by degrees, he whirls it round into a very spin, with no more remorse than if it were a button. Then he draws his sword, slaps his enemy into a settee: and dashes through the window like a swallow.

This is the early model of the Anglo-Saxon Harlequin. Rising above the rude buffoonery of his Italian forebears, he has become an agile, leaping Harlequin — a patchwork Superman who uses his slapstick as a magician's wand to effect startling transformations. And he found his ideal interpreter in the uneducated, eccentric John Rich, who turned the Lincoln's Inn Theatre into a showcase for his acrobatic talents. His figure appears in popular prints of the day, poised in mid-flight, slapstick tucked under his arm. He moved like a ballet-dancer; he could scratch his ear like a dog, and rapidly execute two or three hundred steps in an advance of three yards. His

Marty Feldman, aptly cast as the grotesque Igor, in *Young Frankenstein* 1975

dressing-room was always full of cats, whose feline grace and agility must have rubbed off on their agile master. The French poet, Theodore de Banville, paid tribute to Rich and his company:

Between the adjective 'possible' and the adjective 'impossible' the English pantomimist has made his choice: he has chosen the adjective 'impossible'. He hides where it is impossible to hide, he passes through openings that are smaller than his body, he stands on supports that are too weak to support his weight; while being closely observed, he executes movements that are absolutely undetectable, he balances on an umbrella, he curls up inside a guitar-case — and throughout, he flees, he escapes, he leaps. And what drives him on? The remembrance of being a bird, the regret of no longer being one, the will to become one again.

Today, Ken Dodd puts it another way:

I think we have lots of minds — layers of minds — and in one of our primitive minds there's a great admiration for men who can leap over bars and swing from ropes. I think there's something in the darker recesses of your mind that recognises this animal skill that some people have . . . There's a little Stone Age man in everybody.

Rich knew this, and soon the 'House Full' notices were going up outside Lincoln's Inn Theatre, as the master of fancy footwork pirouetted his way through *Amadis: or the Loves of Harlequin and Columbine*, *Harlequin-Hydaspes*, and *The Magician: or Harlequin a Director (of the South Sea Company)*.

In 1723, seeking safety in numbers, Drury Lane presented no fewer than eight Harlequins in a pantomime called *Blind Man's Buff*. The audience, who were by now quite *au fait* with the Rich 'myth and magic' cocktail, were not impressed by this unnecessary overmanning and hissed the otiose octet off the stage. The next season, the theatres at Drury Lane and Lincoln's Inn both announced pantomimes on the theme of Dr Faustus, and theatre-going became increasingly hazardous as stage staff competed to conjure up the best 'burnings of hellfire'.

An ex-pupil of Rich, Henry Woodward, became the star Harlequin at Drury Lane. Son of a Southwark tallow-chandler, Woodward was an accomplished mime, 'a great master of grimace', who played to the eye 'with a mere monkey's art, twisting and turning and torturing every limb'. He found a visual expression for every line, which he would act out in dumbshow, as if he were playing a game of Charades. At the word 'waiter', he would mime the wiping of a glass or the drawing of a cork; 'tailor', and he would be measuring off several yards of cloth on the flap of his coat; 'undertaker', and he flapped his hat, pursed up his brows, clasped his hands, and with exaggerated solemnity strode across the stage. But as an acrobat, Woodward was not in the same league as his master, Rich. In fact, he pioneered the use of a double to achieve superhuman leaps. A death-defying plunge from gallery to stage was engineered by the simple device of substituting a second, identical, masked Harlequin, whose arrival on stage was camouflaged by thunder and lightning effects. Inevitably, there was a night when the synchronisation was less than perfect and the two Harlequins met in mid-air, to the gallery's delight.

Unlikely stunts and 'happenings' became the order of the day — the more preposterous, the better. At the Haymarket Theatre the announcement of a conjurer's intention to disappear into a pint bottle drew a packed house. The conjurer then took the wise precaution of rendering himself invisible for the entire performance and a riot ensued. Next day, Rich advertised

the recent arrival from Italy of Signor Capitello Jumpedo, a surprising dwarf, no taller than a common tavern tobacco pipe, who can perform many wonderful equilibres, on the slack or tight rope: likewise he'll transform his body in about ten thousand different shapes and postures; and after he has diverted the spectators two hours and a half, he will open his mouth wide, *and jump down his own throat*.

John Rich died in 1761, two months after the coronation of George II. After his death, pantomime became respectable: even those who had reviled the Harlequin shows gave due credit to Rich's 'matchless art and whim, that gave the power of speech to every limb'. The Scottish actor, John Jackson, vividly recalls the scene where Rich's Harlequin emerges from an egg which has been hatched by the heat of the sun:

This was a masterpiece in dumb-show. From the first chipping of the egg, his receiving motion, his feeling the ground, his standing upright, to his quick Harlequin trip round the empty shell, through the empty shell, through the whole progression, every limb had its tongue,

and every motion a voice,
which spoke with most miraculous organ, to the understandings and sensations of the observers.

Rich's legacy, the pantomime, flourishes to this day. The only form of theatrical entertainment that can be guaranteed to 'fill the plush' from December to January, the 'Christmas Panto' also preserves the spirit of the music-hall. As devised by Rich, a fairytale story provides the loose framework into which a particular artist's routine, or speciality act, can be slotted. The logic is inescapable: in the Forest Scene (*Babes in the Woods*, Act Two), Gertie Gitana might say, 'Oh dearie me, I'm lost and alone. I think I'll play upon my saxophone' — which, since she just happens to be carrying it in her shopping basket, she would then produce and embark upon a five-minute solo.

It was pantomime that brought the 'Champion Clog-dancer of the World' to the stage of Drury Lane Theatre (almost a hundred years before *Chorus Line* and *Dancin'*), and London audiences were entranced by as nifty a pair of legs as ever twinkled under seven layers of petticoat.

Mother Goose, Act One, Scene Two:

The curtain rises to reveal a humble widow, seated in a country cart alongside a crate containing live geese, and peacefully driving a pair of donkeys along a country lane. As the cavalcade reaches the crossroads, a motor car horn is heard and a car driven by a huge gentleman, enveloped in furs, dashes into the cart. Over goes the cart, and there ensues a scene of the wildest confusion, amid which one has visions of the widow in all parts of the stage at once, raising the struggling donkeys to their feet, rescuing geese that had escaped from the crate — and finally, grasping by the neck an excited and struggling goose in either hand and alternately slanging the chauffeur in English, French and German . . .

Dan Leno had arrived, and for the next sixteen years he ruled the roost at Drury Lane with a succession of queenly performances that established the 'Dame' in pantomime as a male prerogative, to be exercised in later years by, among others, Charles Coburn, T. E. Dunville, George Graves, Wilkie Bard, Sir George Robey, Arthur Askey, Leslie Sarony, and Danny La Rue.

Harlequin's Leap. From a toy theatre sheet, c. 1820: Harlequin dives through the mirror, confident that two stage-hands are waiting behind it, with a carpet. And two months and thirty yards of sticky tape later . . .

Music-hall comedians, adapting their own comic 'patter' and 'business' to the pantomime situations, brought the fairytale down to earth. Magic, and spangly, stylised costumes were not in keeping with the new-found realism of 'kitchen-sink panto', where household events and everyday occurrences would provide the spark for comic invention. Instead of magical slapsticks, washtubs filled with tattered underwear and tables laden with uncooked, adhesive pastry became the stage 'props', as Dan Leno and his false-bosomed sisters explored the comic potential of what theatre historian W. R. Titterton described as the 'true bread-and-butter stuff, the divine surprises of every day — the fun of getting drunk, of going on the spree, of backing the winner, of meeting a fairy; the dangers of falling in love, of getting married, of coming home late, of having a mother-in-law, of meeting the broker's men; the fun of fights, fires, christenings and funerals; the fun of being a policeman, a porter, a plasterer, or a publican; the fun of losing one's job, the grotesque folly of being an exceptional person'.

Just such a one was Dan Leno, born into just such a world — St Pancras, London, 1860. He made his first stage appearance at the Cosmothica Music-Hall in Paddington, aged four. He was billed as 'Little George, the Infant Wonder, Contortionist and Posturer'. His father died that same year and his mother married William Leno. On his next public appearance the infant wonder was introduced to the audience as 'Dan Patrick Leno, Descriptive and Irish Character Vocalist'. He cleared the house by singing 'Pity the Poor Italian', dressed as a diminutive organ-grinder, with live white rats crawling over him. With his stepfather, and a boyhood friend, Johnnie Danvers, he toured the British Isles. Their act encompassed Comic Songs, Acrobatic Scenes and Eccentric Dances.

In Belfast, Charles Dickens saw the Lenos perform and was considerably impressed by young Dan's dancing. 'Good, little man, you'll make headway,' he said, patting the boy on his head as he came off stage. Of his own dancing skills, Dan used to say 'I can put more beats into sixteen bars of music than a drummer can with his drumsticks'. From his travels in the north of England, he had acquired the knack of the 'clog-dance' — a largely improvised sequence of kicks, rolls, taps, twizzles and shuffles which Dan, being small and light on his feet, could put together in dazzling style. After a series of contests in Leeds, Accrington and Oldham, Dan was declared 'Champion Clog-dancer of the World' and awarded a gold and silver belt, of which he was inordinately proud. Twenty-five years later, in Sunderland, the contestants for the same championship included, from London, Charles Chaplin, and from Ulverston, Stanley Jefferson, who later changed his surname to Laurel. The clog-dancing title eluded them both.

In 1885 Dan Leno appeared at the Forester's music-hall in London, for a salary of £5 for the week. He sang two songs and then — the Big Finish — donned the clogs and did his stuff. To his surprise, the audience were quite unimpressed by the dance, although his singing ('When Rafferty Raffled His Watch') was well received. For subsequent appearances, at Collins' Music-Hall in Islington, the Queen's, Poplar, and the Standard, Pimlico, he was billed simply as 'Dan Leno, Vocal Comedian'. The gold and silver belt was left at home and Dan began to develop the character studies which became his speciality. Asked to explain their origins, he said:

> The characters of my songs are all founded on fact. To get the effect out of such songs is not as easy as it looks. In the first place you have to catch your song, and you will understand the difficulty when I tell you that I have fully 150 songs at home for which I have paid from one to five guineas each, and which are utterly useless. Sometimes I sit up all night studying a song, and trying to see chances of effect in it, until I finally get out of temper and throw it in the fire. I study hard for all my songs, and my favourite way of doing that is to walk for a few miles in the rain, keeping time with my feet to the tune.

From these watery researches came the Ice-cream Man, the Beefeater, the Recruiting Sergeant, the Floor-walker (who spent so much time on his feet that 'he had to turn his legs up at the bottom when his feet had worn away'), and the Railway Guard ('based on a fussy little man I used to see at Brixton Station, rushing up and down, shouting at everybody, and himself doing nothing whatever'). In 1888 he was elevated to the peerage and played the Baroness in *Babes in the Wood* at Drury Lane. Three years later came the final accolade: Queen of Hearts, in *Humpty Dumpty*. His biographer, J. Hickory Wood, identifies Dan Leno's particular magic in regal 'Dame' roles:

> When he acted a queen, she was quite a possible queen, even though she lived in such

conditions that a pair of braces was the natural thing for her to buy the king on his birthday, and the mistake of handing him the *wrong* parcel (containing underwear), to be opened in full view of the court, the not unnatural outcome of her ways of life.

When Leno was Queen, the King was played by Herbert Campbell — a large, solid droll who provided the perfect complement to Dan Leno's quicksilver. It was an ideal partnership and in subsequent seasons the Leno/Campbell double-act provided many memorable scenes. Hickory Wood describes their attempts to gain admission to the ball (in *Cinderella*), having lost their tickets:

The Baroness explains the situation to the haughty flunkey, while the Baron 'stands by', and puts in an occasional remark — short, but generally to the point. They *are* Prince Charming's bosom friends, and what if they *do* happen to have lost their tickets? That kind of accident might happen to anyone. Then come the various stratagems designed to frustrate the flunkey's vigilance, Dan going in *backwards* to look as if he was coming out — Herbert's idea of passing in without being noticed! Finally, an entire change of the situation, when Dandini enters, rebukes the flunkey, and commands him to let the worthy pair pass in at once. Then ensues the triumph of the Baroness. She really doesn't care whether she goes in or she doesn't. Just to show that no flunkey can interfere with her, she *will* go in. Yes, and just to show that she is perfectly free and independent, she will come out again — and keep going in and coming out as long as she likes, with a 'Now I'm in! See?' and 'Now I'm out! Eh?' directed at the flunkey each time she passes him.

Dan Leno as himself *(left)*, as Mother Goose *(centre)*, and as Dick Whittington *(right)*. Leno drawings *(behind)* from a postcard sent to his pal Johnnie Danvers

Dan Leno played his last Drury Lane pantomime in 1903. The final scenes of his life were played out the following year, and, as so often in the lives of the great laughter-makers, the end was tragic. A series of breakdowns, bouts of amnesia, irrationality — then, suddenly, on 31 October 1904, the death of Dan Leno, aged forty-three. The cause was subsequently identified as a tumour on the brain. His friends consoled one another with the thought 'better to wear out than rust out'; while those who had known him only across the footlights mourned in their thousands. Max Beerbohm put their feelings into words:

I defy anyone not to have loved Dan Leno at first sight. The moment he capered on, with that air of wild determination, squirming in every limb with some deep grievance that must be outpoured, all hearts were his. That face, puckered with cares, whether they were the cares of the small shop-keeper, or of the landlady, or of the lodger; that face so tragic, with all the tragedy that is writ on the face of a baby monkey, yet ever liable to relax its mouth into a sudden wide grin, and to screw its eyes up to vanishing point over some little triumph wrested from Fate, the tyrant; that poor little battered personage, so 'put upon', yet so plucky, with his squeaky voice and his sweeping gestures, bent but not broken, faint but pursuing, incarnate of the will to live in a world not at all worth living in — surely all hearts went out to Dan Leno, with warm corners reserved in them for him for ever and ever?

In an age when the timeless essentials of visual comedy were in danger of being swamped by a deluge of comic 'patter', the tiny, frantic figure of Leno — 'an exquisite, reckless, irresistible farrago of fun', as Max Beerbohm described him — provided the necessary link in the chain, and carried the slapstick baton into the twentieth century. His successor, already waiting in the wings of Drury Lane, was, unbelievably, even smaller than Leno. But what he lacked in stature he made up for in agility of leg. *Punch* called him 'first and foremost, both the least and the greatest': Little Tich.

He never grew taller than 4 feet 6 inches. He was born with an extra finger on each hand. His name was Harry Relph and he was the son of the landlord of The Blacksmith's Arms at Cudham, in Kent. When he was ten he could play the tin-whistle, and would entertain customers dancing on the cellar-flaps of public houses in Gravesend.

He learned to dance on points, and in clogs (who didn't?). In 1884 he appeared at the Marylebone Music-Hall billed as:

YOUNG TICHBORNE
Surnamed the Claimants Bootlace
The Eccentric Little Negro Comedian & Champion
BIG CLOG DANCER
The Little Licker of the Loose Leg Business
THE WONDER OF THE STAGE,
HAVING SIX FINGERS AND ONE THUMB
ON EACH HAND —
A DECIDED NOVELTY

The 'Claimant' was, in real life, an Australian butcher who claimed that he was the missing son and heir of Lord Tichborne, tragically lost at sea. The butcher failed to prove his claim and was sentenced to fourteen years for perjury. In the process, he became a national celebrity. As he weighed more than twenty-eight stone, 'Tichborne' became a much-used nickname for huge persons, just as, forty years later, Fatty Arbuckle served the same purpose. The contrast between the gigantic 'Bullocky' Orton and tiny Harry Relph gave the 'Tichborne' label a topical irony. Soon abbreviated to 'Tich', it became common parlance for anyone small.

At Drury Lane, Little Tich was Humpty Dumpty when Dan Leno was Queen of Hearts; in *Little Bo-Peep* he was Hop o' My Thumb; in *Robinson Crusoe* he played a diminutive Man Friday. But he didn't like the pantomime and complained: 'A comedian doesn't get much chance there at Drury Lane. He may be stuck up in his dressing-room for hours while they're procehsing on the stage.'

He was happiest in the music-halls. Invariably top of the bill, he entranced audiences from Accrington to Exeter. His size startled a Portsmouth critic, who noted that Tich was just 'some three feet in height'. His speed of movement was remarked on by the *Birmingham Post* reporter: 'there are certain of his steps and twists in dancing which are done quicker than the eye can follow them'. He was 'seemingly not troubled with bones'; his body seemed 'strung on wire', and his legs could 'wink'.

Like Dan Leno, Little Tich specialised in character songs. J. B. Priestley described them as 'daft miniatures' — a bus conductor, a big-game hunter, blacksmith, barber, pirate, huntswoman, Spanish señora. As a lost-property officer, he sang of his six hundred umbrellas, and twenty-four glass eyes gazing on the wooden legs hanging all around. And, as 'The Charlady', he claimed to 'do' for the House of Commons:

In the Lobby I dance
When I get half a chance —
They call me the Char-ing Pavlova.
But one day I got hurt
For I tripped in my skirt
And I skid on the soap and fell over.

The lyric took on a tragic irony when Tich did this routine at the Alhambra Theatre, in 1927. A bit of comic 'business' required him to stand on the head of his mop, thus making the handle flip up into his hand. On the fateful night he failed to catch it and took a glancing blow on the side of his head. Three days later he suffered a stroke, never spoke again, and died in February 1928.

Little Tich is a key figure in the history of visual comedy. Now, for the first time, the film camera is on hand to record the pint-sized genius in action.

Right: Little Tich. The Big Boots were an indispensable feature of his act for twenty years; he grew to hate them

Far right: He tops a bill which records an early appearance of 'The American Bioscope'

SHEPHERDS BUSH
EMPIRE
MONDAY, NOV. 16th, 1903
Inimitable
LITTLE
TICH
HAYDEN
CLIFFORD
ATHAS & COLLINS
DUNNING
WARREN
THE AMERICAN
BIOSCOPE
THE DESERTER!
CLIMBING THE ALPS IN A MOTOR CAR.
HARCOURT
NEWMAN
BOCCACCIO
MINSTRELS
Signor FRANCIA

In 1902 a pioneering French cameraman recorded a two-minute extract from Tich's most celebrated routine — the 'Big Boots' dance. And suddenly the word-pictures of admiring journalists acquire a filmic reality as the tiny figure clomps about the stage in boots that seem as long as he is tall. In fact, they were twenty-eight inches long, and very heavy. They make a satisfying 'slap' every time foot hits floor. They enable him to lean at a perilous angle and pick up his hat from the floor without bending the knees. He can do the splits, sideways, with straight legs. He can sit, facing the camera, with the boots as a curtain; he opens them to peek through, closes them, and catches his fingers. And for the Big Finish he uses the full length of the boots as stilts, making himself almost seven feet tall. All that's missing from this priceless strip of celluloid are the asides which Tich used as a *sotto voce* commentary on the routine when it was beginning to bore him. 'Comic business with chapeau,' he would mutter, as he lowered head to hat. And '*very* difficult', as he teetered on extended tiptoe. And, when he'd had enough, 'that's about enough of *that*, I think'.

In the year that Little Tich was immortalised on film, Fred Karno's Army had reached Stockport, Lancashire. At the Hippodrome Theatre, Karno was promising Gorgeous Scenery, Brilliant Effects, and Clever Dancing, in a Grand Pantomime, *The House that Jack Built*. Sadly, there's no visual record of this epic production, or of the first appearance on stage of the Chaplin/Melville partnership. They shared one part between the two of them — and one skin — as Dobbin, the lovable, durable pantomime horse (Charlie was the front end, Jack the back). As always, Jack's diary keeps detailed notes of the 'business' to be employed (best laughs starred):

When horse lays down on side after tricks, sides go up and down as if panting. Dame says 'Oh, he's got the wind up.'*
Walking round stage, horse walks in quick short steps, almost nancy.
Front end sits on front of pedestal, crosses legs: back end *stands* on pedestal.* Still in this position, they walk round pedestal. Then back end jumps onto back of front end.*
After short simultaneous dance, dame says 'Come over here' and points to left. Horse crosses to *right*, rests against proscenium arch, crosses legs.*
N.B. For dance, horse does our drunken step, forward heel forward and back. What we know as our drunken step in concerted numbers.

The principle that four legs are better than two was established many centuries before Chaplin and Melville synchronised at Stockport. A picture in a Stockholm museum offers a clue to the pantomime horse's Italian ancestry. The picture conjures up a scene from the seventeenth-century *Commedia dell' Arte* — an episode in theatre history that has suffered from being labelled with a somewhat forbidding title. The coupling of 'comedy' with 'art' sounds ominously highbrow, suggesting serious, academic examination instead of a good laugh. The genre deserves better.

In the Stockholm picture, the players are doing the 'Serenade to Columbine' routine. There's a house with an open window in which the beautiful Columbine can be seen, feigning indifference. A weird-looking gang is approaching the window. There's Pantaloon, who is a doddery old man. He wears a tight-fitting red vest, red breeches and stockings, and soft slippers. The top half of his face is covered by a red mask with a conspicuously hooked nose. On his head is set a soft cap without a brim, like a Turkish fez. He is perched precariously on what appears to be a spindly horse, but on closer examination this is seen to be made up of two men huddled under a voluminous cloak. The 'front end' is dressed in a patchwork suit consisting of pieces of red, blue and green cloth cut in triangles. He wears a small black hat, which hardly covers his shaven head, and a black mask, with wrinkles, which has no eyes but only two tiny holes for seeing through. This is Harlequin. As a concession to his equine impersonation his head is encased in a bridle, with the bit firmly clenched between his teeth. Of the 'back end' of the horse, nothing can be seen except his slippered feet.

Escorting horse and rider is another masked character in a full, white shirt, long, loose trousers and a wide-brimmed circular peasant's hat. He carries a scroll from which he appears to be prompting the aged horseman as they approach the open window.

PANTALOON: Oh, Columbine, my life, my joy,
                Come heed these words from your
                    darling boy:
                My life will end, I'll surely die,
                If in your arms I cannot lie.

COLUMBINE: Impudent Pantaloon, do you think you can capture the flower of my youth with your monstrous proposals? No, no! To couple a virgin with an old man is to extinguish a glowing fire in the snow.

Pantomime horse, from 1580. Harlequin (front legs), Pedrolino (hind legs), Pantaloon (mounted), Zany (prompting)

Pantomime horse, from 1951. Under the skin: Jock Young (front legs) and Charlie Mills (hind legs)

HARLEQUIN: Sing up, Pantaloon, sing well, if you want to win your fair mistress.

PANTALOON: Courage, my friends. I've nearly finished. Give me time, and the sweetness of my voice will penetrate her soul.

And so on. The dialogue is improvised, so the scene can be as long or as short as the players wish. If the audience are responding well, new bits of comic 'business' can be introduced and the basic situation can be extended ad infinitum. If they're not getting the laughs, then the leading player will produce one of the stock 'exit lines', which is the cue for the company to make a speedy departure from the stage.

In these prototype situation comedies, the mask was all-important. As it covered two-thirds of the face, it reduced the actor's scope for 'mugging' and muffled his voice. Consequently, large and unequivocal gestures were needed to convey emotional responses: the body and limbs were used in distinct poses — a kind of mime shorthand to put the audience in the picture. An actor might talk of 'playing the back', or 'playing the head', as if the different parts of the body were separate instruments for creating effect. First and foremost, of course, were the feet. One early Harlequin used his feet to box his enemy's ears. A funny walk was also obligatory, and jokes relating thereto.

HARLEQUIN comes to PANTALOON's house to collect a gift that he must deliver to COLUMBINE. He knocks on the door. PANTALOON opens it.

PANTALOON: Ah, Harlequin, here you are at last. I have the parcel ready — just walk this way.

[*He turns and leads HARLEQUIN into the house, hobbling painfully on his arthritic old legs. HARLEQUIN follows; taking PANTALOON's instructions literally, he parodies the old man's movements.*]

'Walk this way' — an essential first principle of visual comedy is encapsulated in those three words. 'Walk this way' should *not* be interpreted as 'follow me', but rather as 'walk in the way that I do', with a touch of comic exaggeration to get a laugh. It never fails, nor does it weaken by repetition. Here's the Thin Man (William Powell) following the bandy-legged *maître d'hôtel* into the restaurant, with a quizzical look and a passable imitation. Or, Young Frankenstein attempting to reproduce the grotesque Igor's hunchbacked hobble (Marty Feldman). Or Hope and Crosby, on the road again, following the beckoning geisha girl (Hope: 'Walk this way? I could never pass the physical!'). It crops up again in *History of the World — Part One*: scantily clad Trojan woman leading, ogling Mel Brooks following. A two-handed version by Abbott and Costello in *Pardon My Sarong*; three-handed from the Ritz Brothers (*One in a Million*); foursome from the Marx Brothers *passim*. And a nice twist, from Jack Benny, at the lunch counter:

> BENNY: Have you got frogs' legs?
>
> WAITER: No — it's the rheumatism . . .
>
> ALL TOGETHER NOW:
> . . . that makes me walk this way!

'Film comedy is all a matter of *legs*,' declared Jacques Tati, and went on to prove the point most elegantly in his series of films featuring the long legs of Monsieur Hulot. Like Little Tich, whose big boots enabled him to lean forward at a preposterous angle, Monsieur Hulot seems to slant forward as though balancing against a gale. A short raincoat, pork-pie hat, umbrella held like a low-slung rifle, and jutting pipe complete the picture of this human Leaning Tower of Pisa — the inclination being towards disaster. 'He promenades, that's all,' said Tati. 'He takes a walk, innocent and tranquil. He simply looks at things. Is it his fault if we have baptised him with our invented desires and needs? And if, believing ourselves to be serious, we have insisted on being solemn?'

The unmistakable shape of Monsieur Hulot

Tati, born in Paris, was apprenticed to a London picture-framer in the 1920s. But he fell in love with music-hall and decided to become a 'turn'. His first attempts were sporting parodies — a fisherman grappling with a slippery catch; a goalie faced with quickly changing situations; a 'Vimbledon' tennis-player. Colette saw him and was impressed: 'he makes you see invisible partners, and objects in his empty hands'.

In 1931 Tati made his first short film, *Oscar, Champion de Tennis*. Monsieur Hulot was created in 1951 for a film, *Monsieur Hulot's Holiday*, that was five years in the making. In the following twenty years, he made only three more films — *Mon Oncle*, *Playtime*, and *Traffic*. In obsessive detail, Tati charts the growing imbecilities of our technological civilisation, and our guide through the maze is the solemn, concerned figure of Monsieur Hulot, always on the edge of things, mildly curious, always vaguely hopeful that something interesting may develop. The solemnity, like Keaton's, is deliberate. Instead of presenting a normal world ravaged by a comic personality, Tati reveals a world made comic by the sobriety of Monsieur Hulot.

In *Mon Oncle*, his sister lives in a totally automatic, ultra-hygienic house where the garage door opens magically whenever the car passes an electronic eye. No allowance has been made, however, for canine interference, and a dachshund sniffing harmlessly at the eye imprisons sister and brother-in-law in the garage. Tati shows their disembodied faces, yelling inaudibly for help through the garage porthole windows, bobbing about like air-bubbles in a bricklayer's spirit-level. Hulot, meanwhile, is consorting on bomb-sites with his natural allies, mongrel dogs and dirty children, or stretched out contentedly — all 6 feet 4 inches of him — on the pavement, still wearing his hat, and with his pipe jutting up like a submarine's periscope. He can make asphalt look like an air mattress; he can also make it clear that a modern piece of furniture feels uncommonly like asphalt. There are no close-ups in Tati's films. He explained why:

> Music-hall is one of the reasons why I like to shoot from far away, on the *legs*. Take Keaton's legs, for example. You could have a sound-track through the means of his legs. A dialogue. Interrogation. Then decision. Finally fear. But the audience must observe this for themselves. If you bang their nose against the screen, they won't see things in perspective, that the whole *world* is funny. You don't have to be a comic to make a gag.

Putting the boot in: Jacques Tati in *Monsieur Hulot's Holiday* (1951)

Tati in *Playtime* (1968)

Tati died in November 1982. His projected next film had been on the drawing-board for twelve years. The title was *Confusions*:

It's about the fact that you can't take people at face value any more. Men in trench coats with briefcases turn out to be manual workers, while important young photographers and writers dress like plumbers. No one is identifiable — except perhaps the old English guy in the bowler hat.

Which sounds like a cue for the legs of Cleese to make a startling appearance round any convenient corner. Toe comes first, at waist-height, followed by interminable lengths of pin-striped leg, horizontal, joined to torso, vertical, topped with head, bowler-hatted. It was in the Monty Python television series that the 'Ministry of Funny Walks' was first established, with John Cleese adding a new dimension to the 'walk this way' routine — a sinewy, balletic version of the goose-step. In another guise, and tweeds, the legs of Cleese support the frantic frame of Basil Fawlty, manic host of *Fawlty Towers*. Unlike Monsieur Hulot, Fawlty seems to slant *backwards*, usually because his brain has not caught up with the fact that his legs are on the move again, in a desperate dash to head off approaching, inevitable disaster. Occasionally the time-lag between head and heels is so marked that he appears to be in two scenes at the same time — arriving legs make a whirlwind diversionary entrance while departing head is still explaining, ranting, prevaricating, grovelling . . . .

The legs of Max Wall are usually encased in very black tights and very large black boots. In the 1920s, he appeared on music-hall bills as 'Max Wall and His Independent Legs'. He did an 'eccentric dance', which developed from a fairly sedate routine of taps and twists into a simulated lunatic frenzy in the course of which clothes would be shredded, hair torn out, false teeth sent flying. During the war Max Wall refined this taxing routine down to the more sedate antics of Professor Wallofski — he of the tights, boots, pudding-basin wig and manic stare. This ludicrous figure is usually introduced by a tall lady.

LADY: Ladies and gentlemen, tonight it is my privilege to bring to you a pianist of some note — and here he is, the man who has left his brain to the nation, unused: Professor Wallofski.

[*PROF. comes on (funny walk)*]

What are you going to play for us, Professor?

PROF.: Liszt's Hungarian Rhapsody, number two.

LADY: Oh, Liszt! I love him!

PROF.: Do you really? Well, perhaps you'd like me to dig him up?

LADY: Dig him up? I was referring to the man's work, not the man himself!

[*She seizes the PROF. by the lapels, lifts him up to her level. When she drops him, he stays stretched, and walks around in an elongated position. The LADY tries to help, presses down on his shoulders. Too much! Now he's walking around only three feet tall, swinging his arms like a chimpanzee...*]

What follows is not so much a performance of Liszt's Hung. Rhaps. ('which I will play with the aid of an AA map and a spirit-level'), but more a series of ingenious prevarications: the funny walk/march across stage, bottom jutting, spindly legs slip-sliding;

Max Wall: Professor Wallofski

'business' with piano stool ('ooh, look: a little potty inside!'); 'business' with arms (one has become longer than the other); at last the crash of the first chord, except that he's forgotten the lid.

Professor Wallofski first saw service with the Royal Air Force where Max Wall was a Wop/Ag (wireless operator/air gunner), more interested in raising laughs than downing enemy aircraft. His ancestry can be traced to the great Swiss clown, Grock, who topped the bill at the Empire Theatre, Paris, when Max Wall was still in the small print. As well as 'business with piano' (moving piano to stool, instead of the other way round), Grock developed the non-playing of the violin to a fine art. Almost ready to play, he would have to leave the stage on a mysterious errand, carefully placing the violin to his left, the bow to his right. On his return, he would find, to his dismay, that the bow was offering itself to his left hand, violin to the right — a bewildering situation. When that was sorted out, he would listen to the orchestra playing his introduction, and, in a spirit of bravado, toss the bow into the air — and fail to catch it. Annoyed, he would retreat behind a screen, above which the audience could see the bow rising and falling, obviously being caught every time. Out he would come, beaming, ready for anything: music begins, bow confidently tossed into the air — missed again!

Norman Wisdom uses saxophone, piano and drums for his comic props — and occasionally plays them, rather well. His expertise on the drums comes from nightly 'lessons in rhythm' on a machine of his own masochistic invention. The dreaded 'Plinker-Plonker' is a triple-edged torture device; he who sits in it is perfectly positioned for a hammer to strike from above, gloved fist from the side, spiked grab from below. Any passing sadist can be enlisted to put Norman through his paces: when the hammer falls, he must beat the drum; when the fist strikes, he must stop; when the spikes grab, he must hit the cymbal. 'Music, maestro, please...'

A pair of army boots, size seven, set Norman Wisdom on the road to laughter, through tears. He says:

> I was born in very sorry circumstances. Both of my parents were very sorry: they got divorced, they didn't want me. So at fourteen I was walking the streets, sleeping rough, very miserable. Then I joined the army as a band-boy. They sent me to India with the 10th Hussars. I learned how to play the saxophone and the xylophone. In the wash-house, late at night, I taught myself how to tap-dance, and

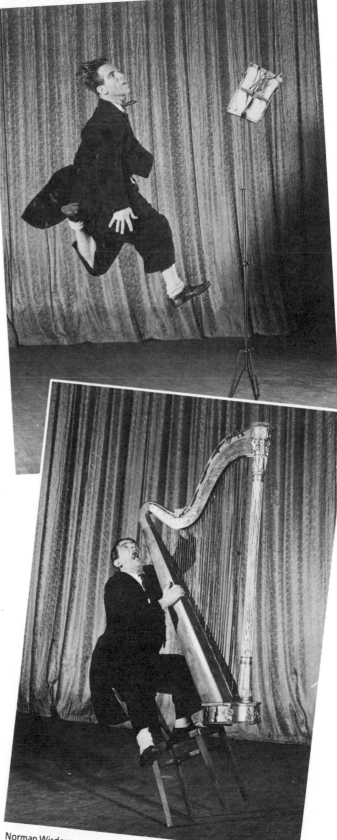

Norman Wisdom: musical mayhem from *London Melody* at the Empress Hall, Earls Court, 1951

John Cleese as Basil Fawlty, on the go. A cartoon by John Jensen

through the turn. And Keaton — torso immobile, face frozen, legs a blur — running for his life from policemen, would-be wives, avalanches.

A late entrant to the race is Michael Barrymore, television comic for the 1980s. This lanky Londoner preys on members of his audience, plucking them out at random for spontaneous interviews — 'I bet you're wishing you'd never come!' More remarkable is the *speed* at which he goes about his business — bouncing off the walls, ploughing through the orchestra, charging into the scenery. When last seen, Barrymore was breaking new ground with a series of 'leg impersonations', specially concocted for the 1983 Royal Variety Performance. Standing on his head, legs in the air, he offers a faultless caricature of Lester Piggott ⟨⟩; Harvey Smith ∨; Larry Grayson ⋁. This last takes the prize as the most ingenious piece of 'leg business' so far devised: the double inversion, one limb ramrod straight, the other cocked at the knee, *limp* at the ankle. Definitely one for the notebook.

then, at the next concert in the officers' mess, I did my stuff. Still in army boots, mind you, and trying to dance while still standing to attention! So, of course, they started laughing at me. Then I got a bit cross, tried all the harder, and started falling over my feet. And they laughed all the more! *Then* I began to think: 'I like this!' I fell about all over the place; they were hysterical. Well, that was it. I never looked back.

Fifty years on, Norman Wisdom is still going strong. In his thirty-shilling 'gump suit', with matching cap, he struts onto the stage with a jaunty, marathon-walker's swagger, chin held high, bottom projecting. For all his optimistic bravado, the audience can be sure of one thing: that very soon he will be splayed all over the floor, limbs scattered. Comic inevitability defines He Who Gets Slapped, and He Who Falls Down.

'Walk this way', the man said — and still they come. Here's Groucho Marx's unmistakable crouching lope, cigar leading. . . . Here's Jerry Lewis, each leg responding to different signals from the brain — one walks, the other runs . . . Here's Chaplin, skidding round the corner, outer leg raised, body heeled over to balance him

Michael Barrymore, showing a leg to the Queen

A · MAGNIFICENT
SHAMBLES

IT'S AN ANNUAL challenge to raise a royal laugh. The Royal Command Variety Performance brings Her Majesty the Queen and her family to the Palladium Theatre, London, to be amused and entertained by today's generation of music-hall artists. It started in 1912, when Sir Oswald Stoll persuaded King George V and Queen Mary to grace the royal box at the Coliseum with their presence. Grand Duchess George of Russia and Princess Henry of Battenberg were also present that night, when the artists included Harry Tate, Wilkie Bard, Chirgwin 'The One-eyed Kaffir', and Little Tich, who was totally overawed by the occasion. And Vesta Tilley caused a sensation by appearing in *trousers*. Queen Mary was seen to avert her eyes from the stage during Vesta's song.

In 1983 the Royal Command Performance took as its theme, 'The Dance'. Ballet star Graham Fletcher paid tribute to Little Tich, in boots too short by half. Billy Dainty conjured up a one-man version of 'The Lancers'. Les Dawson complained that he had been introduced into the evening 'for ballast'. And there were dancers, in all shapes and sizes, from disco to go-go, point shoes to tap. Royal yawns were being stifled behind velvet programmes, royal glances stole to royal watches, when a small man in a roomy black jacket and soft black hat shot onto the stage as if propelled from a gun. What followed was quite unusual. The programme stated simply 'George Carl'. What it didn't say was that George Carl would spend

the next eight minutes splitting royal sides by . . . doing nothing. Or, failing to do anything. Or, reducing an act to a shambles.

Here's his script for the eight minutes. No words, all action:

> Enter (rushin' ballet).
> Biz. with mic, biz. with wire.
> Adjust dress, biz. with no pockets.
> Hat off, bow, hit mic.
> Jacket roll-over.
> Hat rolls.
> More biz. with wire, thumb in button-hole,

> wrestle with braces, thumb in eye.
> Biz. with sleeves (long/short).
> Fetch table, trap thumb.
> Adjust mic. (again), play mouth-organ.
> Biz. with foot (lost control).
> Biz. with gum, stuck to mic., pocket, foot, tongue.
> Play 'Honeysuckle Rose'.
> Band plays 'Can-Can'.
> Mouth-organ falls apart.
> Biz. with table
> (too heavy).
> Off.

It could have been tragic. The Little Man Who Played Before The Queen, only to find that his own limbs, his clothes, his props were conspiring against him, laying traps, subverting him. The microphone won't be adjusted to his height (he tries to *pump* it up, like a bicycle pump). The cable becomes entangled round the stand, his hand, in his coat, in his braces. When he frees himself from its coils and tries to adjust his dress, smooth out the wrinkles, he finds his pockets have disappeared. Panic! Coat off, whirled round, on again, in one continuous movement.

George Carl: pure comedy, equally effective in theatre and circus

Now, one sleeve (or arm) longer than the other (thank you, Professor Wallofski). Adjust, by jumping! Next, the folding table, which traps his thumb (produce giant swollen thumb). Finally, the mouth-organ; cue the band. Of course, they're playing someone else's music. Puzzlement; appeals to the wings; a desperate attempt to join in, and the mouth-organ disintegrates in a shower of tin.

In the event, he stole the show (a blatant case of Broadway robbery) from the elegant hoofers who topped the bill. Next day, George Carl was back in the sawdust ring of the Circus Knie in Zurich, making children laugh.

The comedy of the Inept Performer is, probably, a circus invention. The clowns, running on between the acts, were licensed to parody what had gone before: a bit of wobbly tight-rope walking, crumbling acrobatics, uncontrollable animals. On stage, without the giveaway of the clown costume, it becomes a more dangerous game. The act that 'dies', in reality, is a painfully embarrassing experience for performer and audience alike. To squeeze humour from apparent disaster is dicing with death. Especially if your audience includes crowned heads of Europe.

In 1904 the Shah of Persia paid a state visit to London; his engagements included an evening at the theatre. *Entertaining the Shah* was the show put on at the London Pavilion by music-hall artists. Fred Karno helped to stage it, supplying props and scenery from his Fun Factory in South London. With two companies on the road Karno had decided to broaden his theatrical base. He bought two houses in Vaughan Road, Camberwell, knocked them together and boasted that 'from the House that Karno Built we'll turn you out anything theatrical, from a pantomime, cast, scenery, dresses; everything complete down to a property periwinkle'.

The show for the Shah was not an unqualified success. There was clearly a language problem. Harry Clifton's 'motto songs' mystified their Imperial Majesties, while the Ethiopian Serenaders caused a minor diplomatic incident. Harvey and French did a comic dancing duet, 'Sandy, He Belongs to the Mill', and wished they hadn't. And James Hillier sang:

A tickle in the tunnel is a lark, my boys,
A tickle in the tunnel in the dark, my boys;
    'Tis nice to take your Mary Jane
    A-riding in a railway train,
And have a jolly tickle in a tunnel O!

From his seat in the stalls, Fred Karno watched his pals' increasingly desperate attempts to strike a spark of response from their royal patrons. And it gave him the idea for a show. Imagine a music-hall where each succeeding act is *worse* than the one before — and the first was a stinker. Now, imagine an audience which, not content with booing their displeasure, decide to climb up on the stage and *show* the artists what they think! A performer's nightmare, brought to life in Karno's greatest *coup de théâtre* — 'Mumming Birds', a sketch that eventually became a show in its own right. Here's how Jack Melville remembers it:

The stage is set with two extra sets of boxes, one on each side of the stage. When the overture begins, people come into the boxes. In the two upper boxes, there are noisy patrons, laughing, shaking hands, waving across.

Into the lower right box comes a Fat Boy in an Eton suit, with his doddery grandfather. The boy has a supply of cream buns, bananas, nuts, peas — and a pea-shooter.

The last to appear, in the box opposite the Fat Boy, is the Drunken Swell, in dress suit, monocle, white gloves. An usherette shows him to his seat. He takes his right glove off, swaying delicately, tips the girl, and then starts taking the same glove off (from bare hand). The usherette points out his error, and leaves him. He selects a cigarette from his case and tries to light it from the gas-lamp outside his box. Falls out. The stage manager comes out and puts number boards on a stand near the proscenium. Then the acts begin (they are all as bad as can be imagined).

The Saucy Serio flounces on. She sings (very *arch*):

Although I'm not a forward girl
As plainly you can see,
I know without the counting
How many beans make three.
When I think about you men
It really makes me sad:
The way that you treat us poor girls —
It really is too bad!

Oh, you naughty, naughty men!
You tease us and you squeeze us
But you never try to please us!
You naughty, naughty men!

Then she goes into her 'abandoned dance'. As she passes the Drunken Swell's box, he tries to grab her leg. Misses, falls out. Saucy Serio comes round again as he is clambering to his

Fred Karno's block-buster, 'Mumming Birds': a bit of 'rushin' ballet' for the finale

feet: she turns her back on him and throws her skirts up in his face. He falls back into his box.

Then it's the turn of the Topical Vocalist. He asks the audience for 'Items of Today', and makes up (very bad) rhymes for them. The Fat Boy shoots peas at him, and cream buns.

The Male Quartette come next. They are all different sizes, and wear ill-fitting dress suits. They sing (very horribly):

> *Come, sing to me,*
> *I long for you.*
> *Pray for your love,*
> *Tender and true;*
> *Sunshine is o'er me,*
> *No cloud I see,*
> *While I can hear your voice —*
> *Come, sing to me!*

After the first few bars the Drunken Swell climbs onto the stage and throws the singers into the wings, one at a time. When there is only one singer left (and he oblivious to the fact that he is alone, just reaching for his high note), the Drunken Swell collects a soda syphon from his box and squirts the wretched tenor into the wings.

On comes the Lady Vocalist. She is very big, very grand. The Fat Boy presents her with a bouquet of flowers. The Drunken Swell stands up to bow to her. She lets go the

bouquet, which flies into the Drunk's face (it's fixed by elastic) and knocks him back in the box.

She sings her song: 'And That's a Man'.

Next comes Mad Ralli, the Terrible Turk (he's scraggy, underfed, in fez and big moustache). The Fat Boy throws him a bun, which he eats ravenously.

The stage manager announces that there will be a prize of one hundred pounds to any challenger that the Turk fails to throw in fifteen seconds. The Drunken Swell says: 'I'll take him on!' He is hustled into the wings, returns in red underwear. The Turk does some wrestling biz., the Drunken Swell then tickles him into surrender. Then, Everybody On for the Finale.

It would be a brave producer today who would undertake to extract forty-five minutes of hilarity from that scrap of a scenario. And yet, in its time, 'Mumming Birds' was a riot wherever it played. The classic sketch of 'comic ineptitude', it became the model for many a 'magnificent shambles'. Parody, blended with anarchy, producing chaos — a potent new laughter-making formula. A dancer from Lancashire, Stanley Jefferson, joined the Karno company in 1905 and played every part in 'Mumming Birds'. Fifty years later, by which time he was better known as Stan Laurel, he described the piece as 'one of the most fantastically funny acts ever known — probably the greatest ensemble of the century'. It epitomised the Karno style, which set a new standard of professionalism in slapstick comedy. There was nothing 'hit or miss' about the playing; every laugh was calculated, every bit of 'business' timed to perfection, well rehearsed, carefully plotted. Karno's comics — he called them his 'plonks' — became masters of the slapstick arts, lethal with the custard pie, handy with the slapstick, primed for the fall.

Mumming Birds was booked for a tour of the top-flight Moss Empire Theatres. Karno was paid £165,000. There were no conditions on the contract, no 'star names' to be included, no options or 'get-out' clauses. Karno's name on the poster was sufficient guarantee of a packed house in Aberdeen, Barnstaple or Crewe. 'They used to laugh *before* they went in,' recalls Jack Melville. 'You'd hear them in the queue outside the theatre — "Fred Karno's here, ha ha! We're sure to get a good laugh!" '

With *Mumming Birds* on the road, Karno started to put together a new show. For *London Suburbia* he gave the lead to a new comedian, Syd Chaplin, son of a music-hall singer, Charles Chaplin, who specialised in sentimental ballads — 'Pals That Time Cannot Alter' and 'Yesterday' (by Tosti, not McCartney). Syd was paid £3 a week and the 'guv'nor' was pleased with his work. So when Syd asked Karno to give his step-brother, Charlie, a chance, Karno agreed to take him on. He was paid £3 a week initially: after he had acquitted himself honourably in 'The Yap Yaps', a ten-shilling rise was negotiated.

The new recruit was not well liked in the company. 'I've known him go for a week without saying a word to anybody,' the 'guv'nor' later recalled. 'Occasionally he would be quite chatty, but on the whole he was dour and unsociable. He lived like a monk, had a horror of drink, and put most of his wages straight into the bank as soon as

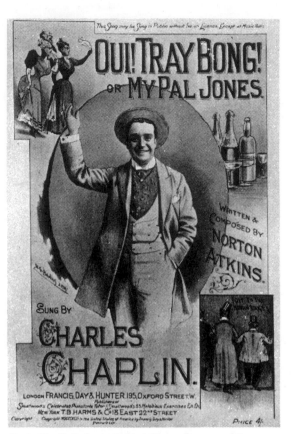

Charles Chaplin Senior: according to his son, 'he was a quiet, brooding man with dark eyes. A bit like Napoleon'

he got it.' Jack Melville remembers Charlie as 'an untidy little devil in those days. He used to sit in his pyjamas all day, playing the violin! He'd made up his mind that he was going to beat that violin — and of course he did; all those beautiful tunes he went on to write. But that used to annoy Harry Weldon. On a Sunday morning, when we all went down to catch the train to the next town, Charlie'd arrive late, looking very untidy, but carrying his precious violin. And Weldon would say, very sarcastically, "Look at the little genius! Look at him; hasn't cleaned his shoes this morning." '

In 1908 Chaplin and Weldon were billed together in a Karno production, 'The Football Match', at the London Coliseum. Working as always on a grand scale, Karno had made a huge back-cloth for the final scene, depicting the packed terraces of a football stadium. 'Live' actors were put in among the painted figures, so that, from a distance, the effect was almost convincing. Loose 'prop' arms were also fixed to the back-cloth, which appeared to wave hats and handkerchiefs. Against this spectacular back-cloth, the plot of 'The Football Match' unfolded. There wasn't much to it, no script as such, but one basic idea capable of endless comic elaboration.

'Stiffy', the goal-keeper, is harried by a villain who tries to persuade him to let in some goals and 'throw' the match. Harry Weldon was to play the comic part, 'Stiffy', and nineteen-year-old Charlie Chaplin was the 'straight man' (the villain). In his autobiography, Chaplin vividly recalls the opening night at the Coliseum:

My nerves were wound up tight like a clock. At the back of that enormous stage, I walked up and down, with anxiety superimposed on fear, praying to myself, There was the music! The curtain rose! On the stage was a chorus of men exercising. Eventually they exited, leaving the stage empty. That was my cue. In an emotional chaos, I went on. One either rises to an occasion or succumbs to it. The moment I walked on the stage I was relieved, everything was clear. I entered with my back to the audience — an idea of my own. From the back I looked immaculate, dressed in a frock-coat, top hat, cane and spats — a typical Edwardian villain. Then I turned, showing my red nose. There was a laugh. That ingratiated me with the audience. I shrugged melodramatically, then snapped my fingers and veered across the stage, tripping over a dumb-bell. Then my cane became entangled with an upright punching bag, which rebounded and slapped me in the face. I staggered and swung, hitting myself with my cane on the side of my head. The audience roared.

Now I was relaxed and full of invention. I could have held the stage for five minutes, and kept them laughing without a word. In the midst of my villainous strutting, my trousers began to fall down, I had lost a button. I began looking for it. I picked up an imaginary something, then indignantly threw it aside: 'Those confounded rabbits!' Another laugh.

Harry Weldon's head came round the wings like a full moon. There had *never* been a laugh before he came on! When he made his entrance, I dramatically grabbed his wrist and whispered: 'Quick, I'm undone! A pin!' All this was ad lib, and unrehearsed. I had conditioned the audience well for Harry, he was a tremendous success that evening, and together we added many extra laughs. When the curtain came down, I knew I had made good. Several members of the troupe shook hands and congratulated me. On his way to the dressing-room, Weldon looked over his shoulder and said dryly: 'That was all right — fine.'

That night I walked home, to get unwound. I paused, and leaned over Westminster Bridge. I wanted to weep for joy but couldn't. I kept straining and grimacing, but no tears would come. I was empty. I walked to the Elephant and Castle and stopped at a coffee-stall for a cup of tea. Then I walked home to Kennington, talking to myself. It was five in the morning before I got to bed, exhausted.

After two weeks in London 'The Football Match' was sent out on tour. The honeymoon was over. Weldon, whose part required him to knock his villainous opponent about a bit, started using the 'straight nap' technique — hitting Chaplin for real, instead of faking the blow. In Belfast the situation came to a head. Chaplin writes:

The critics had given Weldon a dreadful panning but had praised my performance. This was intolerable to Weldon, so that night on stage, he let me have a good one, which took all the comedy out of me, and made my nose bleed. Afterwards I told him that if he did it again, I would brain him with one of the dumb-bells on the stage. I added that if he was jealous, not to take it out on me.

'Jealous of you?' said he contemptuously, on the way to our dressing-room. 'Why, I have more talent in my *arse* than you have in your whole body!'

'*That*'s where your talent lies,' I retorted, and quickly closed the dressing-room door.

Harry Weldon, kitted out as Stiffy, the Goalkeeper for Karno's sketch 'The Football Match'

Back in London, Karno summoned Chaplin and told him he was to play the lead in a new sketch which was to be called 'Jimmy the Fearless' or 'The Boy Ero'. The idea was that young Jimmy falls asleep by the fire, where he's been reading stories of romance and adventure in his 'penny dreadful'. He is then projected into his dream-world where he rescues damsels in distress, wins great battles, discovers buried treasure, woos a fair princess — only to be woken rudely from his dream by a furious Dad who leathers him for letting the fire go out. Clever stuff, subsequently to be recycled for many a stage and screen fantasy, from *Peter Pan* to *Time Bandits*. Karno's version would make use of all the trick scenic effects of the old pantomime tradition: 'transformation scenes', traps, flaps, and flyings. However, to the 'guv'nor's' surprise, young Chaplin declined to take the part of Jimmy, whereupon Karno gave it to Stanley Jefferson, who made the most of it. The rest of the company were mystified as to why the most ambitious member of the troupe had turned down such a plum role. Jack Melville thought it was because the part was too *vocal*:

Charlie never had a good speaking voice. In those days, of course, they had no microphones, and in the big halls like the London Palladium, or the Coliseum, you needed a *big* voice if you were going to be heard in the gallery. That was Charlie's problem; but of course it was a good thing in the long run because it made him concentrate on becoming a pantomimic comedian first and foremost.

In the early days of music-hall, licensing regulations actually prohibited the use of dialogue. To protect the interests of the major theatres and prevent ambitious music-hall managers from encroaching on their 'dramatic' territory, the licensing authorities banned the spoken word from the halls and restricted programmes to song, dance, mime, and acrobatics. Initially, Karno complied with the letter of the law. 'FRED KARNO'S SPEECHLESS COMEDIANS' was the slogan borne aloft by the giant balloon he used for advance publicity. In the early, basic sketches, there was no need for words. The orchestra in the pit provided a noisy musical accompaniment to the action, and the only other sound that could be heard was the crack of the 'nap', the squelch of the pie, the thump of falling bodies. And the occasional groan. As Karno's sketches became more elaborate, a few lines of scene-setting dialogue became necessary, and this in turn led to a certain amount of illegal 'gagging'. Karno's scripts, however, were legendary for their brevity. The back of an envelope was all that Fred needed to encapsulate his pantomime premise. Ben Murray, a comedian from Liverpool, arrived for his first rehearsal with a Karno company to be given script, motivation and direction in ten seconds flat: 'Right, you, boy — you're a waiter. Pick up that tray, carry it across to the table, but trip on the carpet, and do a fall.' Which he duly did, to great effect. 'Since then,' recalled Ben about half a century later, 'I *never* missed an opportunity to bring a good tumble into the act.'

It was a sensible precaution not to put your best material down on paper. Piracy was rife in the music-hall and a good piece of comic 'business' was less likely to be 'lifted' by a rival if it only existed in the mind of its innovator and the skill of its performer. When the laws prohibiting spoken material were relaxed, the question of the copyright to a joke became a thorny issue. On the evidence of Jack Melville's notebooks (1905–08), the galleries of most London theatres were nightly filled with eager scribes, furiously transcribing every 'loose gag' they could catch.

In 1910, Karno recast 'Jimmy the Fearless' for a tour of the English provinces. Chaplin, who'd seen what Stanley Jefferson had made of it, told the 'guv'nor' that he'd like to take a crack at the title role. Karno agreed and Stanley raised no objections, for as Chaplin headed for Bradford, Yorkshire, Stanley found himself en route for New York, with a Karno company that was booked for eight weeks at Hammerstein's Music-Hall.

The American engagement represented quite a coup for Karno. Although English musical comedy had been produced on Broadway with some success, there were doubts as to whether the English sense of humour would engage a New York audience. Dan Leno had made the Atlantic crossing in 1897, also to play at Hammerstein's. Billed as 'The Funniest Man on Earth', he had some difficulty justifying this boast to the New Yorkers. The theatre critic of the *New York Times* had been particularly scathing:

It was absurd to presume that a London concert-hall singer could throw a New York audience into paroxysms of laughter, although it is easy to see how, on his native soil, Leno became the idol of the people who attend the London concert halls. He is just the kind of Englishman you would think would naturally appeal to Englishmen. He has just the manner and the ways which every Englishman finds, for some reason or other , excruciatingly funny. In New York he is worth seeing only as a type — not as a humorist. People unfamiliar with the English comique should find him interesting as a study.

Those warning words have echoed down the years. They should have been posted up above the gangplanks at Southampton Docks and the departure gates at London Airport. Many were called, but few were chosen; many were cold, and some were frozen. Are you listening, Harry Tate, Will Hay, Sid Field, Tony Hancock, Jewel and Warriss, Charlie Drake . . . ?

Fred Karno hit New York in September 1910. *Mumming Birds* was retitled *A Night in an English Music-hall*, and the cast included Karno's son, Fred junior, Billy Reeves and Stanley Jefferson. Shrewd as ever, Karno banked on the transcultural appeal of the 'last-gasp' music-hall — 'No patter, see? Just the old "one-two", the "nap", the "pratfall" — and that's the same in any language, i'n' it?' The show was a resounding success. Even while it was playing, Karno was contracted to send a second company to America to play a six-week tour on the Percy Williams circuit of theatres. Karno sent for Charlie Chaplin and offered him a place in the second wave of his invasion force. Chaplin was cock-a-hoop.

This chance to go to the United States was what I wanted. In England I felt I had reached the limit of my prospects; besides, my opportunities there were circumscribed. With scant educational background, if I failed as a music-hall comedian I would have little chance but to do menial work. In the States, the prospects were brighter.

Chaplin's first encounter with an American audience was inauspicious. As *A Night in an English Music-hall* was still playing to capacity at Hammerstein's, the second company opened at the Colonial Theatre, New York, in a new show, *The Wow-Wows*. From the first rehearsals, Chaplin had reservations about the piece's suitability for New York. A more sophisticated piece than *Mumming Birds*, it parodied the goings-on in an exclusive secret society — the Masons, perhaps. The jokes about initiation rites and secret signals depended to some degree on the audience's knowledge of the conventions that were being parodied. Karno, relying more on his first taste of success than any real knowledge of American ways, insisted that the show was just the thing for a country which, he claimed, was *full* of secret societies. Chaplin was not reassured; in fact, his misgivings were redoubled when he learned that the cast was to include a seventy-year-old Drury Lane clown called 'Whimsical Walker', who had some difficulty mastering his lines. As he carried the major part of the plot, such as it was, his inability to put his lines across — especially to a 'foreign' audience — was going to be a drawback.

Chaplin faced another first night in a tremor of nervous anxiety. 'My first joke was considered a big laugh back home and was a barometer for how the rest of the comedy would go. As "The Hon. Archibald Binks", I entered from a tent, carrying a tea-cup:

ARCHIE: Good morning, Hudson. Do you mind giving me a little water?

HUDSON: Certainly. What do you want it for?

ARCHIE: I want to take a bath.

(A faint snicker, then cold silence from the audience.)

HUDSON: How did you sleep last night, Archie?

ARCHIE: Oh, terribly. I dreamt I was being chased by a caterpillar.

Chaplin (right) with Karno's manager, Alf Reeves, and ladies, en route to the USA

Fred Karno's London Comedians hit Milwaukee. On the return visit
English Music-hall becomes *London Club*

'Still deadly silence. And so we droned on, with the faces of the American artists, who were watching from the wings, growing longer and longer. But they were gone before we finished our act.'

After this chastening experience, things got better. At the Fifth Avenue Theatre, the company found themselves playing to an audience composed largely of English butlers, valets and nursemaids, who found *The Wow-Wows* excruciatingly funny. After six weeks in New York they hit the road, playing Cleveland, St. Louis, Minneapolis, Kansas City, Denver, Butte and Billings. In California they played at Sid Grauman's Empress Theatre, San Francisco. Grauman said to Chaplin, 'any time you're through with the Karno outfit, come back here and we'll put on shows together'.

Back in New York, the second company took over *A Night in an English Music-hall*, which was as big a hit in the gilt and plush of the American Theatre, on Forty-second Street, as it had been in the spit-and-sawdust of Hammerstein's. For the next eight years, almost without a break, the show was playing somewhere in America, occasionally in pirated versions which deserters from the Karno ranks were producing on the sly. In Philadelphia, one such production took an unexpected turn when the stage manager invited challengers from the audience to take on the Terrible Turk. A small, red-faced man rose from

the audience. 'Yes, I'll have a go,' he called out, drawing a horrified 'My God, it's the guv'nor!' from the stage manager, who fled for the safety of the wings. The curtain was called down and Karno left Philadelphia with $3000 in damages.

In June 1912, Chaplin was back in England. After a fourteen-week tour which took in France and the Channel Islands, he was despatched once again to America. This time, Chaplin notes, the Karno company travelled second class on the *Olympic*, in contrast to the cramped cattle boat on which they had made their first transatlantic crossing. From New York they headed west on a five-month tour of 'the sticks', playing sometimes three or four performances a day of the full Karno repertoire: the sketches, 'G.P.O.', 'The Yap-Yaps', 'His Majesty's Guests', 'Early Birds', and the full-length shows, *The Wow-Wows*, and the inevitable *pièce de résistance*, *A Night in an English Music-hall*.

In Philadelphia, company manager Alf Reeves received a curious telegram:

IS THERE A MAN NAMED CHAFFIN OR SOMETHING LIKE THAT IN YOUR COMPANY STOP IF SO WILL HE COMMUNICATE WITH KESSEL AND BAUMAN 24 LONGACRE BUILDING BROADWAY STOP

Chaplin being the nearest approximation to 'Chaffin' in the company, young Charlie was deputed to make the necessary contact. From Kessel, he learned that film-maker Mack Sennett had seen him play the Drunk in the Karno show. And if Chaplin *were* that man (Sennett was never very good with names), would he like to sign a contract with the Keystone film company, to appear in three films a week, for a year? The salary on offer was $150 per week.

At first, Chaplin displayed his usual caution. He had seen several Keystone comedies and considered them 'a crude melange of rough and tumble'. With Alf Reeves, he had often discussed the possibility of making films of the Karno sketches, but, knowing nothing of the techniques of film-making, they had hesitated before taking the plunge. However, the Sennett offer presented the possibility of an introduction to the mysteries of film, as well as a new life in a pleasant environment. Also, despite his reservations about the Keystone comedy style, Chaplin recognised the publicity value of the studio name. 'A year at that racket,' he thought, 'and I could return to vaudeville an international star.' So a deal was struck, to take effect at the end of the Karno tour. He played his last performance with the company on 28 November 1913 at the Empress Theatre, Kansas City. He bought drinks for his fellow-plonks, and was touched to learn that a small presentation was going to be made after the show. In the event, nothing happened, and Chaplin subsequently learned that his 'present' was to have been an empty tobacco box, wrapped in tinfoil, containing some old stubs of greasepaint sticks. Arthur Dando, who hated Chaplin, had planned the stunt, but hadn't the courage to see it through.

There's no record of what Fred Karno said when Fred junior returned from America and reported Charlie's defection. Chaplin wasn't the first, or the last; at £15 a week the Karno players were fair game for dollar-waving impresarios.

Karno's meanness was his undoing. He had just spent £70,000 to build his Fun Palace, the Karsino, on the Thames, where he planned to hold court among the rich and famous. King Manuel of Portugal, the Duchess of Albany, Lord Curzon and Paderewski were among the visitors who came by boat for weekends of champagne, strawberries and entertainment. The 'plonks' were not impressed. Resentful of the 'guv'nor's' affluent lifestyle, they went on strike for more money. At the Empress Theatre, Brixton, Marie Lloyd sang a song of support:

> *Karno, Karno, open your eyes and wake!*
> *You're cutting your best boys' salaries down —*
> *Soon they'll have nothing to take.*
>
> *While you're on your island,*
> *The nobs will sell you a 'pup':*
> *If you don't want to lose the best boys that*
> *   you've got —*
> *Fred Karno, wake up!*

In 1915, the first of Chaplin's Keystone films were released in English cinemas — *Making a Living, Laughing Gas, A Busy Day, Dough and Dynamite*. Soon the new Bioscopes, the Electric Theatres and the Picture Palaces were boasting 'Standing Room Only' whenever a Chaplin film was on the programme. From his flat in Piccadilly, Fred Karno walked across to the Regent Street Bioscope to see his protégé in the new medium. With mixed feelings, perhaps, for along with the frantic chases, brawls and spills that characterised the Keystone house-style, he began to detect another, more familiar element. In Chaplin's *Work*, surely the comic 'business' of the incompetent decorators bore more than a fleeting resemblance to the routines of Karno's own 'Repairs', in which young Chaplin used to play the paperhanger's apprentice? In *The Champion*, a moustachioed villain tries to bribe a boxer (Charlie) to 'throw' the fight, using — apparently — exactly the same stratagems as the identical villain in Karno's 'Football Match'. And the boxing match in the same film follows, gag for gag, the contest that is the climax of Karno's 'Yap-Yaps' sketch.

As the films continued to roll in, at the amazing rate of three per week, Karno material was equally self-evident, either as the comic starting point for a film, or in the detail of the 'business' employed. From 'Early Birds' to *Easy Street*, from 'Hilarity' to *One A.M.*, from 'Skating' to *The Rink*, from 'His Majesty's Guests' to *The Floorwalker* — the connections are unarguable, and reveal the extent of Chaplin's debt to Karno.

Film-maker Mack Sennett: he converted Chaplin to celluloid

Did Karno ever object? Did he ever demand payment, or acknowledgement, for the use of his material? Apparently not — even when, in *A Night in the Show*, Chaplin's borrowings came closest to downright piracy. Here, correct in every detail, are the characters from *Mumming Birds*: the Drunken Swell leering from his box, the Fat Boy in his Eton suit with his bag of buns, and a succession of inept performers who take the stage in turn, to be greeted with scorn, derision, and custard pies.

The silent nature of film has dictated some modification of the scenario — the vocal performers have been replaced with more visual acts . . .

Karno's 'Repairs' sketch

Chaplin's film *Work*, made in 1915 for the Essanay Company

(there's a magician who disappears in a puff of smoke), and a gallery of down-and-outs has been introduced to provide a barrage of rotten tomatoes in the last reel. But the focus of the film is Chaplin, reproducing for the camera his well-established stage performance of the Drunken Swell.

It is curious that Chaplin's plagiarism drew no public reaction from Karno, who had protected his own copyright so vigorously in Philadelphia. Perhaps his legal advisers warned him against the hazards of trying to prove ownership of a piece of 'business'. So much of Karno's work derived from the traditional basics of slapstick, that there was little that could be produced, in the way of evidence, of the originality of his material. Jack Melville's notebooks are brimming with accumulated lists of 'gags', 'business', 'concerteds' and 'sketches', but no authors are credited.

A further complication lay in the very nature of celluloid — and here Karno had already had his fingers burned. After the first Continental tour of *Mumming Birds*, a French film producer had made a 'pirate' film version. Karno took the Frenchman to court, but lost his case when the judge ruled that the action should have been taken against the man who *physically* made the copy, rather than the producer. Recognising the futility of trying to sue the unfortunate camera operator, or the laboratory technician who processed the film, or even the projectionist, Karno dropped the case. 'Once bitten, twice shy'; and certainly the prospect of expensive litigation held little appeal for him in the latter years of the war. The Karsino was doing poor business and theatres were half empty. Perhaps Karno was aware that the names of Karno and Chaplin were linked together in popular mythology and that any hint of a rift would be bad publicity. The association was even being celebrated on the battlefields of the Western Front, where the tattered remnants of the British Expeditionary Force were singing:

We are Fred Karno's Army,
The ragtime infantry.
Fred Karno is our captain,
Charlie Chaplin our O.C.
And when we get to Berlin,
The Kaiser he will say
'Hoch hoch, Mein Gott,
What a jolly fine lot
Are the boys of Company A.'

Jack Melville recalls the birth of this classic soldiers' lament, in the recruiting offices and on the parade grounds, where untrained civilians gathered to 'do their duty for King and Country':

> And of course they were so totally unprepared, and the kit they were given didn't fit, and they had no rifles so they had to drill with brooms or spades or whatever — well, you can imagine what a sight they looked! And so they'd be laughing at one another — "What a right Fred Karno's Army we'd make!" — and that's where the song came from. And the saying, too — it's in the language, now, isn't it? A 'proper Fred Karno's' means a cock-up, a shambles, a disaster.

And the *Mumming Birds* tradition — the shambles of a show — was safe in the hands of the next generation of 'plonks' who invaded the Palladium Theatre in 1932, and kept the spirit of comic mayhem alive for the next thirty years. Originally, there were seven of them, recruited by Fred Karno for a new show called, simply, *Laffs*. A pair of acrobats, Nervo and Knox, specialists in slow-motion wrestling and 'rushin' ballet'; a pair of rollicking 'drunks', Caryll and Mundy; Naughton and Gold, slapstick supremos; and one certifiable maniac, 'Monsewer' Eddie Gray. This troupe of comic saboteurs were licensed to disrupt any attempt at 'serious' performance. During the tightrope act, they might come on, in turn, to argue with the orchestra. A chorus number might be undone by a madman with an axe chasing one of the lovelies up and down the aisles. The scenery might need repainting during a juggler's routine; in fact, any opportunity to slosh water, dough, foam, around the auditorium would be eagerly exploited by the aptly named Crazy Gang, God bless 'em. *Laffs* spawned Crazy Week at the Palladium. The following year Crazy Month was launched, with two new recruits, Flanagan and Allen, providing a nice line in silly interruptions and sentimental songs. Whether as bedraggled charwomen, grotesque fashion models, Shakespearean 'mechanicals', cavemen, or monks (soaring into the flies on uncontrollable bell-ropes), the new recruits to Fred Karno's Army quickly grasped the fundamental principles of cataclysmic comedy.

No one was safe when they were loose.

ALLEN: [*to* FLANAGAN, *observing* GRAY *with malevolence*]:   Who let *him* on?

FLANAGAN: Who let him *live*?

Sandy Powell, as The Guardsman: he used the same uniform on his disintegrating dummy

Sandy Powell didn't stay the course with Karno. He found the going too tough.

I wasn't very confident as a comedian and I think Karno knew this. He used to stand in the wings, shouting at me, when I was on. I think he thought he was encouraging me! 'Faster,' he'd yell, 'get it moving, they're falling asleep!' He'd get so mad he'd start booing, blowing raspberries — anything. I was frightened to come off!

One night, we were playing Collins' Music-hall and I was stood in the wings, waiting to go on. And I felt really sick; I thought I was going to faint. I turned to the guv'nor, who was standing beside me. I said 'Oh, Mister Karno, I do feel ill.' 'Bloody hell,' he said, 'better get on quick!' And shoved me out on the stage!

So Sandy went out on his own, and did very well. He took a leaf from Karno's book and developed a magnificently shambolic 'Vent. Act', complete with disintegrating doll and ill-concealed assistant in the wings providing the 'thrown' voice ('Can you hear me, Mother?').

The disastrous ventriloquist is irresistible. Eric Morecambe was once caught in the act.

ERIC [*to doll on knee*]: Hallo, Charlie, how are you?
[*similarly*] I'm very well, thank you.
ERNIE: Just a moment — I can see your lips moving.
[*a pause*]
ERIC [*baffled*]: Eh?
ERNIE: I can see your lips moving.
ERIC: Of course you can, you fool! Because it's *me* doin' it to him. He can't do it by himself — he's made of wood.
ERNIE: But you're not supposed to move your lips. That's the whole idea. When the dummy talks, *you* keep your mouth shut.
[*ERIC ponders this. Tries it.*]
ERIC: Hallo, Charlie, how are you?
[*silence*]
ERNIE: No, no! You've got to make a *noise*, but without moving your lips. You've got to say 'a gottle o' geer'.
[*ERIC amazed. Tries it.*]
ERIC: Agoriogree.
ERNIE: I couldn't understand a word of that! It was all garbled, unintelligible rubbish. What is he, foreign or something?
ERIC [*quiet, serious*]: No, he's not foreign. He's English. I made him. They take the nationality of the father. I'm English, so he's English.
[*a pause.*] His mother was a Pole!

The Worst Vent. Act ever . . . the Worst Magician? All other contenders pale into insignificance alongside the fez-capped mass of Tommy Cooper. Since the invention of television, it seems, this great man has been dazzling audiences with fumbled conjuring. J. B. Priestley saw him early on, and was impressed:

He is a big man, and he has a large, craggy-featured face, suggesting the boss of some construction gang rather than any kind of entertainer. Seemingly he is never at ease. It is as if he is giving a trial performance in an amateur hour. At times he can be quiet and still, perhaps holding a short length of white rope, waiting for it to do something that it refuses to do. Usually, however, he is very restless indeed, trying some gadget that fails him or hurrying off to bring on some bit of nonsense that he hopes will amuse us, all the while almost terrifying us with a half-mad high giggle, out of all proportion to his size and weight. He will do a sketch of sorts, playing all the characters by rapidly changing hats and finally desperately failing to keep it up.

Thirty-five years later, unbelievably, he was still at large. Moving a little more slowly perhaps, the face gone thicker, the hair sprouting more wildly, he might make an entrance with a huge pile of plates. One falls from the bottom, and shatters. A manic cackle, and suddenly, he throws the remaining plates into the audience! Screams, hysteria — relief, it's only a clever inflatable! He closes the show two minutes in; changes his mind, lurches to his props table.

Magic wand — white tip here, white tip there. The reason for the white tips is to separate the centre from the ends. Now I'll make it disappear.

Wraps wand in paper, loosely. Paper out of control, Cooper loses patience, breaks wand, breaks table. Roaming dangerously, he walks *through* another table (which opens like swing-doors)...

My feet are killing me. Honest — every night I wake up in bed, and they're wrapped around me neck!

Now he's striking matches, which won't light; now he's wrestling with a covered dish, to produce a grotesque cloth turkey. Throws it off in disgust...

I've got something in my eye ... It's my finger!

And for the Big Finish, he produces the same, battered cardboard box that he carried from Collins' Music-hall to the Hippodrome, the Liverpool Empire, Manchester Palace, Bradford Alhambra.

I'd like to recite a little poem:

'Twas New Year's Eve in Joe's Bar
A happy mob was there.
The bar tables were crowded
Lots of noise filled the air.
In the middle of all this gaiety
A door banged open wide:
A torn and tattered tramp walked in
[*Dives in box, produces deer-stalker hat. Dons it.*]
'Happy New Year's Eve, folks,' he cried.
The crowd just looked at him and laughed
And some began to jeer.

But a sailor
[*Dives in box for sailor's hat. Dons it.*]
      standing at the bar said
'Ship ahoy, mate — have a beer!'
[*A pause. Looking in box. Aside:* 'What's next?' *remembers, ploughs on.*]
Then up jumped a banker
(*Homburg hat*)
Who happened to be there.
'Throw that tramp out,' he cried,
'He contaminates the air!'
'Them's harsh words' a sailor [*quick change*] said.
The banker [*quick change*] said 'So what?'
'Them's shooting words,' a cowboy [*quick change*] said,
'Are you aiming to be shot?'
[*A pause. Thinking hard. Under his breath, runs the lines from the beginning, very fast.*]
— I won't be a moment! —
[*sequence of hats, from the beginning, desperate*]
— Oh, yes! —
[*Produces lady's hat, red with yellow rose. Dons it, relieved.*]
Then up jumped a woman
And stared at the tramp
'By goodness, it's Sam!' she cried with fright
And her face went white.

Tommy Cooper, with the essential props: a television top-liner, from 1952 to 1984

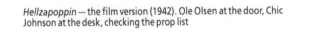

Hellzapoppin — the film version (1942). Ole Olsen at the door, Chic Johnson at the desk, checking the prop list

The pace quickens, the rummaging in the box becomes more desperate, as fireman, Indian, pilot, schoolboy join the throng. Furry animal, with two floppy ears, defeats him ('What's *this*?'): policeman's whistle (off-stage, late) brings the debacle to its denouement, in a heap of hats, the face shiny with sweat, the eyes bright with panic....

Priestley wondered if Tommy Cooper was old enough to have seen, as a boy, the American, Van Hoven.

This man appeared as a conventional conjurer, solemn, and immaculately dressed, but all his tricks went wrong. He was assisted by three solemn urchins, holding eggs and blocks of ice. By the end of the act, now deep in despair, his voice was almost gone, his clothes were a wreck, eggs were falling, blocks of ice were melting, the three urchins were hating him, and we were laughing till it hurt.

Truth is, Cooper couldn't have seen Van Hoven, who never played London, and died while Cooper was still in the Horse Guards, acquiring a modest reputation as a barrack-room comedian. Initially he did impressions but producer Miff Ferrie persuaded him to drop the impressions and go for comedy magic. Wise move.

on a scooter. A man in a hat shares the prima ballerina's spotlight (he needs the light to read his 'Murder Mysteries'). A dancer is launched into the audience, caught by Frankenstein ('what's *he* doing there?'), thrown back onto the stage, caught by a bear. The performing dogs take their turn and, to liven up their act, Chic and Ollie release a sackful of cats onto the stage. Dogs spill from the stage into the pit. Two in a drum, fighting . . . it rolls away. There's water in the piano accordion, wind in the chorus girls' skirts, electricity in the prop swords. A duck flies across the stage, pursued by Ollie with a gun, Chic with a net. The bass fiddle player's bow has been replaced by a *saw*. The bear's in a tree. Ollie shoots it, misses. The bear says 'You need glasses'. Amazed, one dog says to his mate 'Imagine that — a talking bear!' A smoking bomb is formally presented to the leading lady . . . the exits are blocked.

When *Hellzapoppin* was filmed in 1942, the basic 'show within a show' idea was given a celluloid dimension by Chic and Ollie's occasional asides to the audience, and to the projectionist. 'Run that part over again, willya?' (*Aside*) 'He'll do it for me, that's cousin Louie.' During a love duet, a slide is projected onto the screen: STINKY MILLER GO HOME! And the silhouette of the departing Stinky passes across the screen, exitwards. Louie is distracted by the charms of a huge usherette, and the film appears upside down. 'Louie, you dope!' Indians race across the screen behind Chic and Ollie. 'Louie! — you put on the wrong picture!' 'Relatives! I'd fire him if he wasn't your cousin.' 'My cousin? I thought he was *your* cousin!' The cameraman makes a fleeting appearance, and a plea: 'How long do we have to put up with all this?' 'Till we finish the picture.' Exit cameraman. Off-screen, the sound of the fatal bullet.

Perhaps the very success, and durability, of the filmed *Hellzapoppin* undermined the planned Broadway revival of the show in 1977. Jerry Lewis had taken the mantle of Chic and Ollie but it didn't do him any good. Final curtain at the Colonial Theatre, Boston, saw the 'disaster show' end in real disaster, leaving Lewis and his producer Alexander Cohen 'moaning and foaming at the mouth and at one another over what the hell went wrong'. Nothing is as easy as at first it might appear. The comedy of the Magnificent Shambles creates its own special rules and disciplines, and needs to be as well timed and as carefully organised as the seemingly more organised routines. It's a dangerous game: if it isn't funny, you die a double death.

A more likely transatlantic connection can be drawn between Karno's *Mumming Birds*, and the American classic 'crazy show' — *Hellzapoppin* — the brainchild of two genuine comic nuts, Ole Olsen and Chic Johnson, who became a musical double-act in 1914. It's not too fanciful to suppose that, while they were playing Twice Nightly at the Fourteenth Street Music Hall, the duo might have popped across to Forty-second Street to see what the British invaders were up to. At all events, the Karno 'disruptive' element is the key to *Hellzapoppin*, which starts grandly, and then deteriorates. Glamorous chorus girls sashay down a huge staircase, which is then smoothed out into a slide that spills them into the footlights. The corps de ballet are the next victims: sneezing powder in the prop bouquet, flypaper on the feet, carpet tacks on the floor. Meanwhile, a boy on a scooter crosses the stage to be followed by a bear

Los Trios Ringbarkus: Steven Kearney (left) and Neill Gladwin

In 1981 in Melbourne, Australia, two drama students rebelled against the formal disciplines of their course and the 'cultural vacuum' of their native city. Neill Gladwin and Steven Kearney turned from Restoration Comedy to Theatrical Anarchy, and concocted a new version of the Karno cocktail, with added measures of danger and violence. Billed as 'Los Trios Ringbarkus', the duo made their debut at the Last Laugh theatre restaurant in Melbourne. Apologetic to begin with, and very nervous, two trembling figures, in foully stained dinner jackets, edge their way to the central microphone to explain: 'The band seem to be a few minutes late.... Only about five minutes late.... So ... we'll wait.' A pose is struck, and held, tremblingly, for ages. Then, 'Steven's got an idea!' — and the one with glasses, and the madder gleam in his eye, rushes into the wings. Noises off: hammering, banging, drilling. Steven returns with two chairs, proudly. Both sit, and consider their plight. Neill takes out a copy of *War and Peace*, reads aloud from Chapter Three. Steven finds a violin case, opens it, produces box of crackers which he starts to eat, quickly. 'Natasha was listening and considering...' — chomping like a squirrel, mouth now full of crackers — ' "Well, so what then?" she said. "What do you want of him..."' — more crackers, disgustingly, into a mouth that's already bursting — '"You know you can't marry him, because he's young and poor..."' — stuffing crackers into his ears — '"Leave off talking nonsense," said the Countess Bolko ... sko ... vitck ... col ... oski"'

— and in perfect synchronisation with this mouthful of unpronounceable Russian, a spray of partly masticated biscuit is spewed onto the front row of the audience, to their delight.

A musical interlude, Neill playing 'The Harry Lime Theme' on piano accordion, Steven *learning* to play the violin during the course of the first sixteen bars. A bit of chair-juggling, Steven underneath. A volunteer from the audience is brought up, and sat upon, Steven eating his shoe. Panic is increasing; 'Here are some impersonations!' A pair of hands, held downwards, fingers moving. 'Bob Hope?' 'No. D'you want a clue? It's something you'd find in a kitchen.' 'Fish fingers?' 'No — they're moving.' 'Last guess?' 'A spider?' 'No — it's *curtains*!' Next one is easier: hands revolving — 'A clock?' 'Yes! Keep going, you've got a run on!' Now the impersonator is immobile. 'An egg-timer?' 'No.' 'A traffic bollard?' 'In the *kitchen*?' 'A stick of celery?' 'No — it's a *digital* clock!'

Increasingly desperate, 'Los Trios at the Beach' offers tumbling 'business' with deckchairs, and a disgusting picnic of Fosters, mayonnaise, bananas and suntan oil. A new line in impersonations, *banana* becomes dolphin, kangaroo, 'monkey's vomit'. 'You can't say that!' 'Why not?' 'It's *sick*!' And a noisy pastiche of a rock 'n roll concert to finish, talcum powder substituted for dry ice, falling like snow onto a stage already awash with beer, biscuits, suntan lotion and mayonnaise. The final apology, ingratiating but sinister: 'Sorry about the mess.... Sorry about the smell....'

In 1983, Los Trios hit England. They won a prize at the Edinburgh Festival and made a mess of several fringe and university theatres before embarking for San Francisco. In the *Sunday Times*, drama critic Robert Hewison set a respectable seal on their distasteful antics:

For all their 'alternative' ambience (and their assaults on the audience are physical, not verbal) Los Trios Ringbarkus have their roots in vaudeville, but it is the *knowingness* of their act that makes it so contemporary. They are the flavour of the moment: anguished ... violent ... absurd....

CHAPTER FIVE

PROPS·TRAPS·
TRICKS·AND·FLAPS

TAKE A LADDER, for example. Comic potential: enormous. Swing it from the shoulder to crack the head of the follower. Or, you can trip over it, catch fingers under it, climb it, break rungs, fall off. And so on. Here's a good ladder scene from Fausto Nicolini's *Vita di Arlecchino* (eighteenth century):

> I return with a ladder, and say that I had to go to the hangman's house to find one. I lean it against the window of the house. I climb up it, and then do the fall through the window and back out the door and into the street, all in one movement. I say that, thanks to my good luck, I am now inside. I start to look for the door. I say: 'This room is terribly small: I can't find any chairs.' Then I find my ladder. I say: 'Well! My ladder followed me right into the house!'
>
> Then Trivelino enters with a ladder. We lean the two ladders against each other. Between the two of us we do all the *lazzi* of the ladder. He supports me in climbing, foot on shoulder. I get scared and say: 'Oh, that must be the hangman coming back for his ladder.' I then call for help. Someone arrives. We recognise each other. I slap Trivelino and he runs out.

In today's pantomime script, the '*lazzi* of the ladder' would appear, equally gnomically, as 'business with ladder'. The knockabout shorthand takes for granted the performer's familiarity with this most useful prop.

In the circus ring there are no walls to lean the ladder against. This didn't stop Jean-Baptiste Auriol at the Cirque Olympique in Paris, in 1847. Having limbered up with a headstand on the top of a bottle, he would climb to the top of an unsupported ladder, and balance, on one hand, on the top rung. The six Hanlon brothers developed a 'perilous ladder' routine in which brother William balanced a long ladder while the other five did acrobatic stunts at the top. In Cincinnati,

Open-air performances of an Italian comedy, Verona 1772. Oil painting by Marco Marcola

in 1865, brother Thomas fell from the 'human pyramid' and suffered serious injuries. Bone splinters in the brain destroyed his sanity. In 1868, he intentionally dived head-first into an iron stove-pipe and killed himself.

Buster Keaton uses a ladder as a seesaw, or springboard. If he needs a ladder and can't find one, he will remove the porch railing and stand it on end. Master of his filmic environment, Keaton controls the objects that surround him.

Harry Langdon confronts objects and environments as if for the first time. Life is an obstacle course littered with unmalleable impedimenta. A large woman faints in his lap and he is faced with carrying her to bed, up a long, curving staircase (the film is called *The Strong Man*). Starting the long haul, he gets his foot stuck in a flower-pot. Halfway up, he props his burden on the banister for a moment — only to see her slide smoothly to the bottom. He starts again, but this time he sits on the stairs and carries the comatose body on his lap, step by step. Caught in the rhythm of the movement, he continues, still backwards, up a step-ladder at the top of the stairs, right to the top of the ladder, and then down the other side.

Jimmy Jewel has a very special ladder which he keeps in a friend's garage for eleven months of the year. At Christmas, the flats, ropes, traps and springs are broken out and refurbished, and the Jewel 'Haunted Bedroom' is shipped off to Swindon, Sheffield, Newcastle or Liverpool.

Jimmy Jewel (*centre*) and Dave Hill (*right*) in the 'Haunted Bedroom'. 'Look out — he's behind you!'

Whatever the pantomime, you can always work a Haunted Bedroom scene in somewhere, and even for an audience reared on electronic trickery, the scene still works its magic — the handkerchief that climbs a wall, the devil breathing fire in a grate, the sudden snowstorm, the drawer that's pulled from a chest and gets longer and longer, until you see that it's — a ladder! Prop it against a wall, climb to the top, pull a secret rope and — 'Look, the rungs have disappeared! I can't get down!'

Jimmy inherited the scene from his father, a scenic artist and, later, impresario. His speciality was the construction of trick scenery for pantomimes: a miner's cottage that could be magically transformed into a coal-mine; a kitchen dresser that becomes a cow. For *Robinson Crusoe*, at the Alhambra Theatre, Barnsley, Jimmy Jewel (senior) made a ship's cabin which rocked in rough seas. And young Jimmy, aged nine, was given a part in the scene.

> The idea was that Crusoe had taken a few drinks, and so he started to see things. So I was dressed as a little red devil, in a red leotard and mask, with little horns, and I had to keep popping up through different trap-doors that were built into the scenery. For my very first entrance, I had to do what is called a 'lion's leap' — a roll up and over — through the 'star trap' which comes up through the floor of the stage. On the opening night, I broke my shoulder on this trap! I wasn't standing right in the centre of it, and when it came up I hit my shoulder on the edge and broke it!

Nothing daunted, Jimmy continued to endanger life and limb in a career of comedy that has spanned sixty years, and still counting. In the 1930s, he combined with his cousin Ben Warriss in a double-act that topped the bill at all the major variety theatres. Not content with the quickfire 'cross-talk' of the radio double-acts, Jewel and Warriss devised spectacular, three-dimensional comic set-pieces, using scenery and props on a grand scale. At the Regal, Southend, Jimmy invented his celebrated, and perilous, 'Timber' routine:

> There was a song going round called 'Timber'. Silly bloody song, it went:
>
> > *Timber! Timber!*
> > *Can't you hear us calling for timber?*
> > *Swing your axe,*
> > *You lumberjacks,*
> > *Timber's got to come down the river today.*
>
> So I thought it would be a good idea if Ben and I sang this song, and had a load of firewood fall on us. I stayed in the theatre all day Sunday, making two boxes, three foot long by two foot

Harry Langdon in *Feet of Mud* (1924). He's the unfortunate street-cleaner assigned to Chinatown after the local riots

deep with a trap-door on the bottom, a rope, and a pin-hinge on a screw-eye. The rope came off the end, and there was a fellow to work it, one on each side of the stage. I filled the boxes up with firewood — there must have been three hundred bundles of firewood in there! I tried it first of all with a tin hat on, one of those hats that air-raid wardens used to wear. I stood underneath one of the boxes, the stage-hand pulled the rope and down it came. You've never heard such a noise! There was a fellow sitting out front — Fred Gratton — he fell off his chair laughing. So we put it in the act on Monday night. Well, you wouldn't believe the effect it had. The whole house was hysterical! Ben and I had to put towels in the hats, to deaden the noise. And after one lot had dropped, we'd say 'We're not going to stand there, we'll go over the other side, it'll be safer.' And of course the second load would fall on us over there! Well, this routine became the finish of our act — you couldn't follow that.

Val Parnell saw us at the Gaumont,

Holloway, and booked us for a tour — just on the strength of the 'Timber' routine.

Having survived many weeks of raining firewood, Jimmy had another brainwave. This one involved them being pelted with horse-shoes:

The idea was that we would call ourselves 'Jewelitz and Warrissauer at the Pianos': we'd dress ourselves up in tailsuits and wigs, and sit at two 'prop' pianos. The orchestra would play the 'Anvil Chorus', and the stage-hands would throw horse-shoes — real horse-shoes — at us from the wings. And we had some 'cod' horse-shoes, made out of brown felt, which we used to throw into the audience. Then we'd play another chorus — and someone would throw a harness on, which would break the leg of the piano. The next chorus, a cock would crow, and a live hen flew onto the stage. We put it in the piano. Another chorus, the cock would crow again, and I used to pull a string, and a bloody great egg would fall out from under me. Finally, they'd bring a horse on — a *real* horse, mind — which trotted round the stage while we went on playing this thing, until a whole haystack fell in from the flies, completely covering the pianos and ourselves in hay!

Ladders, firewood, horse-shoes, eggs, bales of hay . . . Jewel and Warriss's prop list expanded in response to Jimmy Jewel's creative imagination. A master in the use of comic 'things', Jimmy learned from his craftsman father that, when he has exhausted the comedy of facial expression and body language, the knockabout comedian will turn to props for support. Objects to play around with, to misuse, to fight over, to transform, to be threatened by. By a man's prop basket shall you know him. 'One trunk, one penny-farthing, one tuba, the moon, snow, one canary. . . .' 'Hang on, you've got a cat in that cage — where's the canary?' 'Inside the cat . . . King Tut's skull, one coat of arms' (literally, a topcoat with five arms each side), 'one blow-lamp, one aspidistra — hey, we've got everything here but the kitchen sink!' Enter Ole Olsen with one kitchen sink, to complete the *Hellzapoppin* inventory. Later on they'll need a ladder, of course, which, when carried across the stage by Chic and Ollie goes on and on and on and on.

Take . . . a plank, which has a malevolent life of its own, and follow its adventures on a building site. Eric Sykes did this in 1967, and his film *The Plank* became a minor classic. Because he's hard of hearing — 'totally deaf in one ear, and the other's wonky' — Sykes favours visual comedy. His first job was in a mill, in Oldham. To amuse his mates he sang 'In the Blue of the Night' with a bucket over his head. When he took the bucket off, everyone had scarpered except the works manager, who fired him. He also confesses to being a bit weak in the manual dexterity department: 'I'm useless at most things. Watch me trying to open a can of beans, or mend a fuse, or get the car started. . . .' The dilemma of modern man defeated by the machines of his own invention is the theme of Sykes's second nearly silent movie, *It's Your Move*, in which he joined forces with Tommy Cooper. They play removal men installing furniture in a brand-new house, and demolishing it in the process. Of his partner, Sykes said:

I asked him to be as 'straight' as he could. No comedy. Well, he tried. He had to walk down

Charlie Drake takes a ride on *The Plank*

the street being earnest and honest. But, with that face, and those feet, the more serious he was, the funnier. He couldn't understand why everyone was laughing!

Sykes believes British comedians are tops at the comedy of maladroitness 'because they're so serious. And if they're doing the wrong thing, they're doing it seriously. The secret is that you don't have to be funny, you only have to be incompetent'.

Take . . . a table. Place it in the centre of the ring, or stage. Then fetch another table, slightly smaller. Put it on top of the first table. Continue to build a 'table tower' until you have five tables on top of one another, each table smaller than the one below. Climb to the top, then make the tower sway by moving your weight from side to side. Keep this going as long as possible, travelling a bit further from the vertical each time, until . . . the inevitable collapse of the tower, from which you extricate yourself as best you can. Harry Ritley used the 'table tower' to great effect in Ringling Bros. and Barnum and Bailey's three-ring circus in the 1930s. Jack Melville records an earlier, safer version used in the Karno companies for a Good Exit, after Comedy Acrobatics:

They finish, take curtains, then come back as if to do an encore. Roll up the mat, throw it into the wings. Take big table from centre, and put it down-stage Right, close to Proscenium (with a Dead Clear Run-off behind Prosc.). Then put

Eric Sykes with *The Plank;*
a silent comedy for the Sixties

Jimmy Jewel (senior) in 'The Steeple Sketch' which he wrote and built. A performance from Theldman's Music Theatre

small table on top of big table, then chair on small table (this makes it look very high). Drums roll: one man stands at end of table, almost off stage right. He holds the end of the table, looks up. Other man goes over left. Getting ready business. Drums loud: he runs across stage as if to do some Wonderful Leap — but when he reaches the table, all he does is pick *his* end up, while number One picks his end up, and they *Both Carry Table Off.*

It's a good exit for knockabouts. Gets a Fine Laugh, and leaves stage clear for next item.

Clark and McCullough were circus acrobats who, like Karno, decided that they enjoyed the sound of laughter coming from an audience, and began to inject comedy into their tumbling. With one table and one chair they evolved a thirty-minute routine which started with McCullough climbing onto the table and Clark attempting to hand the chair up to him. It would invariably get caught on the edge of the table, baulking their best efforts. 'Complicated, isn't it?' Clark would yell, circling the disaster area. 'Really a problem for the scientist, but we will attempt it!' The ensuing battle with the chair, the prodigious expenditure of energy (often involving the removal of most of their clothing), the ultimate total noisy collapse of the table, and climactic fist fight, combined to make their act a show-stopper in vaudeville and launched them into a

career in films that was sadly cut short in 1936 when McCullough went mad, and committed suicide in a barber-shop.

The Swiss clown, Grock, took a chair — and sat on the back of it in order to play the violin. One day, as Grock records, the seat of the chair fell out:

And there I was in the middle of the chair, with both feet on the ground. The audience saw that this was not intentional and were all the more delighted. What was Grock going to do now? . . . All that I knew was that I wanted to be on the back of the chair to play the violin . . . The simplest thing would be to jump out. I collected myself, jumped, crossing my legs in the air, and landed on the back of the chair . . . No other artiste has ever done this. Many have tried it, among them fully trained acrobats.

Grock with his violin, one of the twenty-four musical instruments he could play. He was also a wire-walker, juggler and contortionist

Michael Bentine took a chair, and turned it to his advantage. Demobbed from the R.A.F. after the war, he was trying to build a comic career from occasional 'extra' work in films, cabaret, and television 'bits and pieces'. One weekend he was staying with his brother and sister-in-law.

They are two of my favourite people, and we were enjoying a wildcat session of imaginative comedy and a lot of laughs. Suddenly, the old chair that I was standing on to illustrate some comedy point broke off at the back, leaving me with the fractured piece in my hands. 'Blimey, I'm sorry, Bro!' I said, knowing how broke we all were and wondering how much a new chair would cost. 'Not to worry!' said my brother. Then, grinning broadly, he took the chairback from me and held it like a submachine gun. 'You'll be shot at dawn, of course!' he chuckled. Then and there, using the oddly effective shape that the broken back of the chair made, Tony, Mona and I took hysterical turns to mime all the different articles that its silhouette suggested.

When we finished, weak with laughter, Tony said: 'You'd better keep it as a souvenir, Michael! I'll turn the bottom half into a stool.'

Walking home to Barnes that night, Bentine played with the chairback. En route, he began to realise that this single prop could provide the basis of an original comedy routine. Three months later he had worked a series of visual pictures into an organised, fast-flowing sequence of visual gags: and when Val Parnell, all-powerful supremo of Moss Empires, saw Bentine's 'chairback business' in performance, he booked him for a new revue, *Starlight Roof*, at the London Hippodrome. From this vantage point Bentine launched himself into radio, through *The Goon Show*, and television, with *The Bumblies*, *Potty Time*, and *It's a Square World*. All on account of a broken chair. Intriguingly, one moment in Bentine's transformation mime called for the chairback to be used as a giant key, to open a door . . . .

A chairback becomes a key, a clothes-horse and a broom become a coach and horses, a kitchen dresser becomes a fully operational cow. The prop transformed is the staple of English pantomime, in the tradition codified by the great nineteenth century clown Grimaldi. In Grimaldi's hands, every prop took on a new, comic life. He would stand a broom upright, fix a tin-lid to the pole, grasp a brush and a ladle — and become a one-man band. Or, he would force a mop-stick through a cheese, place the ends in the hands of his wretched accomplice, Pantaloon, pile cheeses on his back, and wheel him off by the ankles as a wheelbarrow. Another time, he would clothe Pantaloon in a bearskin, with an ass's head and the tail-feather of a swan, and bring the strange beast to life. He burlesqued the flamboyant uniform of the Regency Hussars, donning two varnished coal-scuttles for boots, candlesticks for spurs, and a lady's muff for a helmet — and all this with a row of tight-lipped genuine articles occupying the stage box! A 'Vegetable Man' was constructed with turnip head, cabbage body, carrot arms; a coach was assembled from saucepans, Cheshire cheeses, coal-scuttle and broom-handle; an elephant arose from a chest of glass, a bull's head, a barber's cue and powder puff, a chair and an umbrella . . . . 'But what use is it,' asked a contemporary admirer, 'to mention these things? It was the style in which he joined and sub-joined them, looked, studied (what a brown study was his!), and then rushed, in triumphant joy, when a new idea flashed over the extent of his countenance.'

As Grimaldi's tricks became increasingly more elaborate, so the stage carpenters had to invent new machinery to achieve his effects. This is, perhaps, one of the reasons why Grimaldi never appeared in the circus ring. His comic 'business' depended more and more on the paraphernalia of

Grimaldi plays the Bold Dragoon, in *Pantomime of the Red Dwarf*. It was staged at the Theatre Royal, Drury Lane in 1812

Below stage: the workings of the Star Trap. Counterweights held the platform down: when released, the performer was projected on to the stage as if by magic

stage machinery — traps, springs, flaps and hoists — whereby Clown and his cronies could be made to appear and disappear through the floor and walls of the scene. There was the 'star trap', which projected Clown through the stage floor, to appear as if out of nowhere. And the 'vampire trap', consisting of two spring leaves which returned to their original position after the performer had dived through, giving the impression that he had penetrated a solid surface.

Other devices made possible the instant conversion of one object into another. A handwritten fragment of a pantomime text in the British Museum explains how a post-chaise can be transformed into a wheelbarrow. The chaise is to be merely a 'profile', but when its door is opened a piece of hanging canvas gives the appearance of substantiality. On entering, Pantaloon steps into a (concealed) wheelbarrow. When he loosens a brace, the upper part of the chaise is hauled up, while the lower part sinks through a 'cut' in the stage floor into the 'cellar', leaving the wheelbarrow exposed. Similarly, a quack's pill could be changed into a duck, a drum into a temple, a public house into a teapot, and a

dish of gooseberry fool into a grinning idiot.

From the back of the gallery these transformations were spectacularly convincing. To a seasoned observer in the stalls, however, the effect fell somewhat short of magical. Writer Percy Fitzgerald, who saw Grimaldi at Drury Lane in 1820, later recalled:

Part of the stock-in-trade of the old Clown was a number of tricks or mechanical contrivances. A Clown was supposed to have a genius for inventing them, they were expected of him. How well I see them now! Nothing more clumsy, or less delusive, could be conceived. You heard a rattle, and an immense chest came rolling in on wheels, the cord very palpable. Harlequin then slapped the ground, and there came a sudden flapping of doors, pulling of cords etc . . . A legend was shown — 'ENGLAND'S HOPE' — and a little boy dressed as Cupid walked out. Often the cords would not work, and a flap stuck fast, and then the thing was wheeled off contemptuously out of the way. It is astonishing how clumsy makeshifts were accepted, even at first-class theatres.

Along with his 'constructions', Grimaldi also developed the down-to-earth business of the pantomime. A new stage weapon was introduced to rival Harlequin's explosive slapstick — Clown's red-hot poker. Sneaking up on his intended victim, Grimaldi would ask the audience, 'Shall I?'. The inevitable reply produced the inevitable result, with a show of pain from the victim that was nothing compared to Grimaldi's own expression of agony when, later in the show, he sat down on his own poker. Butter was another favourite prop; it could be applied to the doorstep of the unfortunate shopkeeper, who would then be summoned by a ring on his doorbell, to take the predictable slippery pratfall. The 'kick in the pants' was another regular ploy. Indeed, so many variations of the comic 'attack from rear' were being practised on Clown's victims that the audience's enjoyment of the simulated violence occasionally gave way to sympathy for the sufferer, and the cry 'Look out! He's *behind* you!'

Grimaldi, laden down with spoils

became part of the pantomime tradition, used as a weapon in the audience's armoury to warn a popular actor of imminent danger from behind.

Not every punch was pulled, nor was every pratfall a painless experience. Grimaldi, although considered by his contemporaries to be a relatively unacrobatic Clown, was a skilled swordsman (with fish, as well as foil) and choreographer of mock fights. He was also well accustomed to being knocked about. The theatre critic of *The Times* wrote:

> It is absolutely surprising that any human head or hide can resist the rough trials which he volunteers. Serious tumbles from serious heights, innumerable kicks, and incessant beatings come on him as matters of common occurrence, and leave him every night fresh and free for the next night's flagellation.

The demands of his profession and a series of domestic tragedies brought Grimaldi to a premature old age. At forty he was struggling, and men had to be positioned in the wings to catch him as he staggered from the stage, and chafe his aching limbs. In 1823, he played his Farewell Performance at Drury Lane. Unable to remain standing for long, he was helped to a chair close to the footlights, where he addressed his audience for the last time:

> Ladies and Gentlemen, I need not assure you of the sad regret with which I say it; but sickness and infirmity have come upon me, and I can no longer wear the motley! Four years ago I jumped my last jump, filched my last custard, and ate my last sausage. I am not so rich a man as I was when I was basking in your favour formerly, for then I always had a fowl in one pocket, and sauce for it in the other . . . .

George Cruikshank's portrait of 'Grimaldi Thieving' is the only surviving visual clue to Grimaldi's special comic identity. In it, the Clown's distinctive costume is virtually concealed under an overcoat which bulges with the fruits of his larceny. A live duck's head pokes out from every pocket, there's a piglet under one arm, a goose under the other. On his back is a basket bulging with vegetable produce; on his head a stolen Beadle's hat. The bulging eyes, the painted face identify the villain on the lookout for more booty to store into that 'leviathan pocket of his', as Fitzgerald described it, 'that receptacle of all sorts of edibles, and occasionally of kettles full of boiling water, and even lighted candles'.

Harpo Marx sizes up his victim (Edgar Kennedy) in *Duck Soup* (1933)

when in come Pantaloon and his servant [Groucho and Chico?] — at opposite doors, both in search of the glutton, and both resolved to pounce on the rascal headlong. They rush forward accordingly; he slips between them with a 'Hello, I say' — [a squawk on Harpo's hooter?] — and the two poor devils dash their heads against one another like rams. They rebound fainting asunder to the stage-doors; while the Clown, laughing with all his shoulders, nods a health to each, and finishes his draught. He then holds a great cask of a snuff-box to each of their noses, to bring them to; and while they are sneezing and tearing their souls out, jogs off at his leisure.

The 'constructive' ingenuity of Grimaldi also lives on in the films of Charlie Chaplin, who loved to play with the interchangeability of things. In his burlesque of *Carmen*, he uses Don Jose's dagger as a toothpick, and also as a knife to eat with.

Escamillo's plate is so clean when he has finished eating that Chaplin is able to use it as a mirror. He plays a game of billiards with scallions as balls, and his duelling sword as a cue.

In *Behind the Screen*, Chaplin constructs a xylophone from the remnants of lunch — empty pie tins and a pair of chewed bones. In the same film he uses two beer bottles as a pair of binoculars. Collecting chairs, he turns himself into a porcupine. In *The Fireman*, he deals out dinner plates as if they were a pack of cards: in *The Immigrant* he shoots dice in the style of a baseball pitcher. In *The Pawnshop*, he uses a ladder as a lasso, pinning his adversary between two rungs. He has difficulty in sweeping up a long piece of string on the shop floor, so he uses it as a fantasy tightrope. Later, he serenades Edna Purviance in the kitchen, with a length of dough garlanding his neck and a serving spoon substituting for a ukulele. And, in one of the best-remembered moments in the history of film, he 'transforms' a customer's alarm clock, in the process of assessing its worth. He takes a stethoscope to it, as if it were a sick baby. Then he attacks it with a tin opener, to examine its innards. A pair of dentist's pliers are needed to

That same 'leviathan pocket' was to provide another lovable villain, Harpo Marx, with a fruitful store of fun, some hundred years after the death of Grimaldi. Even the detail of the lighted candle recurs, this time burning at both ends, in response to Groucho's warning about late nights. Ever literal, from the inner depths of his tatty raincoat Harpo produces a cup of coffee; a feather (to knock Groucho down with); an axe to cut the cards (and the card-table); a stuffed moose-head; flags of all nations; and a complete four-course dinner. For, like Grimaldi, Harpo's appetite is insatiable. Compare this account, by Leigh Hunt, of a scene from *Harlequin and Friar Bacon* (1820), with Harpo, demolishing his first square meal for days, in *Room Service* (1938):

Down he sits, contriving a luxurious seat, and inviting himself with as many ceremonies as if he had the whole day before him; but when he once begins, he seems as if he had not a moment to lose. The dumplings vanish at a cram; — the sausages are abolished; — down go a dozen yards of macaroni; and he is in the act of paying his duties to a gallon of rum

extract defective bits. Springs and coils spill out onto the counter like tadpoles; he squirts them with his oil-can until they're subdued. All avenues explored, he shovels the detritus into the astonished customer's hat and returns them with a cold stare. No sale. Grimaldi's law is eloquently re-established. A clock can be a baby, a can of sardines, an open mouth, frogspawn, anything. The identity of an object lies only in the attitude you take towards it.

Chaplin's stage training with Karno shaped his attitude to film. The comedy owed little to the technical tricks of the camera, which was used to record events more or less as they happened. It was, after all, a machine which reproduced whatever was presented to it while its aperture was open, and recorded that data faithfully. And from the early days the audience's expectation was for real things, in motion. The first Vitascope machines showed people, ferryboats, a street parade, steam engines. When film was projected onto a screen, in life-like proportions, audiences stampeded and fled from their seats in real terror as a locomotive bore down on them. The shock depended on the audience being caught unawares and on the breaching of the code of propriety which, normally, distances the spectator from the spectacle.

The French film pioneer, George Méliès, discovered by accident the camera's capacity for lying. Filming crowds in the Place de l'Opéra, in Paris, his camera stopped momentarily then started up again. On the developed film, men were transformed into women, prams into bicycles, carts into buses. Magic! Further intentional experiments revealed the possibilities of superimposition, reversal, the freeze-frame. Images could be removed from the flow of time and the flux of appearances, and they could be rearranged to create illusion. In *The Indiarubber Head*, Méliès inflates his head, which swells to gigantic proportions. Then he lets the air out . . . . His contemporary, Louis Lumière, also toyed with technical trickery. He filmed a wall being demolished, then reversed the film to show it springing back into place. But Lumière was not a conjuror, his experiments were geared to displaying the scope of the camera as a machine. Thomas Edison, inventor of the Kinetoscope, had high hopes for the future of the new medium but became disillusioned.

I had some glowing dreams about what the cinema could be made to do in teaching the world things it needed to know — teaching it in a more vivid, direct way . . . . When the industry began to specialise as a big amusement proposition, I quit the game . . . .

In Britain, the movie pioneers were technicians, not showmen. Cecil Hepworth, a keen amateur photographer, was the son of a magic-lantern exhibitor. In Walton-on-Thames, he created the first British film studio. It was a semi-detached house called The Rosary. The rent was £36 per year. Here, within the narrow confines of his back garden, front sitting-room, kitchen, scullery and bathroom, Hepworth proposed to write, produce, develop and print for distribution, a regular supply of short comedy films. A cottage industry — very makeshift, very British. The scullery housed a second-hand gas engine which provided the power, the two bedrooms were fitted out as film processing and drying rooms, and the dining-room became the front office. The studio was the back garden, where an 8 foot by 4 foot wooden platform was erected, with upright posts to support the scenery, which Hepworth himself painted.

Hepworth's first films were short comic incidents and glimpses of everyday suburban life. As his confidence and ambition grew he began to devise stories which his family and neighbours would be required to act out in the 'studio', or 'on location' in the road outside, at Walton station, or on the towpath of the River Thames. As Hepworth records in his autobiography, this was film-making on the most primitive and personal level — light years away from the overmanned industrialisation that today's directors complain of.

There were only two or three of us in the little company at Walton, and we did everything ourselves. First we thought of a story; then we painted the scenery, if it wasn't to be all in the open air, which it was usually. Then we acted and photographed it.

Hepworth's *Beating the Bobby* uses some familiar 'copper-baiting' routines from Karno and Sennett. But it also shows the director originating some effective 'sight gags' and making the most of his props. The first scene shows some scruffy schoolboys coming out of a tobacconist's shop in Walton High Steet. They are about to light up when the 'Bobby' hoves into view. He confiscates their fags, lights one himself, and walks away to enjoy his smoke. The boys follow

Chaplin in *The Pawnshop*. A two-reel comedy made in 1916 for the Mutual Film Corporation: 'the happiest period in my career'

him, intent on revenge. They find him chatting up a girl . . . so, they creep up behind him, put fireworks in his pockets and escape over some railings as the fireworks explode. The policeman talks to a milkman . . . the boys put water in the milk, which causes a dispute between policeman and milkman, and the Bobby gets a jug of watery milk poured over him. He gives chase . . . the boys hide in a bush and trip him up as he rushes past. His sweetheart appears and takes him into her house . . . but the boys have been there first and put something nasty in his dinner. The first mouthful causes the Bobby to rush out and be sick. The boys meanwhile dress up a tailor's dummy as a pretty girl, put it on a park bench, and smear glue on the seat beside it. The policeman walks by; the boys pull a string which makes the dummy's arm appear to beckon. He sits. The boys then reveal themselves and laugh at their victim. He tries to give chase but is stuck fast. Two fellow-policemen come to his aid but cannot detach him. They decide to carry him, bench and all, to the local carpenter to be sawn out.

Chaplin with Anna Pavlova, the Russian ballerina, on a visit to his studios. They admired one another's dancing

Beating the Bobby was sold 'by the foot' to exhibitors and was sufficiently popular to warrant extra prints being struck off in the bedroom laboratory. *The Suffragette's Downfall* was a topical hit in 1909, and soon other would-be film makers were clamouring for a place on the bandwagon. At Waddon, in Surrey, the Cricks and Martin studio produced a series of trick films, featuring a comic character called Scroggins — *Scroggins Goes in for Chemistry, and Discovers a Marvellous Powder: Spring Cleaning at the House of Scroggins*. They also employed music-hall comedian Fred Evans in a number of 'Charley Smiler' comedies. At Moonshine Studios, Bertie Wright played an amorous and over-zealous boot salesman in *Bertie Bungles* and *Bertie Buys a Bulldog*, while at Clapham Park, Lupino Lane, soon to follow Chaplin's route to California, was cutting his teeth on a series of short 'Kinekatures'.

For all its unsophisticated enthusiasm and occasional ingenuity, the British product was no match for the combined skills of Chaplin, Sennett and Roach. In fact, so worried were British producers about their failure to win an audience, that in 1920 they launched a British National Film League. The Prince of Wales, supported by Sir Arthur Conan Doyle and Mr Ramsay MacDonald, spoke at a luncheon to inaugurate the League. Exhibitors were exhorted to present British Film Weeks all over their country and, to ensure that there was sufficient product available, the film renters ransacked their vaults for anything remotely British to back up the 'Show a British Picture' campaign. Weighed down by mediocrity, the League collapsed, and by 1924 most of the British studios had closed, or were on the verge of closing. Even the introduction of a quota law, whereby every exhibitor was bound to show a certain proportion of home-made films, failed to persuade the public that Scroggins, Pimple, or Mr Butterdun, were in the same league as 'Our Charlie', who, in 1920, made plans to visit his homeland. This caused quite a stir. 'HOMECOMING OF COMEDIAN TO RIVAL ARMISTICE DAY' trumpeted the *Morning Telegraph*, while *The Times* tried to temper the welcoming enthusiasm with 'A CALL FOR SANITY':

In heaven's name, let us recover our sanity. I dare say Mr Chaplin is a most estimable person, and I am not interested to inquire why the homesickness which so touchingly affects him at this juncture did not manifest itself during the black years when the homes of Britain were in danger through the menace of the Hun. It may be true, as has been argued, that Charlie Chaplin was better employed playing funny tricks in front of a camera than he would have been doing manly things behind a gun . . . .

Ouch. Still, there were cheering crowds at Waterloo Station. 'Here he is! Good old Charlie!' they shouted, and the rallying cry was taken up by the throng outside the Ritz Hotel, which the prodigal had chosen as his headquarters. 'It had just been built when I was a boy, and, passing its entrance, I had caught a glimpse of the gilt and splendour inside. Ever since I had had a curiosity to know how the rest of it looked.'

Chaplin plays host to Churchill in Hollywood. Between them stands Ambassador Moore; on the left, Churchill relatives and Alf Reeves, who was Karno's manager in the USA

For the crowds who stood in the rain outside the Ritz waiting for a glimpse of the dapper little figure — barely recognisable without the emblematic moustache, bowler, cane and baggy pants of his screen persona — the vigil took on an almost religious aura. After all, had not the Great Man been quoted as saying: 'My name is quite well known in Tibetan lamaseries, where the name of Jesus Christ has never been heard'? A remark that was to be echoed half a century later by another celebrated Englishman, who appalled New York with his claim that 'The Beatles are more popular than Jesus Christ' (J. Lennon, R. I. P.). Worldwide fame, commonplace in the age of the satellite and the microchip, in 1920 was reserved for the handful of film stars whose films were sold abroad. So, the Great and Good queued to shake the hand of Charlie Chaplin: H. G. Wells, Somerset Maugham, Sir James Barrie, Sir Edwin Lutyens, Sir Philip Sassoon, Lord Rocksavage, Prince George of Greece, and the Marquis de Talleyrand-Périgord.

Surprisingly, among these new-found, well-heeled friends who frequented Chaplin's suite at the Ritz, there was no sign of the stocky, balding figure of Fred Karno. In his own account, Chaplin admits that he was now setting his sights on 'that rarer sphere of *ducal* living'. No place in this rarefied atmosphere for the down-to-earth Karno, for all his ambitions to be accepted in the 'white tie and tails' set. Fact is, he could never resist cocking a snook at pomposity and snobbery. For a

Full Dress Gala at the Birmingham Hippodrome, Karno devised a Grand Opening scene, in which white-wigged footmen unrolled crimson carpets down the gangways, while the orchestra played the National Anthem. On the final, majestic crash of cymbals, the curtain rose to reveal, alone on stage, a small, live, Scots terrier, back to audience. His tail was wired in the vertical position and underneath it was fixed a single red bulb, flashing on and off!

In the Karno troupe, the departure of Chaplin had created opportunities for some of the lesser lights. Jack Melville played 'The Deceitful Husband' in *The New Slavey* — a 'Humorous Burlesque on the Troubles and Worries of Domestic Life in 3 Elaborate Scenes'. No script survives of this prototype situation comedy, although the list of props in Jack's notebook confirms that it was 'business as usual' at the Palace, Watford, twice nightly.

3 cups, saucers (*breakable*)
1 tray with tea-pot glued to it (*confetti inside*)
1 fly-paper (*very sticky*)
1 hat, with two wasps hanging from front brim
1 white glove (*for 'on the other hand' routine*)
1 umbrella (*to be used as a pen*), with ink-well
1 white dicky (*spring-loaded*)
4 squares of canvas (*for off-stage ripping*)
1 funnel and tube (*for never-filling whisky glass*)
2 whisky bottles (*cold tea*)

Chaplin in *Modern Times* (1936), the epitome of gadgetry comedy

1 baby's nappy (*the 'eternal triangle'*)
1 old-fashioned corset (*to be played like an accordion*)
1 round cake tin with no bottom (*'cinder sifter for gas fires'*)
1 bouquet
1 feather-duster
2 oranges (*juicy*)
2 custard pies (*fresh each performance*)
buckets etc. as usual (*don't forget the* mop)

It was a messy business, never more so than when the custard pies were flying. On stage or screen, a face-full of 'gunge' was the most effective visual punch line to end a scene. Fatty Arbuckle was on the receiving end of one of the first film custard pies, in *Mabel and Fatty's Married Life* (Keystone, 1916). Mabel Normand launched that

one, but in their subsequent encounters Fatty got his revenge. As well as a good aim, he had the physical dexterity to hurl two pies in opposite directions at the same time. The pies were delivered to the studio from Greenberg's Bakery. At first they were the genuine article but these tended to disintegrate in flight, so Greenberg invented a ballistic version that had a double thickness of pastry and a filling of flour, water and whipped cream. There were two flavours — blackberry for blonde recipients, lemon meringue for brunettes. Sennett staged a battle of custards for *Keystone Hotel*: but this was topped by Laurel and Hardy's *Battle of the Century*, when a record 3000 pies were despatched. In more recent times, *Beach Party*, *The Great Race* and *Smashing Time* have kept Greenberg's in business; while in England, the Christmas pantomime season brings a heavy demand for flan cases, shaving foam and cochineal. In 1983 the Prince of Wales achieved another royal 'first'. At a Manchester community centre Katie Slater (fifteen years old) slammed a festive custard into the future King's face. She spent a cheery Christmas in the Tower.

In *Modern Times*, Chaplin plays an ingenious variation on this well-worn theme. The factory management have installed a feeding machine, designed to speed up production by feeding the assembly line workers while they're on the job. Of course, the machine runs amok and Charlie becomes the object of the first mechanised lunch-assault, as the machine pelts him with mashed potato, spills soup over him, sprays sweet-corn, proffers bolts for beef, and the inevitable pie — into the face, not the open mouth. Between each course an automated 'mouth-wiper' swings into position to remove stray crumbs. Whatever happens, the mouth-wiper returns, on cue.

Industrial society may not be able to feed a man but it will teach him to be mannerly.

A more successful feeding-machine was devised by Buster Keaton for *The Scarecrow*. Buster and his brother sit down at the breakfast table. Sugar-bowl, salt and pepper cruets are suspended above the table on pulleys, to be lowered as required by a tug on the string and swung across the table like trapeze artists. A tiny table-wagon delivers rolls; another pulley flies the ketchup bottle from fridge to table, and back. After the meal, a hinged trap in the table flips a bowl of flowers. Keaton loved gadgets. At the age of fourteen he spent some weeks perfecting a complicated device to wake a deep-sleeping friend.

Domestic gadgetry is the theme of Hal Roach's *It's a Gift*, which starred the Australian comedian Snub Pollard (originally Harold Fraser), he of the inverted Kaiser Wilhelm moustache. Made three years after the Keaton film, it extends the range of automated aids to include a feather-alarm (it tickles the feet, a snooze-button activates a razor, which decapitates the feather); an egg-deliverer (chute from hen to saucepan); bed-maker (covers become curtains at the tug of a tasselled cord); trouser-raiser (step in, pulley hoists them up); and a folding bed which becomes a fire, flaming dangerously. Leaving the house, Pollard removes the 'B' from his GARBAGE can, and wheels out his bullet-shaped 'magnet car'. Motor power comes by simply pointing a giant magnet at passing vehicles, which take him in tow. Not content with this ultimate energy-saving device, Pollard has invented a miracle fuel for cars — MOOZ (ZOOM backwards). A drop from an eye-dropper is enough to send the fleet of test cars roaring off in every direction. The final tableau is a magnificent wreck: a heap of smoking rubble, shredded drivers festooned on lamp-posts, balconies, rooftops. The 'magnet car' meanwhile sprouts wings, and Pollard flies off into the sunset.

Take . . . a car, a train, a boat, a plane. The internal combustion engine produced a whole range of motorised props and new toys to play with. Limitless opportunities for fast and violent fun. Mack Sennett drove brand-new cars into walls, over cliffs, through houses (vertically and horizontally). Laurel and Hardy concertinaed one car, sliced another neatly in two. Harold Lloyd bought a new car to match his nice white trousers, and wrecked

Snub Pollard, who became a star comedian at the Roach Studios. The heavy moustache and eyebrows were his trademark

it in minutes. W. C. Fields took his revenge on careless motorists by driving them into the ditch ('How d'you like that, road hog?'). And Billie Bevan, another Australian wooed to Hollywood, produced one of the most memorable 'motor-car sight gags' in *Easy Pickings*. His car has broken down, and he's pushing it to the garage. En route, he picks up all the other cars that are parked along the sidewalk. Sweating and heaving, he shunts his accumulation of autos uphill, and topples them over a small cliff.

For the circus ring, the Russian clown, Popov, has created a motorised cottage. Full to bursting with domestic oddments, it has a washing machine lid on top, a front door with a letterbox, windows with wooden frames and fanlights, and a tiled roof with chimney and gutters. In America, Lou Jacobs built a car that was only 3 feet long, and 18 inches off the ground. This tiny car would buzz round the ring and stop at a miniature filling-station manned by a dwarf. A door would open, and a shoe, which was as long as the car, would emerge, followed by the rest of Jacobs. He was over 6 feet tall and had trained as a contortionist.

In the theatre, Harry Tate took pole position, with his famous sketch 'Motoring'. This short scenario, in which the proud owner of a motor car has to suffer all manner of indignities, was first aired at the London Alhambra, in 1925. On the page, it looks a trifle thin:

Scene: A London street. Battered car on the kerb: Tate in the driving seat, Idiot Son beside him. A uniformed Chauffeur sits in the rear. Business with levers. Tate getting angry.

CHAUFFEUR: Why, sir, you've got the brake on.

TATE: Which is the brake? [*to Son*] Why didn't you tell me? We might have run into something.

[*More business with levers. Nothing happens.*]

TATE: What's the matter now? [*to Chauffeur*] Have you got any oil in that lamp?

[*Shot fired behind car*]

TATE: It's no good, the whole thing will have to come down. [*to Chauffeur*] Hand me that screw-driver.

[*Chauffeur gives him an axe.*]

TATE: Is that all you've brought? Where's the tool-box?

[*Tate gets under car. Shot fired. Tate emerges with eye blackened.*]

CHAUFFEUR: Why, whatever is the matter, sir?

TATE: Matter? I got my eye in the gear-box.

It's no use, we'll have to push the confounded thing.

[*All get out of car, start to push. Enter Policeman.*]

POLICEMAN: Stop!

[*All look in amazement.*]

POLICEMAN: Now then, sir, I want your name, address, and licence number.

TATE: What for?

POLICEMAN: For furious driving.

TATE: Furious driving? But we've been stuck here for the last half-hour!

[*All argue. Tate pushes Son away. In doing so he picks up Son's cap, puts it on. Son puts Tate's cap on. Tate sees this, takes it back, puts it on (on top of Son's cap). Son kicks Tate. Policeman collars Chauffeur. Car falls over. Curtain.*]

What turned this rudimentary routine into a show-stopper was the character that Tate assumed: an ever-so-slightly exaggerated portrait of an Edwardian 'Sporting Gent'. According to J. B. Priestley, 'Types like him, though not quite so outrageous, could be found, boasting at the tops of their voices, in saloon bars throughout Edwardian England. Tate's man had a large, wobbly moustache, a loud voice, staring eyes, an enormous sense of his own importance, a hectoring manner, and an unfailing capacity to saddle himself with irritating people and a ripening anarchy.'

Jewel and Warriss were the proud owners of a prop car — a Model T Ford which started and stopped on its own. It worked on a time switch, with six pedals to control the effects. A shot from a revolver appeared to start it up; remove the steering wheel and it still trundled round the stage independently. At the end of the act, when the driver got in, the back would fall off. One night in Bristol, Ben Warriss pressed the wrong pedal and the car took off into the wings, ploughing through scenery and stagehands. 'Fortunately,' says Jimmy, 'nobody was badly hurt.'

Take . . . a streetcar. Harold Lloyd, in pursuit of his girl, who's going to marry a rival, leaps from car to motorcycle (ridden through a ditch, flipping diggers out one by one), to streetcar,

Above: The Keystone Kops in *Kars.* At the Sennett Studios, vehicles were written off daily

Below: Harry Tate and Company in 'Motoring'. A postcard, with a typically bad-tempered autograph

which loses contact with the overhead wires and runs wild through the streets. Lloyd climbs on the roof to fix the trolley; is swung out over the passing traffic and drops into the front seat of an empty car, which is being towed away backwards. Charlie Chaplin, meanwhile, being drunk, mistakes a lunch counter for a streetcar, clutches a hanging salami as a strap to balance himself, and tries to give the waiter his fare. On the sidewalk, Lloyd Hamilton is trying to do up a shoelace. He puts his foot up on a handy box, but it collapses. He sees an ash-can, at just the right height, but it's swung into the air as he approaches. An elderly gentleman is stooping to clean mud from a lady's foot; Lloyd tries to use the gent's bottom as a step, but is violently repulsed. The rear wheel of a water-wagon beckons, only to douse him with an alfresco shower. In desperation, Lloyd hails a streetcar. It stops, he puts foot to running-board, ties the lace — and imperiously waves the streetcar away.

Take . . . a train on *A Trip to Switzerland*, with the amazing Hanlon-Lees — 'the unconscious prophets of the crash of civilisation'. In the 1880s, the Hanlon-Lees astounded theatre audiences in Paris, London and New York by creating a Pullman sleeping car, with rotating wheels beneath it, which is then blown up on stage. The train splits into two, the screaming passengers fly into the air, and land in conveniently placed trees.

Film offered even more startling uses of the train as prop, in a tradition that runs from Keaton's epic *The General* to *Supertrain*, taking on board *Broadway Limited* (Hal Roach), *The Big Noise* (Laurel and Hardy), *Oh Mr Porter* (Will Hay), *Twentieth Century* (John Barrymore), *Around the World in Eighty Days* (David Niven), *Two Way Stretch* (Peter Sellers), *Some Like it Hot*, *The Magnificent Two* (Morecambe and Wise) and *The Wrong Box*, in which

Harry Langdon in *Tramp Tramp Tramp* (1926). He was a circus acrobat and tumbler, who came late to movies.

Sir Ralph Richardson survived a cataclysmic head-on collision, in the first-class lavatory.

In *Tramp*, *Tramp*, *Tramp*, Harry Langdon, fugitive from justice, throws his ball and chain (still attached to ankle) into the tender of a passing train — but hasn't the speed to jump in himself. He starts running . . . . Forty miles later the train stops and Langdon sits on a wheel to take a breather. His chain lies on the line. When the train starts up again it cuts through the chain. Langdon, unaware of his freedom, picks up the ball and sets off wearily alongside the train . . . .

The Marx Brothers wreak railway havoc *Going West*, picking up a farmhouse (with farmer on roof doing repairs) en route, and finally demolishing the train on which they're travelling, to fuel the engine.

Playing with trains . . . every schoolboy's dream ambition, most vividly realised by Buster Keaton in *The General*. A 'Boy's Own Adventure' becomes a comedy classic. An intensely *moving* picture, full of memorable imagery. Buster on the roof of his beloved engine, speeding through the spectacular Oregon landscape, leaning into the wind at an impossible angle, like Little Tich in his big boots. Buster, perched on the cow-catcher, playing 'spillikins' to remove the logs from the line ahead. Buster trying to escape the cannon on his own tender, which is now pointing straight at him; at the moment of discharge, a curve in the line puts the cannon-ball on a different trajectory. Phew! And the climactic collapse of Rock River Bridge, the pursuit train spilling into the water, belching steam. A moment of real drama, no place for laughs. Keaton's railway adventures began in *Our Hospitality*, on a runaway train, with Buster straddling engine and tender (which have become disconnected), one foot on each. The gap widens, but just before he's torn in two, the tender leaves the rails, taking Buster with it, and rolls down the embankment — into a river. Ever resourceful, Buster adapts to the new circumstances, finds a shovel, and paddles away into the distance.

Take . . . to the water, in anything that floats. Here's Keaton again, launching his home-made cabin cruiser, which climbs diagonally across the screen to go up-river, and vice versa down-river. Or Laurel and Hardy, fitting out their newly acquired fishing boat. Of course, Ollie will paint the masthead; Stan is banished to the cabin to keep him out of harm's way. Of course, he manages to get his head stuck between mast and bulkhead. And, of course, the only way he can extricate himself is by sawing through the mast. The shots that follow are visually superfluous, the

Buster Keaton, all at sea, with Kathryn McGuire; *The Navigator* (1924)

imaginative viewer having already envisaged the graceful parabola against the sky, the traditional tableau of Ollie, spreadeagled in the mud. And that's the closest he gets to the water. On the highway, Stan suggests they raise the sail to speed up the towing. A gust of wind produces another off-screen debacle, nothing salvageable from boat or car, except Stan's hooter . . . .

Meanwhile, here's Jacques Tati paddling his own canoe, which is hinged in the middle, for easier handling. If it folds up on the water, however, the luckless Monsieur Hulot will be folded up in it — and his attempts to extricate himself transform the ends of the canoe into the snapping jaws of a giant fish. The beach clears instantly.

Take . . . a plane, as the pace hots up and the daredevils of motion comedy head for new horizons. Snub Pollard, in pursuit of a set of false teeth (let's not go into *that*!), hijacks a plane, demolishes a barn, and acquires a pig (on the wing). Climbs out to free pig, falls off — onto a passing oil derrick. Caught *en passant*, by the foot, in a rope — which swings him round in a great arc and deposits him in the front seat of the plane he was pursuing! *Sold at Auction* was made at the Hal Roach studios in 1923, setting the standard for aerobatic comedy, *sauve qui peut*. For the next half century the skies were full of airborne incompetents: George Formby (*It's in the Air*) ; Abbott and Costello (*Keep 'em Flying*); Harpo Marx (*A Night in Casablanca*); Laurel and Hardy (*The Flying Deuces*); Jimmy Edwards (*Nearly a Nasty Accident*); W. C. Fields (*Never Give a Sucker an Even Break*); Jack Lemmon (*The Great Race*); Terry-Thomas et al. (*Those Magnificent Men in their Flying Machines*); Michael Crawford (*Some Mothers Do 'Ave 'Em*); Fred MacMurray (*The Absentminded Professor*); and Robert Hays (*Airplane*).

Extended ladder business from *It's a Mad Mad Mad Mad World* (1963)

The last reel brings the pursuers onto a wobbly fire-escape, six floors up, and thence . . . to a *ladder*. Kramer adds a new dimension to 'ladder business', as defined by Auriol, the Hanlon-Lees, Jewel and Warriss. He puts his ten protagonists on the end of a fireman's ladder, fully extended and swinging from side to side like a giant metronome. A 'perilous ladder' routine with a vengeance, from which all shall fall — Sid Caesar into an office block and down the stairwell; Phil Silvers through a bedroom window and onto a fold-up bed, which folds up; Buddy Hackett and Milton Berle into a tree and thence through a plate-glass window; Terry-Thomas and Mickey Rooney onto electricity wires, which bounce them into a lily pond; Spencer Tracy into a pet shop and the slavering embrace of a pack of mongrels. Dissolve to the hospital ward where the frustrated adventurers languish, trussed up and mummified.

'I'd like to think,' says Tracy sadly, 'that *some* time — maybe ten or twenty years from now — there'd be something I could laugh at. Anything.'

It's a Mad Mad Mad Mad World decreed producer Stanley Kramer in 1963, when he paid tribute to the silent pioneers of motion comedy with an epic 'chase' movie, to end all 'chase' movies. Chance, and the lure of money, bring together an ill-assorted gang of fortune-hunters, who use any and every mode of transport in pursuit of the loot. Cars, trains, lorries, planes — forwards, backwards, upwards, downwards; flying through buildings, driving on water, hurtling across the open spaces of the Cinerama screen against a soundtrack that buzzes with the frenzied hysteria of human greed.

Which is the cue for Ethel Merman to make an entrance, blasting into the ward on full throttle, only to be up-ended in a glorious 'floating on air' pratfall, by that most fundamental of comic props, the *sine qua non* of skiddy subversion, an ambush for the unwary, the coefficient of comeuppance, the Great Leveller — 'Look out, it's right in front of you!' — the slippery skin of the humble banana. No self-respecting prop list is complete without one.

CHAPTER SIX

· SPARRING ·

PARTNERS

GEORGE FOOTIT was an equestrian acrobat who served his apprenticeship in his father's Great Footit Allied Circus. He joined Sanger's Circus and, by 1880, had become one of the most famous horseback clowns. He went to France where, in a card game, he lost his horse. Dismounted, he began to experiment with the traditional clown entrées and formed a partnership with an *émigré* Cuban, Raphael Padilla, who had been sold into service in Portugal. Padilla, who was black, became 'Chocolat', and 'Footit and Chocolat' went into business as a double-act.

In the ring, Chocolat presented himself as a would-be man of the world, a fool attempting to be dignified but rarely getting away with it. Impeccably dressed in silk stockings, satin breeches, stylish jacket and hat, he became the butt of Footit's arbitrary and savage bullying. Their relationship was analysed by a Victorian journalist:

Sour-faced Footit putting the boot in. Chocolat is unconcerned: his turn will come

> Footit is the despotic master, pig-headed, narrow-minded, ill-natured, goading, cowardly toward his superiors, bossy around those below him. Chocolat on the other hand is the hapless Negro scapegoat who obeys without complaining, but who still acts lazy and whose impassive mask leaves the spectator vague as to whether he has before

him an absolute fool without a brain in his head, or an intelligent but unfortunate individual who is aware of his moral forfeiture, who understands everything, but says nothing because . . . he knows it would not do any good!

Roles were clearly defined from the moment Footit loudly declared 'Monsieur Chocolat, I shall be obliged to slap you.' A man of his word, Footit would then deliver a punishing 'straight nap', felling his elegant partner. According to Footit's biographer, Parisian audiences 'were delighted to see that this gentleman, who was so chic, was destined to be a victim of the impertinent slaps of the clown in multicoloured tights, whitened face, and conical hat!'

Footit loved to parody the Montmartre street-singers, whom he considered to be boring in the extreme. Coming to the centre of the ring, he would announce that he was going to sing 'La Petite Maison'. Clearing his throat he would begin to sing:

A la maison nous n'irons plus,
A la maison nous n'irons pas,
A la maison nous n'irons jamais pas,
A la maison nous n'irons plus . . .

This awful dirge would bring Chocolat into the

ring, curiosity aroused. Footit sings on. Chocolat becomes impatient. He hits Footit on the shoulder. Footit sings on, unperturbed. Chocolat hits him harder. Footit stops singing long enough to slap Chocolat. Then he starts singing again, from the beginning:

> A la maison nous n'irons plus,
> A la maison nous n'irons pas,
> A la maison nous n'irons jamais pas,
> A la maison nous n'irons plus . . .

Chocolat comes again to Footit; kicks him, gently. Then a bit harder. Ten kicks, twenty kicks, a hundred kicks, first with the right leg, then the left. All the while Footit sings on, regardless. Finally, Chocolat collapses from exhaustion. Now Footit pauses, notices Chocolat on the ground, gazes at him disdainfully. After an apologetic gesture to the audience, he bows, announces the first couplet again, and begins to sing:

> A la maison nous n'irons plus,
> A la maison nous n'irons pas . . .

At least two people are needed to carry Footit from the ring. And still he keeps on singing.

Equally violent was the encounter between Secchi and Alfano — a classic clown routine, sometimes known as 'Dead and Alive'. The protagonists bet five francs to see who can stand on his head the longest. Secchi cheats, Alfano retaliates, and they come to blows. A lethal punch apparently kills Alfano, but when Secchi tries to remove the body before the police arrive, he discovers it to be more alive than dead. If he pulls Alfano's legs together, the arms spring apart; like a puppet come to life, Alfano's extremities impede all Secchi's attempts to gather up the corpse. The movements of the two clowns are coordinated in a sequence of acrobatic stunts — all perfectly motivated by the peculiar circumstances of Alfano's 'death'. Secchi finally succeeds in removing his partner from the ring by borrowing a wheel, putting the ends of the axle in Alfano's hands, and pushing him off like a wheelbarrow.

The ground rules for the comic double-act, as laid down in the sawdust ring, were further developed in the Victorian theatre, where the post-Grimaldi Harlequinade focused on the love-hate relationship between Clown and Pantaloon — artful 'Joey' and the weak-kneed 'old 'un'. An account in the British Museum conjures up their frantic antics:

> If Clown receives a slap of the face, he pays himself instanter, by knocking down the offerer of the insult. If Pantaloon in turning a corner, by accident runs against his brother motley, and is struck down by the collision, he bears no ill blood, but lays his hand to the leg of the fellow, and pulls him down after him, with the amiable desire of 'making all straight with him'. Clown is not offended by the kind solicitude of Pantaloon, as some of dully-framed human beings might be; — not he! He throws a somersault, springs to his feet, gives a horse-laugh, which would frighten the best animal in Christendom, to show that he thinks nothing of the affair — he takes a prodigious leap, that seats him comfortably on Pantaloon's shoulder — and whirling over his adopted hobby, tumbles into a baker's truck which is just entering.
>
> Under all circumstances, Clown and Pantaloon pull together. Though they baste one another — a proof, merely, as in an Irish scrimmage, of their partiality for one another — they allow no-one else to 'step between them and their fighting souls'. Like Beatrice and Benedict, they wage a merry war with one another, and all the world.

Height and shape were important factors in the evolution of the double-act. Clown must be short and solid, Pantaloon tall and thin. Shakespeare, it is said, created the model for Abbott and Costello when he paired Sir Andrew Aguecheek with Sir Toby Belch in *Twelfth Night*. And Fred Karno put tubby little Jack Melville alongside gigantic Fred Kitchen for his sketch 'The Bailiffs', which was premiered at the Argyle Theatre, Birkenhead, 1907. 'He knew what he was doing,' chuckled Jack. 'Even before we did anything we were sure to get a laugh, just standing there, like David and Goliath!' The Bailiffs of the title are Simpkins (Kitchen) and Meredith (Melville). Their task is to 'distrain upon the property' of a householder — but first they have to gain access to the house. Easier said than done.

SIMPKINS and MEREDITH approach the front door, which is at the top of a flight of steps. MEREDITH is carrying a bag.

SIMPKINS: Well, here we are.

MEREDITH: Is this the house?

SIMPKINS: The number's on the warrant.

MEREDITH [searching for it]:   Oh dear, I wish I'd brought the piano.

SIMPKINS: Why, what do you want a piano for?

A twentieth-century revival of the classic confrontation: Clown (Bob Hoskins) versus Pantaloon (Andy Andrews)

MEREDITH: Well, that's where I left the warrant — on the piano!

[*SIMPKINS beats MEREDITH about the head*]

SIMPKINS: Here's what we'll do. You stand over there, on the alert. I'll knock on the door, and when she opens it, you come off the alert, give me a push, and — Meredith, we're in!

[*SIMPKINS goes up the steps, knocks on the door. He turns, signals MEREDITH to be ready: While he's looking away, LUCY (the maid) opens the door, looks out. SIMPKINS turns back, sees the open door just as LUCY is closing it. SIMPKINS makes a rush, gets his fingers trapped in the closing door. MEREDITH rushes up the steps to free him, both fall backwards down the steps, land in a heap.*]

MEREDITH: You might have been in, there, laddie.

SIMPKINS: I *was* in [*measuring his finger-tip*] — *that* much.

[*They get up, dust themselves down. SIMPKINS picks up his bag.*]

The Poluski Brothers as Blake and Holmes — the detectives — in *The Sleeping Beauty*

MEREDITH: What's in the bag, laddie?

SIMPKINS: Disguises. I thought they might come in handy.

[*He empties bag, takes charlady's skirt, shawl and bonnet, starts dressing himself up.*]

MEREDITH: What's the plan, laddie?

SIMPKINS: I'm going to knock at the door, and ask to clean the steps. She's got to give me a pail of water. So, when she goes to get it, you give me a push, and — Meredith, we're in!

[*SIMPKINS goes up the steps, knocks again. LUCY opens the door.*]

SIMPKINS: Good morning, lady. Don't you know me? — I'm Rosie the charwoman. I'll clean your steps for a copper or two.

LUCY: No, I shan't bother. It looks like rain.

SIMPKINS: Please, lady — I haven't had a bite all day.

LUCY: Oh, very well then.

[*She goes, closing the door. SIMPKINS puts a leg against it, leans, warns MEREDITH. LUCY opens the window, and hands out a pail. Pause. Double take. Resignedly, SIMPKINS takes the pail, starts washing the steps.*]

SIMPKINS: Well, that's that.

MEREDITH: So I see, laddie.

The Brothers Griffiths: a double-act for the stage and for the ring

SIMPKINS: You'd better have a go now. Can you throw a fit?

MEREDITH: I'll try, laddie.

[*He starts rolling and groaning. SIMPKINS watches in disgust.*]

SIMPKINS: You're the worst fitter I've ever seen. For goodness sake put more feeling into it.

[*MEREDITH obliges. SIMPKINS runs up and down the steps, in panic, knocking at the door en passant. LUCY opens the door, sees MEREDITH.*]

LUCY: Why, whatever is the matter?

SIMPKINS: He's fainted on your doorstep, lady — fetch some brandy quick.

LUCY: We've got no brandy.

SIMPKINS: Well, two pale ales — anything...

Karno's Bailiffs are the first in a long line of comic partnerships in music-hall and pantomime. The Griffiths, the Two McNaughtons, the Poluski Brothers, and Lupino and Evans were among the many duos assured of a seasonal spot in Christmas pantomimes, where the Broker's Men (*Cinderella*), the Robbers (*Babes in the Wood*), the Chinese Policemen (*Aladdin*), the Two Pirates (*Sinbad the Sailor*) are parts tailor-made for tumbling twosomes. At Southport, for the 1985 Christmas season, Les Dennis and Dustin Gee played both the Broker's Men and the Ugly Sisters in Cinderella. This double duty took its toll: Dustin Gee collapsed with a heart attack and died on 3 January 1986.

Starting in 1914, two hard-headed Australians, Roy Rene and Nat Phillips, pioneered two-handed 'business' in the Antipodes as 'Stiffy' (no relation to Karno's inept goal-keeper) and 'Mo'. They opened modestly at the Princess Theatre, near Sydney's Central Station, with one of the routines fundamental to double-acts — 'Just a Moment'. Stiffy is preparing to sing a song, shooting his cuffs, clearing his throat, when Mo rushes on.

MO: I say, just a moment, have you heard, Arthur's dead.

STIFFY: What did he die of?

MO: Well, d'you know that iron staircase outside my house?

STIFFY: No, I never saw it.

MO: Neither did Arthur.   [*Exits — but returns as STIFFY opens his mouth to sing*]

The idiot paired with the bully-boy: Barry Lupino (Funnykin) and Will Evans (Pompos) in *The Sleeping Beauty*

Mo, alias Roy Rene, alias Harry Van Der Sluice. He continued as a solo act after the death of Stiffy (Nat Phillips) in 1932

Stiffy and Mo. Mo died in Sydney in 1954

Mo: I say, just a moment, take a look at this ring. What do you think? I gave the fellow a five-pound note for it.

STIFFY: Why, this ring was made in King's Cross!

Mo: So was the five-pound note!   [*Exits, but returns with a bale of hay*]

STIFFY: Just a moment, where are you going with that hay?

Mo: I'm taking it to your wife.

STIFFY: Why take hay to my wife?

Mo: I've heard she eats like a horse.   [*Exits*]

For seven years, Stiffy and Mo played top of the bill in all the Australian capitals except Perth and Hobart. Nat Phillips used to complain bitterly that theatres where they played were full of aspiring duos, furiously transcribing the best gags. 'As a matter of fact,' said Phillips, 'there are only forty thieves in this profession. Roy and I want the other thirty-eight exterminated!' Mo cultivated a deliberately unshaven look, which involved sticking black crepe paper to a few days' growth of beard. He was an outrageous scene-stealer, forever mugging and doing funny walks during his partner's best lines. Their dressing-room was always furnished with substantial, unbreakable items.

At the Princess Theatre, in Melbourne, the young violinist, Nancye Bridges, had the misfortune to be sharing the bill with Stiffy and Mo: and allowed herself to be inveigled into taking part in one of their sketches. The scene was a high society 'musical evening', with titled ladies and gentlemen in full evening dress listening to a recital of Bach. A few bars in, Mo bounded into the scene, an unsavoury interloper. Lurching up to the unfortunate violinist, he leered horribly, and announced through a fine spray of spit: 'Strike me lucky — it's Lily from Little Lon!' Miss Bridges was mortified, doubly so because her mother was in the audience, trebly so when she learned that the street referred to was currently Melbourne's 'red light' area. Thereafter, Mama limited playing engagements to concert halls, where a 'better class of artist' would be encountered. Mo continued to flourish and played a leading role in Olsen and Johnson's *Hellzapoppin* at the Empire Theatre in Sydney.

The 1930s saw the stalwarts of Fred Karno's Knockabout Army facing a double threat. The cinema, which in its infancy had fostered the art of mime and visual comedy, was now in the process of discovering sound, which would favour the 'gag-men', and the 'cross-talk' merchants. The writing was on the wall for those 'speechless comedians' who relied more on acrobatic skill than a well-filled joke book. A sketch from the Karno portfolio epitomises the shape of things to come: 'The Means Test Committee' — plenty of *jokes*, no *business*.

The scene is a bare council office. Behind the desk sits HARRY WELDON *(the 'commissioner') in black suit, pince-nez glasses.* JACK MELVILLE *(scruffy layabout) stands in front of the desk.*

WELDON: What's your name?

MELVILLE: Allsop.

WELDON: Any relation to the Allsop who sells beer?

MELVILLE: Yes. Customer.

WELDON: How long have you been on the dole?

MELVILLE: Since it started.

WELDON: Where do you live?

MELVILLE: In a house. Big house.

WELDON: Where?

MELVILLE: Up a hill. It's the workhouse.

WELDON: Have you lived there all your life?

MELVILLE: Not yet.

WELDON: Are you an inmate?

MELVILLE: When I'm in, mate, I'm an inmate.

WELDON: What was your last job?

MELVILLE: I was on the Railway.

WELDON: What did you do?

MELVILLE: Open the carriage doors.

WELDON: What for?

MELVILLE: To see if they were shut.

WELDON: Where were you born?

MELVILLE: In Newcastle.

WELDON: Why Newcastle?

MELVILLE: I wanted to be near my mother.

WELDON: Have you ever been in the Army?

MELVILLE: Yes, but they chucked me out.

WELDON: Why?

MELVILLE: I lost my tambourine.

WELDON: Are you married?

MELVILLE: Yes, sixteen wives, no kids.

WELDON: Ridiculous — no man in England is allowed sixteen wives.

MELVILLE: Yes, he is. Doesn't it say in the Marriage Service: 'Four richer, four poorer, four better, four worse'? Well, four fours are sixteen.

In 1926 — a sign of the times? — Karno had been declared bankrupt. The Fun Factory and all the company props and scenery were sold off. Karno's unsecured liabilities totalled £16,646. His realised assets amounted to £338. The following year the first millionaire 'plonk' arrived from America to publicise his new feature-length comedy *The Gold Rush*. There was still no contact between Charlie Chaplin and his 'guv'nor'; however, Sydney Chaplin *did* meet up with Karno and announced that he had been invited to produce two films in London for British International Pictures. The first of these, he suggested to Karno, was to be a screen adaptation of *Mumming Birds*. How he proposed to improve on his brother's 1915 version of the same piece (*A Night in the Show*) is not known; in the event, this was never put to the test. Sydney's film failed to get off the ground and some years later a disappointed comedian called George Carney received £227 10s damages from B.I.P. for breach of contract to employ him in the film.

After lying low for a number of years, Karno once again began to toy with the idea of film-making. A New York agent had been trying to persuade him to come over to provide material for an up-and-coming vaudeville act — 'The Marx Brothers'. At the same time, Jesse Lasky, who had once been a theatrical agent in London and was now a film producer, had written several letters to Karno suggesting he should try his luck in the States. So Karno embarked for New York, hoping to improve his fortunes in the New World.

In New York he discovered that the prospects

of working with the Marx Brothers were illusory and that Jesse Lasky had gone to the West Coast. He decided to follow him there. On arrival in Hollywood he booked himself into the Roosevelt Hotel and then headed for La Brea Avenue, to look up Charlie Chaplin. Arriving unannounced, he found his erstwhile protégé, dressed in his working clothes of ragged pullover and baggy slacks, on the back lot.

'Guv'nor!' cried the astonished Chaplin, 'what a surprise!' He took Karno home to his Beverly Hills mansion, where he played the organ for two hours, and then announced that he was going to dinner with Marion Davies. Whether Karno dared to raise the thorny question of Chaplin's celluloid piracy is not recorded. Chaplin makes no mention of the meeting in his autobiography.

Next, Karno paid a call at the Roach Studios to look up another 'plonk' who had made good in the movies — Stan Laurel. Like Chaplin, Laurel had gone to America with a touring version of *Mumming Birds*, and had decided to stay on. It took him longer than Chaplin to break into films, during which time he appeared in vaudeville as a solo comedian. In 1917 he was spotted by Hal Roach who gave him a part in *Nuts in May*. Soon after this he made an appearance with an actor called Oliver Hardy, in a film called *Lucky Dog*. The association was so casual that, on the evidence of later interviews, both men forgot it entirely. In the scene they play together, Hardy is the 'heavy', holding up a man in the street and taking his money. Laurel, passing by, stops just behind Hardy, with the result that Hardy stuffs the money into Laurel's pocket. When he finds out, he turns his gun on Laurel, and the first words spoken between them are given in a title: 'Put 'em both up, insect, before I comb your hair with lead!'

The 'guv'nor' was greeted warmly by Stan Laurel, who never concealed his immense professional admiration for Karno. He introduced him to Hal Roach, who suggested that Karno might like to 'sit on the lot for a few weeks, and learn how we do it'. Which he agreed to do, readily accepting a fee of $1000 per week for his movie apprenticeship. He was installed in an office and given carte blanche to attend script conferences,

rehearsals and filming, and to contribute ideas for scenes and 'business'. However, within a few weeks Karno became painfully aware that his well-paid sinecure was little more than a gesture of gratitude from Stan Laurel. No one paid any attention to him, and his suggestions and comments were mostly ignored. Besides, as Jack Melville recalls, Karno was never very adept at articulating his ideas.

> He had a funny way of always saying 'See? See what I mean? See?' — because with him what you *saw* was all that mattered. He was much better at showing people what he meant, rather than telling them.

In the end, Karno blew his top. He had finally persuaded Roach to let him direct a scene, which he had devised, in which a banker is sitting in a hotel lobby, with a tiny black dog on his lap and his silk top hat on a table beside him. Enter a waiter, who knocks the hat off the table with the tail of his coat. Apologising profusely, he picks up the hat with one hand and the dog with the other hand, and carefully brushes the dust off the hat — with the dog. It was a good gag, and Roach had every intention of including the scene in his film. Unfortunately, on the day the scene was to be

Fred Karno visits Laurel and Hardy at the Hal Roach studios

shot, the dog, which Karno had chosen, escaped
from his handler, ran out of the studio gates and
was run over by a passing car. When the news was
brought to Karno on the set, he exploded.
Convinced that he was the victim of a conspiracy,
he walked out of the studio and headed for home,
via New York City. A splenetic press conference
produced the farewell headline: 'FRED KARNO,
DISGUSTED WITH AMERICA, DECIDES TO 'OP IT'.

Although the Roach Studio breathed a
communal sigh of relief at Karno's departure, the
few weeks that Roach had had Laurel's 'guv'nor'
on his payroll had done nothing to diminish the
American film-maker's respect for Karno's
achievement. On a subsequent visit to London,
when he saw Karno's *Real Life* at the Hackney
Empire, Roach told English reporters:

> Your Fred Karno is not only a genius,
> gentlemen, he is the man who originated
> slapstick comedy. We in Hollywood owe much
> to him.

Roach himself must take the credit for an
important shift in the evolution of the comic
double-act. What had been rarely more than a
convenience pairing of two comics was to
become, under Roach's direction, a fully
developed human relationship, with a history and
a future. The accidental juxtaposition in *Lucky
Dog* had given Roach the idea that Stan Laurel
and Oliver Hardy together would be funnier than
either on their own. In both he saw a childlike
quality, and it was his belief that 'visual
comedians essentially imitate children'. Hardy,
shyly lowering his head, glancing through
eyebrows, twiddling his tie in embarrassment;
Laurel shrugging, beaming, close to tears.

In the early Laurel and Hardy films the roles
were not well defined. In fact, in *Sailors Beware*,
they are hardly on the screen together. Hardy is
the purser on a cruise ship, ingratiating himself
with the lady passengers and trying to foil a
stowaway jewel thief. Laurel is a cab driver
whose vehicle has been accidentally taken on
board; his adventures include losing dice to a
midget, and taking a poke in the eye from a
flapper. In *Do Detectives Think?* Laurel is still the
frantic tearaway of his solo films, rushing through
the frame in pursuit of villainy, reacting
hysterically to the unexpected: a revolver shot
causes him to leap piggyback onto the shoulders
of the person next to him (even if it's the lady of

Big Business (1929). Tit-for-tat violence: Laurel and Hardy demolish
James Finlayson's house while he vandalises their car. The comedy lies
in the pauses between the outrages

the house). Hardy at first seems to be trying to keep up with his partner — an impossible task. So he lags behind, out of touch, unable to compete.

What was needed was for Hardy to take authority. To tap Laurel on the shoulder, as it were, and order him to stand back: 'Let *me* handle this.' Waiting, blinking, *reacting* to Hardy's self-inflicted havoc, Laurel was better placed to assume the childlike role Roach wished upon him: Laurel the innocent, Laurel the put-upon, Laurel the tearful go-stand-in-the-corner booby.

Putting Pants on Philip (1927) sees the beginnings of this new relationship. Laurel is Hardy's nephew, newly arrived from Scotland, wearing a kilt, of all things. Hardy, taking charge, marches Laurel to the nearest tailor to be measured for trousers. The Scotsman's undue modesty provides the comic key to the scene that follows, with Laurel flinching tearfully from the tailor's measuring tape, and Oliver reassuring, scolding, finally aiding the tailor to wrestle his victim to the floor to ascertain the all-important 'inside leg'.

In the films that followed, at an astonishing rate, Hardy is confirmed as He Who Leads, Laurel as He Who Must Follow, and who gets his finger slapped away from the doorbell if he steps out of place. If it's James Finlayson's doorbell, in *Big Business*, the summons provokes a comic confrontation of classic proportion, in which Finlayson's home is disassembled and the partners' car torn apart in a back-and-forth ritual of solemn tit for tat. If it's the doorbell of 1127 Walnut Avenue, it's at the top of a monumental flight of steps, and there's a piano to be delivered (*The Music Box*). First two flights, no problems. Then they encounter a lady with a pram; they lift the pram to help her pass — and the piano's on the move, downwards. Back to where they started. The lady laughs a lot. Stan, miffed, aims a kick at her backside, gets a punch on the nose. Oliver, very amused at this, gets a milk bottle broken over his head. Back to work . . . and four flights later they reach their destination. Leave the piano, to ring the doorbell ('Let *me*, Stanley') — and it's gone again, all the way down. Third time lucky. Piano secure, Hardy rings the bell — pulls it out! There's obviously no one at home, so 'we'll take it through the window'. Of course. Business with block and tackle, and balcony awning; block falls onto Hardy's head. He dives through front door. Piano falls from window into patio pool. Ollie follows. Then Stan. A horse watches from across the fence, amazed.

The introduction of synchronised sound, which caused the demise of Keaton and Langdon, posed few problems for Laurel and Hardy. Their first all-talking film, *Berth Marks*, was apparently made without a script, so that a long sequence of the partners trying to undress in the upper berth of a train suffers somewhat from the overuse of one line of dialogue — 'Will you stop *crowding*' — repeated, ad nauseam, by Hardy. But *Men of War* eliminated the clumsiness of their first foray and blended visual and verbal humour. As sailors on furlough, the boys take two girls to a soda fountain. As they can only afford three sodas, Hardy, the decision-taker, explains to Laurel that they'll have to share one — 'and you can drink your half first'. Unseen by Hardy, Laurel drinks the whole glass. Hardy, smiling winningly at the girls, takes glass in hand to drink, sees it's empty, and smile clouds over. 'Do you know what you've done?' he asks Laurel. A sheepish nod. 'Why did you do it?' — at which Laurel breaks down and cries 'I couldn't help it, my half was on the bottom!'

By the time *Hollywood Party* was made (1934), sound was back in its rightful place as *punctuation* between comic events. Laurel and Hardy's encounter with the 'Mexican Spitfire', Lupe Velez, is remarkable for the deathly silence that precedes each manoeuvre. The trouble begins at a bar, where Lupe sits, perched on a stool. Her shoe falls off. Hardy, ever the gentleman, returns it to her — and, for his pains, gets a blow on the head with a stiletto heel. This leads to the breaking of a few eggs, into the lady's other shoe. Who then returns the compliment, with eggs, broken in the hand, then decanted into Hardy's pocket. Sticky hands are then wiped on a nearby lapel. A long pause follows. Laurel, who has watched all this from his rightful place on the sidelines, moves into the arena. He takes a peek into Hardy's pocket (just to check), then whispers advice into his partner's ear. Emboldened, Hardy takes two eggs, one in each hand, but before he can use them the wily Mexican has cracked both, with her stiletto. She places two more, unbroken, in Hardy's pants. A smile, and a hefty egg-cracking slap, almost as an afterthought. There is then a long, drawn-out sigh from Hardy. A bit of repositioning, and an egg is carefully balanced on a barstool. Now comes the first line of dialogue.

HARDY: Siddown.

LUPE: Alright.

She sits. There is great merriment from all three.

Early to Bed (1928). Laurel is Hardy's valet. He's trying to put the boss to bed. Hardy wants to play

Then, a full-blooded 'straight nap' to Laurel, and
an elbow in the guts for Hardy.

LAUREL: Owwwwwww!

HARDY: Oooooooof!

Viewed without the benefit of a cinema-full of
laughter, the empty spaces on the soundtrack
stand out. With hindsight, it's clear that the
timing of gags, and the spaces between them, was
being adjusted to the new film medium and to the
audience's response. Stan Laurel, who was the
creative dynamo of the partnership, devised a
scheme to show 'rough-cut' versions of their films
to a preview audience, where he would measure,
with a stopwatch, their laughs. The cuts in the
film would then be adjusted to fit.

But the *visual* gag remained their trump card,

in perfectly constructed sequences; the essential
ups and downs of physical comedy, reworked and
extended to perfectly logical conclusions. Like
Early to Bed, where Laurel, working as a butler in
Hardy's house, has been provoked into breaking
up the place. Hardy tries desperately to stop him.
He corners Laurel, who is holding a precious vase
in front of an ornate panel of three panes of glass.
Hardy throws a brick at him. It misses, and
shatters one pane. Laurel takes this in, thinks, and
throws the vase through the second pane. Hardy
makes threatening gestures; Laurel backs away in
fear, knocks over a standard lamp — and the lamp
goes through the third pane. Or *Bacon Grabbers*

(American equivalent of 'The Bailiffs'), where the partners have to repossess Edgar Kennedy's radio because he hasn't kept up the payments. Eventually, they succeed in repossessing it. On their way to the sheriff's office they pause for a breather, putting the radio — an elegant console model — down on the road. A passing steamroller demolishes it. Kennedy is cock-a-hoop. His wife then appears with the good news that she has paid the outstanding instalments and the radio is theirs. Laurel and Hardy rejoice. The steamroller, meanwhile, continues on its course — and crushes their car. Fade out.... Or *Double Trouble*, with *both* in a phone booth when the phone rings. A drunk joins them — 'It's for me.' A tight squeeze, hats, flowers, telephone passed from hand to hand, faces pressed against the glass, noses bent, milk spilled, Stan trampled.... Finally, the booth is overturned. A passer-by inquires: 'What happened — did you get in a fight?'

They made one hundred and five films together and, for both, the partnership proved more durable than marriage. Hardy married three times, Laurel no fewer than six times — three times to the same woman, Ruth Rogers. But between the partners, all was sweetness and light.

Laurel said:

> We seemed to sense each other. I loved editing and cutting the pictures, something Ollie wasn't interested in — he preferred to spend his afternoons playing golf. But whatever I did was tops with him. There was never any argument between us, ever.

No arguments, no rivalry. Uniquely among film double-acts, both partners share the laughs; the big fat man is as funny as the short thin one.

According to Bud Abbott, this combination was unworkable. He claimed that:

> Every comic needs a straight man, a 'lecturer'. There are only seven original jokes in the world. It's the way you sell and deliver 'em that gets the laughs. And without somebody to bounce off, the funniest guy in the world is all at sea.

The partnership of Abbott and Costello emerged from the seedy world of burlesque theatres in the 1930s. Bud Abbott had worked with a number of comics before he saw Lou Costello doing the 'Lemon Table' routine at the Eltinge Theatre in New York and invited him to

Costello terrorised, as ever; *Abbott and Costello Meet the Invisible Man* (1951)

team up. There was never any doubt about who did what. Bud said:

> Lou is the funniest man in the world — when he wants to be. I know every move of his body; I know just how he's going to react. When we go out on stage, we haven't decided what we'll do. Lou can choose from a thousand routines, and I'll have the questions for him.

From the Steel Pier, Atlantic City, 1934:

BUD: Didn't I see you at the race-track today?

LOU: Yeah, I was there. I like to bet on the nags.

BUD [*grabbing him*]:   Don't talk like that about horses! Do you realise that I have one of the greatest mudders in the country?

LOU: What's your mother got to do with horses?

BUD: My mudder *is* a horse.

LOU: What? I will admit there's a resemblance.

BUD: My mudder won the first race at Hialeah yesterday.

LOU: You oughta be ashamed at yourself, putting your mother in a horse race.

BUD: I take very good care of her. If she don't feel like running, I scratch her.

LOU: And what do you give the old lady for breakfast — oats?

BUD: Don't be old-fashioned. Modern mudders don't eat oats. They eat their fodder.

And so on. Cross-talk was the basis for the act; Abbott the know-all, Costello the idiot. Any attempts to improve his mind will, inevitably, founder. At the doctor's, for example:

DOCTOR: Mister Abbott, I don't understand how you can run around with a nincompoop like Lou Costello.

BUD: I wouldn't dream of inflicting him on anybody else.

DOCTOR: Mister Abbott, you're a bad influence on this boy. I resent your derogatory and insulting treatment of him. Just because he happens to be a poor illiterate boor with the intelligence of a delinquent doesn't mean you can abuse him.

BUD: Now, look here . . .

LOU [*interrupting*]:   Now, just a minute, Abbott — you had this coming to you for a long time.

DOCTOR: I want you to notice this boy — his blank, expressionless countenance, the receding forehead, the antediluvian physiognomy of this boy — can you blame him for being a slovenly, unkempt, grubby-looking crumb?

LOU [*delighted*]:   How do you like them apples?

DOCTOR: You must admit you've seen more intelligent specimens in *cages*.

BUD: I wouldn't say that . . .

LOU: Oh, you can say it — you just don't want to remember it.

No love lost between these partners. The idiot relies on the wise guy for guidance, support, help: but all too often the despairing cry 'Abbotttttttttt!' falls on deaf ears, and He Who Will Be Put Upon is left floundering in the giant washing machine, assaulted by the dentist, persecuted by the psychiatrist, nailed by the cop. A visit to the sanatorium, for a much-needed rest cure, brings to Lou's bedside a succession of loony visitors — gunmen, gamblers, gardeners, firemen — all seemingly bent on driving the patient further out of his wits. When the duo appeared in *Rest Cure* at the Broadhurst Theater, New York, in 1939, Brooks Atkinson wrote in the *New York Times*:

> Abbott is the overbearing master-mind whose feverish, impatient guidance of the conversation produces the crisis. Costello is the moon-faced zany with wide, credulous eyes, a high voice, and puffy hands that struggle in futile gestures. Both men work themselves into a state of excitement that is wonderful to behold.

The films Abbott and Costello made for Universal Pictures in the 1940s saved the studio from bankruptcy, and became the model for the next generation of double-acts, on both sides of the Atlantic. In the United States, Wheeler and Woolsey, Clark and McCullough, Martin and Lewis; in England, Jewel and Warriss, Murray and Mooney, Morecambe and Wise. All adhering to the principle of the 'straight man' and the comic but varying the balance of the relationship between the two.

In the Jewel and Warriss partnership, Ben Warriss is a bully in the Abbott mould. In the 'Tank Sketch', Jimmy Jewel is the gormless, gullible idiot who wants to buy a pen that will write under water. Ben is the sadistic salesman who insists that the customer must give the pen a full underwater trial, to which end he reveals, behind a curtain, a tank ten feet high and full of

Jimmy Jewel with his partner and cousin, Ben Warriss; a Royal Command Performance in Blackpool, 1955

Martin and Lewis: the schnook and the smoothie. *Living It Up* (1954)

water, into which the luckless Jimmy, forcibly stripped to his underpants, is promptly plunged. Pen and paper in hand, the victim flounders like a monster goldfish, mouth pressed to glass. If he bobs to the surface, probably to express his evident satisfaction with his purchase, a firm hand pushes him back under the water. On a good night, Jimmy could expect to spend as much as fifteen minutes submerged. On a bad night, at the Pavilion, Rhyl, the tank split and the water flooded the orchestra pit and fused every light in the theatre. 'If I hadn't grabbed the edge and hung on,' says Jimmy, 'I would have been swept through the glass and cut to pieces.'

At the Club 500 in Atlantic City, an impromptu performance, replacing a lousy singer, launched the partnership of Dean Martin and Jerry Lewis. Stepping into the breach, they improvised a forty-minute variation on the well-worn 'Just a Minute' routine: Martin the suave crooner, Lewis the frenzied busboy creating noisy diversions and interruptions around the singer, conducting the band with his shoe, burning their music, up-

ending tables, accosting customers, spilling soup. In terms of energy expended, the partnership might have seemed uneven. But Lewis liked to give credit where it was due.

Imagine a day at the circus. . . . There at the centre ring, is the flyer winging his way high up on a trapeze while thousands watch his every move, not realising that if it weren't for the catcher below, the flyer would be nothing.

And Dean was my catcher — the greatest straight man in the history of show business. His sense of timing was so flawless, so infinite and so fragile it almost looked as if he didn't do anything at all. Which, of course was the magic, giving form and substance to the act.

The twosome went on to play the Copacabana in New York and Slapsie Maxie's in Hollywood, where producer Hal Wallis saw them and signed them up for five years. In all, they made thirteen films for Paramount, which topped the box-office ratings, but almost invariably bombed with the critics. Milton Shulman wrote in the *Evening Standard*:

> In more enlightened times it would be considered impolite, almost indecent, to be amused by such ugliness, lunacy and deformity. . . . The team represent a deterioration in humorous taste not far removed from what might be expected if the printing-press were suddenly abolished or if Attila the Hun reconquered Europe.

In their formative years, Morecambe and Wise took plenty of critical stick. In 1954 one critic wrote: 'Definition of the week. TV SET: the box in which they buried Morecambe and Wise.' Fifteen years later, they bounced back: OBEs, Freemen of the City of London, performing to royalty, award-winning series. What made them so resilient?

ERNIE: You need to have experienced the hard knocks, working in Variety. That chipped the rough edges off us. And the most abrasive treatment of all, was the Glasgow Empire. That was a tough place all right. Very nationalistic. They always opened the show with an act in kilts — like Mackenzie, Reed and Dorothy with their accordions. Or a cripple.

ERIC: There's nothing more guaranteed to get an audience's sympathy than a cripple playing an accordion, especially if it's a bit too heavy for him . . .
    But I knew top English comedians who would rather have open-heart surgery like mine, than face Glasgow.

ERNIE: I can remember coming off at Glasgow one night, to the sound of our own footsteps! And the fireman said: 'They're beginning to like you'.

They got together in 1939 for a touring talent show, 'Youth Takes a Bow'. Ernie Wiseman was a clog-dancer earning £5 a week. Eric Bartholomew did impressions and comic monologues, for £7 a week. When the show disbanded, they decided to team up.

ERIC: And we've been together ever since — except for the war. Ernie was in the Navy, you know. He was a deck-hand on a submarine!

Eric went down the mines, as a 'Bevin boy', until he was invalided out with a suspected heart condition. After the war, as Morecambe and Wise, they joined Lord John Sanger's Variety Circus.

ERNIE: Dinner jackets and gum-boots.

ERIC: Never again.

They appeared in E.N.S.A. concerts and at the Windmill Theatre. They toured variety theatres for forty-eight weeks of the year.

ERNIE: 25/- for digs. A 'combined chat', which was a big room with a double bed: we shared a bed, slept together for years!

ERIC: All those stories about theatrical landladies are rubbish! I *never* met a landlady who said 'Yes'.

Morecambe and Wise reversed the accepted convention that the short, fat man should be funnier than the tall, thin, bespectacled one. Besides, Wise's 'straight man' is warmer and more sympathetic than Abbott, or Martin. Morecambe is less stupid than Lewis, less neurotic and panic-stricken than Costello.

ERIC: Of course, I always fancied myself as a cross between Alan Ladd and Glenn Miller — which is why I used to wear rimless glasses, a raincoat and a trilby. And Ernie looked like Mickey Rooney (which is a station just outside Leeds).

As the act developed, the partners began to devise more elaborate set-pieces. For a Royal

Morecambe and Wise: *The Intelligence Men*, their first film for the cinema (1964)

Subtle disguise for the spies (*The Intelligence Men*)

Variety Performance they appeared as 'Marvo and Dolores'. Eric was the inept conjuror, in a hugely bulky tailcoat, apparently densely packed with bird life. Ernie was his dimpling lady assistant.

ERIC: There were feathers everywhere! Every time I moved, feathers came drifting out of my sleeves, up from the back of my neck! And there's me, whispering urgently into my sleeve 'Send the budgie up!'.

ERNIE: He put me into a frame, at which he was going to throw knives. Suddenly, a lovely chorus girl appears on the side of the stage. He looks at her, then he looks at me, a battered old bag. Makes his mind up, throws his knives *at* me, kills me, walks off with the girl.

In the 1960s they tried their hand at film-making, with disastrous results. The absence of an audience was disorientating to these very outgoing performers, whose rapport with the audience, in theatre or TV studio, was what energised the act and brought it to life. On location, the partners found themselves 'talking into a void' and never adapted to the new medium.

In their continuing TV series, the distinction between 'straight man' and comic became blurred as Ernie added pseudo-intellectualism, conceit and chirpiness to his knowingness, and Eric became more cunning and aware. In real life, Eric's two heart attacks brought them closer together. On screen, they occasionally shared a bed.

ERIC: We've done sketches where we share a double bed; and no one has ever suggested there was anything immoral in it. I think we're the only double-act, apart from Laurel and Hardy, to share a bed. The audience accepted it from Laurel and Hardy — now they accept it from us. And it's a great gift.

A double-act for the 1980s are Cannon and Ball, an explosive combination, widely tipped as heirs presumptive to the two-seater throne. You won't find these two sharing a bed; from kick-off to final whistle it's heads down, feet in, and 'don't hit me *there*, I've got a carbuncle'. The pair first worked together on the factory floor in Oldham, near Manchester. They were welders. Then they became singers: a duo called The Harper Brothers.

CANNON: We used to do six songs, with gags in between. But after a while I realised the gags were going better than the songs. But the problem was getting Bobby to change. He'd always thought of himself as a singer, you see.

Once persuaded, Bobby Ball took to his new comic role as to the manner born. Like a flea with St Vitus's dance, he hops around his elegant partner, twanging his braces, or thrusting his hands deep into the pockets of his wrinkled trousers, making rude gestures, mugging, grimacing, complaining.

BALL: For years you've pretended to be my friend, but you *hate* me, you really *hate* me!

CANNON: You're useless.

BALL: Tom, I know I've let you down, but *if you ever talk to me like that again — I'll kill you!*

This last said with boiling aggression, head poised to butt, fingers to poke. Ball is the vulnerable, put-upon 'little fellow' who, when provoked, becomes a manic imp, lurching between defiance and pathos. A distillation of Costello/Lewis/Jewel, less of the idiot, more of the hooligan. Cannon is as smooth as Martin (*and he can sing*), but prone to impatience (Warriss), and irritability (Abbott). He affects a low opinion of his diminutive partner.

CANNON: Look at him — the first scent of an audience and he's off like a Jack Russell down a rabbit-hole.

Any opportunity for degrading He Who Will Be Put Down is seized with alacrity. A few honeyed words — 'with your brilliant voice control' — has Ball eating out of his hand, and gratefully accepting the job of providing the animal noises for Cannon's song.

CANNON: And you'll find the heads behind the fence.

BALL [*aghast*]:   What *heads*?

Animal heads, of course, for lightning changes between verses, and the inevitable confusion:

BALL: I can't find the frigging *hen*!

Every outburst is followed by physical and mental collapse.

BALL: Tommy, I'm goin' all *limp* . . . You're bringing me out in a *rash* . . . I'm sweatin' on my *braces*.

When Cannon sings, Ball will play a nice trumpet obbligato in the background.

CANNON: And don't overlap into my words — lay back.

[*Ball lies on the floor*]

CANNON: Not like that, you fool, just take it easy.

Next time through, there are still too many notes.

CANNON: No, no, no! I only want a little bit in the middle!

BALL: So do I, but we won't get it here.

CANNON: When I sing 'The Very Thought of You', you should go (*sings*) 'Da dee dah dah'.

BALL: I've got it.

But he hasn't. Four bars later the little man sings 'Da dee dah dah'.

CANNON: No, for God's sake, do it on the trumpet!

BALL: What if I fall off?

As the tempo quickens, Cannon is provoked into tearing Ball's trumpet into little pieces, to Ball's open-mouthed horror. He tries to play on, even though he's been reduced to the mouthpiece. Cannon fetches a waste-bin from the wings, throws the mouthpiece into it. Ball is aghast.

CANNON [*with great confidence*]:   The very thought of you . . .

[*BALL, operating the foot-pedal on the waste-bin, produces a punch-line cadenza and flees for his life*]

BALL: Don't, Tommy, I've got a gum-boil there . . .

In 1983, Cannon and Ball made a film, *The Boys in Blue*, in which they play a pair of bungling village policemen, in the 'Sergeant Lightning' mould. On location, they weren't bubbling with confidence. Ball said:

The film world is not an easy place and we are just keeping our fingers crossed. It's totally different for us — we are live performers at heart. When you make a film you play at about a quarter strength to what you do on stage, and there is no audience to feel your way by. Nothing to respond to. The cameramen and technicians aren't allowed to laugh.

Director Val Guest was reassuring:

Don't worry — it's just a mixture of Disneyland and Laurel and Hardy. You're

'The Boys in Blue': Cannon and Ball as the village bobbies, with the lord of the manor (Roy Kinnear)

going to be film stars — as well as everything else.

After eighteen years in double harness, Cannon views their relationship as a marriage:

In time, a marriage becomes companionship. You reach a point where the arguments become less and less — and we've reached that point.

Their television programmes usually end with the partners going their separate ways. Ball goes off left, in waders and fishing hat, for a solitary weekend on the river-bank: Cannon goes right, in Bermuda shirt and shades, to join his flash friends in Marbella, or Cap Ferrat. Under the end credits, there's a last-minute reconciliation — Cannon relents, beckons ('come *on*'), Ball runs to join his pal, cock-a-hoop.

The split, in real life, can never be less than traumatic. According to Jerry Lewis:

Any two men that did what Martin and Lewis did would be arrested — only because what they had was a great relationship: a relationship that came off the screen — a young guy looking at his big older brother, and having a friendly father-figure. You don't have ten years of that — and just wipe it off the slate. It's like a marriage — and if it ends, you can't just write it off, pretend it didn't happen.

If sometimes I avoid talking about it, that's because sometimes it's very painful. Because I had some marvellous years with my ex-partner — and yet I wouldn't have it any other way than it is right now. But when I think about it, I get kinda sad, because it was good. But he was dumb. Next question?

Eric Morecambe tells a good story about a double-act that split up, both partners going solo:

They meet, years later, at the Express Dairy in Charing Cross Road.

PAT: How are you doing these days?

MIKE: Oh, not badly. I've just done a season at Las Vegas — twenty weeks, full houses, I made a million dollars.

PAT: Oh, really? I didn't hear about that.

MIKE: And I'm doing a film now — a big one, they're paying me two million dollars.

PAT: Oh, really? I didn't hear about that.

MIKE: And I've cut a record, which has sold thousands. I'll get a golden disc.

PAT: Oh, yeah? I didn't hear about that.

MIKE: And last week I was at the Palladium, and, oh boy, did I die the death! The audience actually booed me!

PAT: Oh, yes — I heard about *that*.

CHAPTER SEVEN

· INSPIRED ·
LUNACY

IN HIS YOUTH, Eric Morecambe used to sing a silly song.

> *I'm not all there.*
> *There's something missing.*
> *I'm not all there —*
> *So the folks declare.*
> *They call me Loopy, they call me Loopy —*
> *Nothing but a great big BOOPY!*
>
> *Courting couples in the park*
> *On any night you'll find.*
> *If you stare they'll break away*
> *'Cos love's not always blind.*
> *But they let me stand and watch 'em*
> *And they never seem to care —*
> *'Cos I'm not supposed to be ALL THERE!*

The comicality of idiocy goes back a long way. In the Islamic court of Haroun-al-Rashid (ninth century), the cavortings of Bulhul the Madman had the moguls in stitches. The line between the fool natural and the fool artificial is often blurred. The *thanigratha* — tribal loonies of the Crow Indians — were chosen from the natural eccentrics, the show-offs, the wild boys. Once classified as *thanigratha*, they were licensed to extend their crazy antics and they became professionals. As the saloon bar sign says: 'You don't have to be mad to work here — but it helps'.

For the 'crazy' comic, the visual impact is all-important. Eric Morecambe used to caper on in a floppy beret, with chalk-white face, cut-down evening dress, red socks, and a bootlace for a tie. 'Daft as a brush', he would hear the audience mutter. Billy Bennett cut an eccentric dash, in the Victorian music-hall, in a shrunken tail-coat and a strangling wing-collar which had the effect of making everything to the north of it bulge grotesquely — Adam's apple, tongue, cheeks,

Scenes from *A Night at the Opera* (1935), the first film the Marx Brothers made at MGM. Irving Thalberg was the producer

eyes. In a gravelly monotone, he would harangue the audience with surreal doggerel:

> The League of Nations met at Berwick Market
> To discuss on which side fishes ought to swim.
> There were Hottentots and Prussians playing
>   honeypots on cushions
> And a Greek with bubble-and-squeak upon
>   his chin.
> Some rolled up in taxis that were empty:
> Some arrived to say they couldn't come.
> The Hindus had their quilts on; the Hebrews
>   had their kilts on;
> A Scandinavian rose and said 'Bai Gum'. . . .

Jimmy James had two loonies to support him in his music-hall persona of The Drunken Swell. To the left, in ankle-length overcoat, mop wig and squashed hat, was Hutton Conyers; to the right, in shrunken trousers and deerstalker hat, was slack-jawed, ashen-faced Bretton Woods.

JAMES [*aside, to the audience*]:   It must be going to rain, if they come this far up the river!

To Conyers belongs the most celebrated catch-phrase of the lunatic fringe. In a rare burst of vitality, he would accost the elegant James and put him on the spot.

CONYERS [*aggrieved*]: Here, are you puttin' it about that I'm barmy?

JAMES: Why — are you trying to keep it a secret? [*to the audience*] You wouldn't think these are the two fellers that cut the cables at Bath Races, would you?

When it transpires that Conyers is carrying two man-eating lions in a shoebox, Woods is despatched for reinforcements, and coffee.

JAMES: Get on the phone. I'll keep him talking till they come.

CONYERS: I've got a giraffe too.

Jimmy James, *Sober as a Judge*. He was born in Stockton-on-Tees, 1892; died 1965

Billy Bennett, *Almost a Gentleman*. He was born in Liverpool, 1887; died 1942

JAMES: Where do you keep it?

CONYERS: In the box.

JAMES [*to WOODS in the wings*]:   He's got a giraffe in that box.

WOODS [*from off-stage*]:   Is it black or white?

JAMES: I'll ask him. [*to CONYERS*] He wants to know if the giraffe is black or white.

WOODS: No, the coffee I mean.

JAMES [*to the audience*]:   I hope there's room in the van for the three of us . . .

Craziest of the Crazy Gang was the odd man out, the soloist thrown in with three double-acts — 'Monsewer' Eddie Gray. Off-stage and on, 'he was a holy terror', recalls Charlie Chester. 'In summer, he would sit in his dressing-room, with the door open, stark naked except for his moustache, dicky front, socks and shoes. Passing chorus-girls got a very nasty fright!' In full costume, Gray added a battered topper, steel-rimmed spectacles and tatty evening dress to the famous 'Kaiser Bill' moustache. White face, a deadpan expression. Only the *eyes* gave him away: the manic gleam of a diabolic trickster whose every move was infuriatingly unpredictable. Tommy Trinder will never forget the night he shared a stage with Gray.

We'd rehearsed a new gag. I was to ask him 'What did you have for breakfast?' He'd reply 'Haddock.' I'd say 'Finnan?' and he'd say 'No — thick 'un!' Of course, when it came to the performance, it didn't go quite like that. When I asked him what he'd had for breakfast, he said 'Cornflakes' — and then just stood there looking at me without blinking an eye, watching me die. . . .

Trinder also credits Gray with the invention of a now-celebrated practical joke.

I was walking with him down Berwick Street one afternoon, and we were passing a letter-box when the Monsewer suddenly stops and starts talking to it. He's shouting into the slit 'Well, how did you get in there? Don't panic, I'm sure we can get you out. How tall are you? Were you *registered*?' Of course a crowd gathers, and once he's got them all going, the Monsewer shouts 'I'm going for help' — and legs it round the corner! Mad as a hatter!

Marty Feldman's eyes qualified him for this frightful fraternity. A thyroid operation in his youth left him with two bulging, independently operated eyeballs. A broken nose completed the picture. Cheerily billing himself as 'the gargoyle with legs' or 'the frozen nightmare', Marty carved himself a niche in television and films as the Pest in the Mac — the little man with organ-stop eyes and manic grin, who latches onto the unsuspecting passer-by and won't let go. The character was drawn from life; the streets of London and New York are full of 'em.

There were those that said that Tommy Cooper should never have been let out. J. B. Priestley saw him early on and made a diagnosis:

That craggy convulsed face, the sudden daft grin, those rolling eyes, and, perhaps above all, that almost insane high giggle, together make us feel, in some dark corner of the mind,

Graham Chapman and Marty Feldman, 'Waiter, there's a loony on my table'. *At Last the 1948 Show*

that we might have here some dangerous lunatic capable of something appalling....

Max Wall excites the same fear when he capers on in tights and boots. The huge, bewigged head, the sunken melancholy eyes, the Neanderthal jaw. He used to sing a song, which removed all doubt:

I'm mad, I'm mad,
It's sad, but it's true,
I froth with wrath,
Bite chair legs in two....

And Ken Dodd, with hair on end and eyes on stalks, makes the surprising confession:

It's fifteen years since I went out of my mind. I'd never go back.

For Spike Milligan, it was a bomb that did it. Interviewed by the distinguished psychiatrist, Anthony Clare, Spike confessed:

I was always a neurotic. I knew I'd just have to have that mechanism inside me tripped — and this mortar bomb blew me up in the war in Italy, and it did it .... Now I realise that there's a vast spectrum of neurosis: a lot of people are uncertain, insecure or frightened in the world. It sometimes gives you brilliance like Van Gogh or El Greco — both neurotics — it's a gift and a pain at the same time.... You get the pain much worse than anybody else, but you see a sunrise much more beautiful than anybody else...

I suppose I'm the way I am because comedy needs a vast spectrum of emotion. There are no heights unless there are depths....

For Milligan, a traumatic experience was the spark that fuelled his comic drive. But others warn of the danger of too much introspection — Pagliacci on the psychiatrist's couch. Jerry Lewis, who played the screen idiot for a decade, came to the conclusion that

Too much self-analysis can be a bad thing. For some comedians, a visit to the psychiatrist could be disastrous. Suppose you go there, and find out something that has been tormenting you: then if the psychiatrist shows you that

that same thing is of no consequence, you might lose what it is that makes you funny.

John Cleese, who spent three and a half years in group therapy, sympathises with those artists who 'find their inspiration through their own special experience of suffering — which makes them cling to the suffering itself. Some performers think that psychiatry would destroy their art. They'll never consider it, for fear that sanity would take away what makes them good performers.'

Woody Allen has spent twenty-five years in analysis. The experience colours his work:

The standard ploys of the professional funny man are jokes about anguish and dread:

Woody's comedy is a form of autobiography. From night-club monologues in which he fantasised on experiences from his early life — schooldays, parents, girls — he graduated to film and produced a series of surreal satires. The Allen's-eye view on crime (*Take The Money and Run*), sex (*Everything You Always Wanted to Know About Sex But Were Afraid to Ask*), history (*Love and Death*), the future (*Sleeper*) and, central to every situation, the tiny, panicky figure of our hero. His *sanity* in a world gone mad is the key to the comedy; the sanity is intense because it's sanity under the severest pressure, at breaking point. In real life, success imposes its own strains. The author/director/producer couldn't be persuaded to go to Hollywood to collect his Oscar for *Annie Hall*. 'I'm afraid of the dark,' he said, 'and I'm suspicious of the light. I have this desire to return to the womb . . . anybody's.'

Today, Woody uses his weekly sessions on the couch as a source of therapeutic insight — and good jokes. Among his favourites:

A man goes to the psychiatrist to ask for advice about his brother. 'He thinks he's a chicken,' he explains. 'Well, you'd better turn him in,' says the shrink. 'I can't,' says the man, 'I need the eggs.'

John Cleese. Rolling eyeball business. Tim Brooke-Taylor aghast.
At Last the 1948 Show

finality, mortality, human suffering, anxiety. . . .

Woody's bespectacled, beleaguered screen persona has gate-crashed the American audience's subconscious in a remarkable way, as psychiatrist Dr Dee Burton discovered, when a survey of dreams turned up the fact that hundreds of people in New York and Los Angeles habitually had dreams about Woody Allen. 'Many of the dreamers apparently gain a feeling of self-acceptance from seeing someone respected, rich and famous, presenting himself as a very awkward person, anxious and neurotic, forever having difficulty with the opposite sex.

Thirty years ago the couch was hardly the place for a giggle, and attitudes to psychiatry were hedged around with fears and phobias. When Bud Abbott decides that Lou Costello needs treatment, the visit to Dr Mildew's office puts the patient in a flurry of anxiety, aggravated by finding himself sharing the waiting room with a man who has a propeller on his head ('he thinks he's a B-29'). Dr Mildew, needless to say, is wild-eyed, Germanic, aggressive.

BUD: This is your patient, doctor — Lou Costello. He's been acting very strangely.

MILDEW [*eyeing his victim*]: He does look a little, how shall we say . . . [*laughs immoderately*] Now, young man, lie down on the couch.

[*Lou obeys, reluctantly*]

Tell me now, have you had any dreams?

Woody Allen in *Love and Death* (1975) cocking a snook at the Russian epic novel and the Swedish art movie; *(bottom)* with Diane Keaton

LOU: Last night I dreamt I wanted a salami sandwich.

MILDEW: Did you do something about it?

LOU: I got up and cut myself a salami sandwich.

MILDEW: Did the dream repeat itself?

LOU: No, but the salami did...

MILDEW: I have probed the subconscious and come up with the solution — he needs sleep.

BUD: Thank you, doctor. Send the bill to Mister Costello.

The double-act, in the interplay between the nincompoop and the wise guy, is an ideal showcase for displaying the comedy of idiocy. 'A heart-throb tailed by a monkey' is how Jerry Lewis describes the Martin and Lewis partnership. And the lasting image of Jewel and Warriss is put-upon Jimmy cowering, hands locked protectively over his head, eyes goggling, tongue protruding: 'Don't hit me — *please*....'

Two's company, three's a crowd — at least when the Three Stooges are in action, falling all over one another, slapping and kicking, creating traffic jams in doorways. The trio made hundreds of two-reelers for Columbia Studios in the 1930s, and filled every frame with frenzied action and mutual violence. They reduce the give-and-take of knockabout comedy to its most primitive fundamentals, punctuated only by grunts, squeaks and moans. Their horseplay is a *ritual*, perfected by hours of painstaking practice. Bald-headed Larry is the maddest of the three, mop-headed Moe does the thinking, such as it is, and wild-haired Curly holds the middle ground.

The trio apply for work

THE BOSS: Are you brothers?

TRIO: Yeah, we're tripalets!

BOSS: How old are you?

CURLY: Twenty-eight.

LARRY: Nineteen.

[*MOE pokes CURLY in the eye*]

CURLY [*screaming*]: Nineteen!

[*MOE turns to LARRY*]

LARRY [*hastily*]: Twenty-eight!

MOE turns to CURLY

CURLY [*mystified*]: Twenty-eight?

[*MOE punches CURLY in the belly*]

CURLY [*a gasp*]: Nineteen...

[*LARRY grins complacently. This angers MOE,*
who gives CURLY a slap on the head for good
measure.]

They get the job.

The Three Stooges worked variations on their 'slapping and poking' routine for more than forty years. In the process, two of the original gang were worn out. Shemp Howard replaced his brother Curly in 1947 and, on his death, Joe Besser joined in. In 1959 he was replaced by Joe de Rita.

In the beginning, there were five Marx Brothers. But the two sane ones soon gave up the unequal struggle and left the field clear for the loonies — the triumphant triumvirate of Chico (born Leonard, 1891), Harpo (born Adolph, 1893) and Groucho (born Julius, 1895). It would be historically tidy to imagine that the Italianate stage names were part of a conscious attempt to conjure up the spirit of the *Commedia dell' Arte*: Pedrolino, silent, 'pale as the moon', romantic; Zany, sulky and suspicious; Harlequin, the wily trickster. But in a Marxian context such connections are superfluous. They exist in their own right, a tearaway trinity to whom nothing is sacred. In their world, things and people exist solely in order to be subverted, overwhelmed, ridiculed. It was a master-stroke to make Harpo dumb, with the result that he exists in the films in his own private world — a world of silent slapstick, where he can make his own rules and be as mad as he pleases. His determined pursuit of everything in skirts is all the more frightening for being conducted in silence, but the wild eyes, popping out on stalks, and the devilish leer are enough to induce what often sounds like genuine hysteria in his victims.

The brothers were first let loose in a series of lightweight musical comedies that never did anybody any harm. *The Cocoanuts*, premiered on Broadway in 1925, was ostensibly written by George S. Kaufman, who later complained that the show as performed bore little relation to the script he had written 'owing to the on-stage ad libs and antics of the Marx Brothers'. This was putting it mildly. True to tell, the brothers rode roughshod through Kaufman's script, and all subsequent attempts to tie them down. Plot never impinged on their consciousness, although occasionally they might make minor concessions to the setting in which they found themselves by adopting bits of a costume — a mortar-board, jockey's cap, doctor's gown, battledress. But a scene only existed in order to be demolished. Scripted dialogue was poached, scrambled, and

punned. Performers served only as victims for goosing, corpsing, insulting, assaulting.

The Cocoanuts became a film in 1929 and launched a series of Marx Brothers' comedies that are still being recycled on video today. *Animal Crackers* (1930), *Monkey Business* (1931), *Duck Soup* (1933) and *A Night at the Opera* (1935) are the best of the bunch — classics of crazy comedy, fast and furious. The images fall over one another, clamouring to be remembered. . . . The unwelcome interior decorators (Harpo and Chico), invading Groucho's midnight tryst with man-trap, Esther Muir, and wallpapering everything in sight, including Miss Muir. . . . Or, the stowaway's cabin, rapidly filling up with four Marxes; two maids; an engineer — 'I've come to turn off the heat.' 'Well, start on *him*!' (Harpo, entangled with maid); cleaner with mop; four stewards with food; a manicurist — 'Long or short?' 'Better make it short, it's getting crowded in here'; maintenance man; passenger looking for his Aunt Milly; porters; waiters and, finally, the statuesque Margaret Dumont, arriving for her secret appointment with Groucho. She opens the door and the human contents spill out like junk from a wardrobe. . . . As the pace quickens, three figures flit in and out of Thelma Todd's apartment, sometimes stopping for a quick cuddle on the sofa, or to deliver a massive block of ice (what's the connection?). . . . Another bedroom, and endless permutations of beds being recycled via the balcony and the room next door, to prevent the hotel manager knowing the full extent of the suite's occupancy. . . . A fight in the hay ('where are all these farmers' daughters I've been hearing about for years?'), with Chico calling the rounds, Groucho the blow-by-blow commentary, Harpo as Napoleon, on a horse, backwards. . . . A costume ball ('the beer is warm, the women are cold, and I'm hot under the collar'), where somebody is *inside* a detachable bustle, clamping himself to the rear of any passing lady. . . . The captain's table, with three uninvited guests circling ravenously, filling their pockets with hors d'oeuvres. . . . An operating theatre, where three mad surgeons, endlessly handwashing, rush around not examining Mrs Upjohn . . . a train, feeding on itself as the trio demolish the carriages to fuel the boiler . . . an opera sabotaged by piratical invaders from the flies . . . a horse-race that must be stopped . . . a

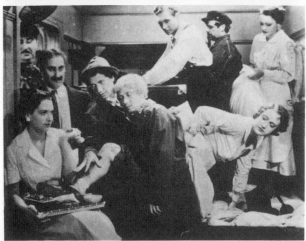

Scenes from *A Night at the Opera* (1935). The show toured for two months in vaudeville theatres before the start of filming

Right: Harpo Marx with Louis Armstrong: an informal studio encounter, sadly never filmed

The Crazy Gang mauling Shakespeare. Royal Command Performance (1956). *(From left)* Eddie Gray (Wall), Teddy Knox (Prologue), Jimmy Nervo (Lion), Jimmy Gold (Moonshine), Charlie Naughton (Thisbe), Bud Flanagan (Pyramus)

circus that must be saved . . . a war that must be won. Because there *is* a plot, somewhere in the middle of this hurly-burly: a touch of romance, a story of villainy and heroism, flattened under the onslaught of the brothers' explosive anarchy. If you can't stand the pace, a word of advice from the cigar-smoking, moustachioed spokesman for the family:

Listen, I *have* to stay here — but why don't you folks go out in the lobby for a smoke till this thing blows over?

The Crazy Gang were exact contemporaries of the Marx Brothers and matched them for unpredictable, disruptive anarchy. They never took to film, although they made five; but on their home ground, the stage of the Palladium or the Victoria Palace, they were irrepressible. The juggler would find his clubs had been lubricated. The chorus girls would find their knickers had been sewn up before the quick change. Stage managers were chased onto the stage in their underwear; musicians would be sprayed with soda syphons. Their antics spilled over into the auditorium, where patrons would be accosted by leering ushers selling out-of-date programmes and 'dirty postcards' (blank, but *stained*). A trumpet solo by Nervo would be cut short by the curtain falling; undaunted, he would climb back over it. Curtain then rises, with Nervo perched on it, still playing. From the flies he would then slide down the full length of it. Naughton and Gold would saunter on, with a plank of wood and two trestles, and then spend some minutes trying to make the plank fit the trestles ('Turn it round the other way').

Flanagan and Allen played new variations on the old 'cross-gags'.

FLANAGAN crosses the stage, carrying a suitcase. ALLEN watches him, curiously.

ALLEN: Where are you going?

FLANAGAN: Taking my case to court.

[*He disappears into the wings, returns shortly with a larger suitcase. Crosses the stage.*]

ALLEN: Where are you going now?

FLANAGAN: Taking my case to a higher court.

[*He disappears into the wings, returns quickly carrying a coathanger. ALLEN opens his mouth to speak, but FLANAGAN's too quick for him.*]

FLANAGAN: I lost my suit!

[*He runs for the wings, giggling.*]

And the last laugh would invariably be collared by the moustachioed Monsewer, juggling with balls that disappear into the flies, to return multiplied a hundredfold ('this is the trick I usually broadcast!'); balancing billiard cues; massacring Shakespeare; fracturing French; hectoring the audience; teasing his fellows — and all, as critic James Agate described him, 'with the air of an income-tax inspector taking a busman's holiday'.

The Second World War saw the Crazy Gang temporarily disbanded. Flanagan and Allen joined E.N.S.A. and sang patriotic songs in garrison theatres to an audience of fresh-faced squaddies. Among them was Gunner Milligan of the Royal Artillery, plotting his revenge on the faceless villains 'who had sent me this cleverly worded invitation to come and get killed. It was a proud day for my family when eight military policemen dragged me screaming from the house, tearing off my nun's clothing. . . .' In later years

Milligan became philosophic about his wartime experiences, which included that cathartic encounter with a German mortar and, in Naples in 1944, an equally fortuitous introduction to Gunner Secombe, Harold. Historian Milligan records that at about this time,

> Aircraftman 2nd Class 223033 Sellers, P., was in Ceylon, being interviewed by his Commanding Officer. Sellers, it appears, had complained: 'Captain — I heard tigers roaring last night!' Now the tiger is an animal unknown in Ceylon. Still, he says he heard tigers, it wasn't a dream. . . . You see, it was happening to all of us. Michael Bentine was also in the R.A.F., and he was going slowly round the twist flying Polish airmen who didn't know the English for 'Jump', or 'Drop the bombs'. . . .

In a world gone mad, the quartet did the only sensible thing and created their own refuge — a gloriously barmy ritual of surreal nonsense, broadcast on the BBC's homely Home Service under the apt title, *Crazy People*. This was later modified to *The Goon Show*. The first script conference, according to Milligan, took place in a Soho restaurant. The service was sluggish, so Secombe announced: 'I'll attract the waiter's attention.' He pulled his raincoat over his head so that he looked like a headless body waiting to order, and hung out his hands in a ghost-haunting gesture. Meanwhile, Milligan had signalled to Sellers and Bentine, and the three of them tiptoed out into the street. They watched through the window as Secombe tried to explain himself to the quivering *maître d'hôtel*.

Subsequently, a pub in Westminster, the Grafton Arms, became their base. Landlord Jimmy Grafton was appointed KOGVOS ('Keeper of Goons and Voice of Sanity'). Spike 'lunacy is our planet' Milligan hatched the scripts, with occasional contributions from Larry Stephens and Eric Sykes. Peter Sellers took the lion's share of the characterisation. He was (in folk memory, still is) Major Bloodnok, military idiot, coward and bar; Henry Crun, geriatric embodiment of fossilised Imperialist thinking; Hercules Grytpype-Thynne, plausible public school villain and cad; and Bluebottle — 'a short, shivering youth wrapped heavily in rice-paper and dental string'. Milligan played Minnie Bannister, spinster of the parish; Comte Toulouse-Moriarty of the House of Roland; and Eccles, the Original Goon, modelled on Disney's idiot cartoon dog,

Goofy. Harry Secombe took the part of Neddie Seagoon, true blue British idiot, hero and scapegoat. Michael Bentine became the first Goon dropout when, after clashes with Milligan, he asked to be written out in November 1952. By then nearly four million listeners had become addicts. The Goon message of Unorthodoxy was getting through. Milligan encapsulated it:

> It is against bureaucracy and on the side of human beings. Its starting-point is one man shouting gibberish in the face of authority, and proving by fabricated insanity that nothing could be as mad as what passes for ordinary living.

The dictionary definition of 'surrealism' makes a brave stab at pinning down the intellectual basis of Goonery: 'pure psychic automatism, expressing the real process of thought. Thought's dictation, free from any control by the reason, independent of any aesthetic or moral preoccupation'. Or, as Bluebottle might put it: 'Ye he he! Heuheuheuheuheu he!'

Spike Milligan sounds the alarm; *Postman's Knock* (1962)

FX: SOUND OF TRAIN CHUGGING THROUGH THE DRIVING BLIZZARD

SEAGOON: As I sat in my bath in the back of the snow-plough — a foul trick was played.

GRYTPYPE: Hands up, Neddie. Moriarty, tie his hands — then hide them where he can't find them.

SEAGOON: What a fiendish move — you naughty men — I'll write to *The Times* about this —

FX: SOUND OF PEN SCRATCHING ON VELLUM

SEAGOON: Dear Sir — I wish to complain about an outbreak of hand-tying on snow-ploughs while taking hip baths.

GRYTPYPE: Give me that letter — you'll not send that, lad — now. . .

FX: SOUND OF FURIOUS WRITING

GRYTPYPE: Dear Sir — today I heard the first cuckoo — there, sign that —

FX: PEN

GRYTPYPE: Good — Moriarty, post it — that'll put them off the track.

MORIARTY: I'll just tie his hands again — ahhh — there.

GRYTPYPE: Good — now cut the knot off so he can't untie it.

MORIARTY: Right — here — put it in your pocket. Now, together — one! two!

SEAGOON: No, don't throw me out!

MORIARTY: Three.

SEAGOON: Helllll [*going off*] pppppp —

FX: SOUND OF UPWARD RUSH OF TRAIN — STEAM — ROAR OF THE WHEELS GOING INTO THE DISTANCE (*pause*) THEN JUST THE HOWL OF THE BLIZZARD

SEAGOON: I lay gasping on the railway bank. Suddenly, from a nearby frozen pool I hear —

ECCLES (*off*):   In the good old summer timeee — in the good old summer timeeee —

SEAGOON: I say, don't you feel cold in there?

ECCLES: Nope — I got my overcoat on.

SEAGOON: Listen, that tricycle against the wall — whose is it?

ECCLES: Mine — a present from an admirer.

SEAGOON: Could you drive me to town on it?

ECCLES: Oh, the tricycle ain't mine, the wall was the present.

SEAGOON: Well, drive me on that.

ECCLES: Right — hold tight.

FX: SOUND OF MAD ENGINES RUNNING PAST

ANNOUNCER: The sound you are hearing is Neddie and Eccles driving a wall at speed. We thought you ought to know. Meanwhile, at Pevensey Bay station. . . .

The Goons ruled the airwaves from 1952 to 1960, when they went their separate ways. While Sellers extended his chameleon talent as a film actor, and Secombe cut out a career in bel canto, Milligan kept the flag of Goonery flying in an extended series of television farragos, economically labelled *Q5*, *Q6*, *Q7* etc. On BBC-2, Spike explored a Plague of Liberaces, the First Irishman in Space ('10, 7, 3, 9, 6, what's next, Mick?'), the Home Mortician's Kit, the Idiot Scout Troop ('the four hanging from the beam are learning to untie knots'), the Electric Banana, and the Liquefaction of Harry Secombe ('Can't you top him up with a little tap water?' 'No — it's against his religion.'). The first working Goon to draw the old age pension, Milligan has become a

The revolution, so far. The Goons, fourth series, 1953. Sellers was 28, Secombe 32, Milligan 35.

guru figure to the succeeding generation of British comedians, for whom *The Goon Show* scripts are holy writ. In 1981 Elton John paid £14,000 for a batch of Milligan originals, announcing 'I have boughted dem because I love dem'. Other confessed devotees include the heir to the throne of England, a Mrs Ethel Terrible of Catford, and Messrs Cleese, Chapman, Palin, Jones and Idle.

The adolescent in the 1950s was not well served by the entertainment industry, which had yet to acknowledge the existence of a 'young generation' with its own particular appetites. The British film industry offered predictable Hollywood retreads, recording artists were fat and forty, and television in its infancy had no place for the zany, or the surreal. *The Goon Show* on Friday nights became a haven for rebellious, nonconformist teenagers, champing at the bit. And the most amazing and revolutionary aspect of these broadcasts was that, overnight, *silliness* became 'okay'. After all, it had the blessing of the BBC. The floodgates were open; the way was clear for throwing off parental and educational restraints, for kicking over the traces, letting the hair down, and babbling in strange tongues:

Bim bom biddle skiddle skoll
Needle nardle noo...
I'm walking backwards for Christmas,
Across the Irish Sea...

That you could make a living from silliness on a professional level was a further revelation, shortly to strike the elite of the Goon-weaned generation, who were clowning their way through Oxbridge in the 1960s. At Cambridge, Humphrey Barclay produced the 1963 Footlights revue — *A Clump of Plinths*. He recalls:

We were all totally unshowbizzy then. Especially John Cleese. There was a bizarre logic about his humour — a strong element of fierce nonsense running through it.

John Otto Cleese towered head and shoulders over the rest of the cast. Schooled at Clifton College in Bristol ('I was an immensely weak boy, and consequently was bullied a lot'), he was studying Law at Cambridge, and so was typecast in the role of the Prosecuting Attorney in 'Judge Not'.

ARNOLD FINCH is charged with assaulting SIDNEY BOTTLE, a dwarf. The PROSECUTING ATTORNEY rises.

PROS. ATT.:   My Lord, in this case my learned friend Mr Maltravers appears for the defence, and I appear for the money.

[*The first witness is PERCY MOLAR.*]

USHER: Call Percy Molar.

VOICE OFF: Call Percy Molar.

DISTANT VOICE OFF: Call Percy Molar.

VERY DISTANT VOICE OFF: Call Percy Molar.

[*PERCY MOLAR makes an entrance, in a loud check suit, and revolving bow-tie.*]

MOLAR: Hello, hello, hello, hello!

PROS. ATT.:   You are Percy Molar, a music-hall comedian?

MOLAR: That is correct.

PROS. ATT.:   Are you married?

MOLAR: Yes I am. My wife, my wife...

PROS. ATT.:   Describe your wife to the court.

MOLAR: My wife, she's so fat, when she walks down the street it looks like five dogs fighting in a sack!

PROS. ATT.:   Would I be right in imagining that your wife recently returned from the West Indies?

MOLAR: Yes.

PROS. ATT.:   Jamaica?

DEFENCE: Objection!

PROS. ATT.:   I'll rephrase the question. Did you meet your wife in a revolving door?

MOLAR: No, she went of her own accord!

PROS. ATT.:   Please listen to the question — did you meet your wife in a revolving door?

MOLAR: Yes — and we've been going around together ever since!

The part of Percy Molar was played by Tim Brooke-Taylor, a bright spark from Buxton, Derbyshire. He did his public-school survival course at Winchester College:

I hated it. The Latin used to make me cry. Honestly! I remember in my first term being sent out on runs — and beaten with birch twigs, to encourage us to go faster. So comedy was a release, an escape route.

Brought up on *Much Binding in the Marsh*, Norman Evans in pantomime, and Terry-Thomas in variety, Tim shared with his Cambridge contemporaries a nostalgic feel for the lost world of music-hall.

We favoured a broader style of comedy, as against the more 'precious' style of undergraduate humour. I think we all had a

Officer material: *(from left)* Tim Brooke-Taylor, John Cleese, Graham Chapman; *At Last the 1948 Show*

reverse chip on our shoulders and were trying to slough off all the trappings of privilege — the public school attitude, and accent.

A Clump of Plinths became *Cambridge Circus* and was booked for the Lyric Theatre in London. Critic Milton Shulman described 'Judge Not' as 'as funny a skit as I can remember', and Brooke-Taylor and Cleese became professional funny men. Not 'comedians' in the traditional, theatrical mould; the graduate jesters of the 'Swinging Sixties' had a new approach to their chosen career, geared to the times. Adaptable and versatile, they would be able to turn their hands to every aspect of the business — writing, producing and performing, in all the media. And the comic style for the new era, matching contemporary trends in music and fashion, was brash, unrestrained and colourful. And very, very silly.

The next landmark in the evolution of inspired lunacy can be located in the archives of Rediffusion Television. A flickering black-and-white kinescope announces 'Let's Speak English', and on the screen appear four bowler-hatted, pinstripe-suited worthies, sitting formally around a tea table. Dialogue ensues.

No. 1:   I am a chartered accountant.

No. 2:   I am a chartered accountant.

No. 3:   I am a chartered accountant.

No. 4:   I am a gorilla.

No. 1:   The teapot is on the trolley.

No. 2:   The teapot is on the trolley.

No. 3:   The teapot is on the trolley.

[*No. 4 gets to his feet, picks up trolley and places it on the table, smashing teacups ad lib.*]

No. 4:   The trolley is on the table — and it goes through the window.

[*He bungs it through the window. He then pours tea over the astounded trio, smashes furniture, pulls down walls. Then he takes his seat again. The punch line comes from No. 1. In close-up, he has remarkably prominent eyes, pupils dangerously askew. He has a large, hooked and broken nose, ears like jug-handles.*]

No. 1:   I am a chartered accountant, but I'm thinking of becoming a gorilla!

[*He grins, diabolically*]
[*Blackout*]

This quaint quartet was assembled in 1967 for

a television series enigmatically called *At Last the 1948 Show*. No. 4 was Cleese, No. 3 was Brooke-Taylor. No. 2 was a new recruit from Cambridge, class of '63, Graham Chapman. Schooled at Melton Mowbray College ('we did revues, there were plenty of chances for going over the top'), he had recently qualified as a doctor of medicine ('but I wanted more adventure, some disruption in my life'). No. 1 was an eccentric from the other side of the tracks, Marty Feldman. Of East End Jewish stock, he had left school at fifteen, worked as a market trader, jazz trumpeter, and comedy script-writer, often in collaboration with Barry Took. For some years he fought shy of becoming a performer, because of his unique physiognomy. He needn't have worried. His face was his fortune.

At Last the 1948 Show also boasted a simpering blonde lady announcer, who linked the sketches with the catchphrase: 'And now for something completely different. . . .' And there was music. Under the closing credits, the tall figure of Cleese, in immaculate white tie and tails, is flanked by giggling choristers as he sings, solemnly,

I've got a ferret sticking up my nose.

How it got there I can't tell,
But now it's there it hurts like hell,
And what is more it radically affects my sense of
*   smell.*

I've got a ferret sticking up my nose.

It starts singing when I wear my formal
*   clothes. . .*

From these auspicious beginnings in Wembley it was but a small step to White City and the studios of BBC Television, where the same four protagonists reported for work in 1969. Marty Feldman's eyes had won him instant celebrity and his own series, *Marty*, for which Tim Brooke-Taylor was conscripted to be his sidekick.

Chapman and Cleese joined Marty's ex-partner Barry Took for serious discussions about a new strand of comedy programmes. A number of working titles were under consideration: 'Owl Stretching Time', or 'Whither Canada?', or 'Bum, Whack It, Buzzard, Stubble and Boot', or 'The Royal Philharmonic Orchestra Goes to the Bathroom', or 'Man's Crisis of Identity in the Latter Half of the Twentieth Century'. In the end, it was called *Monty Python's Flying Circus*. Nobody quite knows why.

Cleese and Chapman headed the bill, with four new collaborators. From Cambridge, class of '64, came Eric Idle. He'd seen the light during his formative years at a 'semi-orphanage in the Midlands', where he discovered that 'there's something involved in being up to your neck in mud which makes people laugh'. And from Oxford, class of '64, came Michael Palin and Terry Jones ('I was very impressed with the corduroy suits. . .'). From Occidental College, Los Angeles, came Terry Gilliam, a primitive cartoonist. Gilliam created his own style of 'cut-out' animation for the opening titles of the programme and punctuation between events. Fast, crude, and noisy — a nightmare world of decapitation, defenestration, and deflation. There was an occasional BBC-style announcer, set up only to be knocked down, like Wallace Greenslade in *The Goon Show*. And if things got really out of hand, the Voice of Authority was introduced, in the guise of a moustachioed military man, with a complaint:

> This is getting silly. It started off quite nicely, but now it's getting too silly for words. So, on the command 'Cut!', I want you to cut to the next scene. Are you ready? — Wait for it! — Cut!

Monty Python's Flying Circus played to good houses from 1969 to 1975. The television series spawned feature films, stage shows, books and records. The word 'Pythonesque' was coined to describe the flavour of their comedy, and regular characters from the series became heroes for the next generation. 'The Gumbies' are monosyllabic idiots in gumboots, trousers rolled up to the knee, handkerchiefs knotted on the head, arms swinging dangerously close to the ground. 'The Pepperpots' are strident, domineering ladies in housecoats, dabbling in French existentialist philosophy. The Batley Townswomen's Guild provide dramatic reconstructions — 'The Battle of Pearl Harbour', for example. 'Last year we did "The Camp on Blood Island", so this year we thought we'd try something in a lighter vein.' Hats, handbags and fox furs fly as the ladies set to in a sea of mud. The aggrieved owner of a dead parrot becomes a folk legend, with his despairing cry:

> It's expired! This is a late parrot! It's a stiff! Bereft of life it rests in peace — if you hadn't nailed it to the perch it would be pushing up daisies! This is an ex-parrot!

Hot on his heels come the ingratiating barfly ('nudge, nudge, wink, wink, know what I mean?'), the ingratiating *maître d'hôtel*, the Spanish Inquisition, the naked organist, the mad chef, the

Minister for Silly Walks. Chartered accountants get predictably short shrift, while figures of authority are regularly debunked or debagged. Schoolmasters, officious civil servants, judges, surgeons, *bossyboots* — all the demons from Monty Python's collective subconscious have to be called up, and exorcised. Ordinary suburban life, too, is in danger of invasion and desecration. Victor and Iris's quiet evening at home is turned into a nightmare by the arrival of uninvited, strange guests who change the record, sit on the cat (killing it), bring in a goat — 'oh, sorry, it's done number twos on the carpet'. The *coup de grâce* is delivered by a score of singing Welsh miners and a naked fairy.

Celebrity sat uneasily on Monty Python's shoulders. They resisted all attempts to classify their comedy and place them in the historical tradition of British clowning. Eager researchers of Pythonology were fobbed off with nonsense and fairytales that only occasionally contained the germ of a truth. Their debt to postwar Goonery, for example, was obliquely acknowledged in a pseudo-official account of their coming together. The Python's tongue, as always, is in his cheek.

The MONTY PYTHON team met while serving in the R.A.F. during the last war. They were attached to the now legendary and effeminate 243 squadron which flew over 400 difficult missions over Europe dropping tons of makeup to the Allied troops.

After the war they all wore very loose suits, and met up again at an R.A.F. reunion in 1947. There the idea came up for a 'whacky, new kind of show to take the lid off all the sacred cows of everything in Britain'. After explaining their idea to the top brass at the B.B.C. the boys were given jobs as commissionaires in the newly extended car park at Alexandra Palace. But it wasn't long before 'Doc' Chapman and Terry 'Pud' Jones left the group to become robbers.

In the late 50s Mike 'Smudger' Palin and Terry 'Please don't kick me when I'm Down and Out' Gilliam left the B.B.C. to run an R.A.F. Benevolent home near Hove and it was here on a wintry day that a chance meeting of a few old service buddies was to lead to a breakthrough which was to influence so many people in later years.

But still Python was a long way off and it wasn't until a Bring Back Flogging Dinner Dance at Esher in 1966 that the boys came up with an idea that was to change everything.

They decided to rejoin the R.A.F. After a moving passing-out ceremony beneath the tower at Cranwell which has meant so much to generations of men who gave everything to fight for the freedom of Britain's skies, the boys left to do Monty Python.

Despite the very Englishness of Pythonery, a spark of transatlantic lunacy was struck in 1974, when KERA, a local TV station in Dallas, started showing episodes from the first series. Confounding the sceptics, the message began to seep through to the younger section of the audience, and a small but enthusiastic cult following was generated. The moguls of ABC television then decided to give Monty Python an airing on the network. Their marketing executives pointed to the long line of English comics who'd failed to match Chaplin's success with American audiences; so, hedging their bets, the ABC 'adapted' the programmes for network screening. Sketches were re-edited in an attempt to impose order, vulgarity was censored, non sequiturs were eliminated, punch lines deflected. When the emasculated version was viewed by the Pythons, they applied for an injunction to prevent the ABC from transmitting the videotape. In the historic court case that followed, a Justice of the Supreme Court ruled in favour of anarchy and lunacy, accepting the Pythons' complaint that the quintessence of their comedy had been drained off in the editing. However, the judge ruled that an injunction preventing transmission of the programme on the day after Christmas would be unreasonable. The show was duly broadcast, with a Pythonesque disclaimer....

In the 1980s the Pythons went their separate ways, becoming actors, authors, directors, impresarios. They came together for a farewell concert at the Hollywood Bowl in 1982, and the following year saw the team working on their Ultimate Project, the summation of Python philosophy, their answer to the Eternal Questions — *The Meaning of Life*.

There's everything in this movie
Everything that fits
From the Meaning of Life in the Universe
To girls with great big tits.

Or, putting it another way:

If you fear death and are a middle-class bore at dinner parties, who after making a twit of yourself at public school went into the farce of big business, having served your country well enough in war to have a stupidly proud sense

The maître d'hotel (John Cleese) offers a snack to the fattest man in the world (Terry Jones); *The Meaning of Life* (1983)

of her history, if you eat and drink to neurotic excess but respect whatever church you pretend to belong to, if in other words you are a typical product of middle-aged Britain, then hurry at once to see yourself mirrored, satirised, burlesqued, travestied and beaten to a pulp in the new Monty Python movie. (David Hughes, *The Sunday Times*)

The bleakness of the Python vision lost them a few friends, who preferred the more palatable eccentricities of the early days. *The Meaning of Life* takes no prisoners and shows no mercy. The message is clear from the moment the 'kidney pirates', armed with surgical choppers, descend on an unsuspecting citizen to claim his organs *by force*. Religion, birth control, the Law, militarism, patriotism, colonialism, class, business ethics, consumerism, American tourists, and education are all grist to the Python mill — the commentary provided appropriately by six melancholy fish, who view the dismal behaviour of mankind from their tank in a seafood restaurant.

The mad chef (John Cleese), restrained by the waiter (Terry Jones); *And Now for Something Completely Different* (1971)

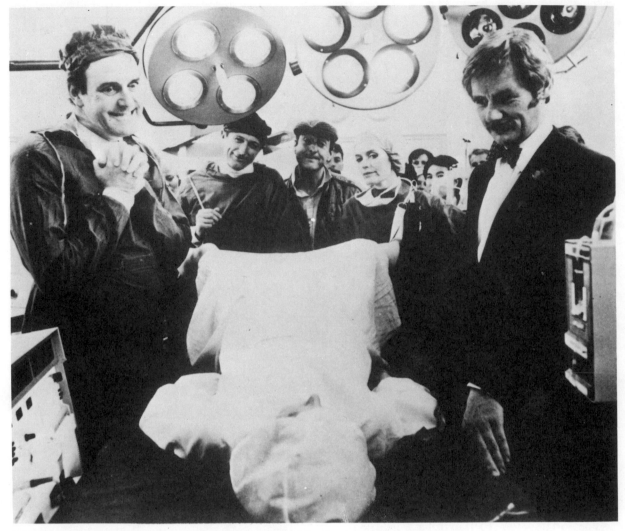

The appalling obstetricians (John Cleese, Graham Chapman) show off their handiwork; *The Meaning of Life* (1983)

George Harrison, ex-Beatle, now a Python producer and investor, keeps his finger on the Python pulse. He says,

Let's face it. There are certain things in life which make life worth living, and one of those things is Python. Especially to someone like me. When you've gone through so much in life, and you're supposed to decide what is real and what isn't, you watch the television and you see all this *madness* going on, and everyone is being serious and accepting it, and you're ready to bang your head on the wall — then someone says 'And now for something completely different . . .' That saves the day.

A sentiment echoed by H. L. Mencken, the distinguished American commentator:

The liberation of the human mind has never been furthered by dunderheads: it has been furthered by gay fellows who heaved dead cats into sanctuaries and then went roistering down the highways of the world, proving to all men that doubt, after all, is safe . . . .

CHAPTER EIGHT

·VISUAL·
VULGARITY

DOWN TO BASICS. The absurdities of anatomy, appendages and orifices. The ins and outs of fundamental comedy, the acrobatic antics of the two-headed beast. As Woody Allen describes it: 'the most fun I've had without laughing!'

The phallus comes to the fore — an exaggerated, leather simulacrum of the male organ, indispensable equipment for the players in the early Greek and Roman pantomimes. In Aristophanes' play *Lysistrata* (411 B.C.), the women of the warring Athenian states decide to refuse their husbands sexual relations until they stop fighting. The deprived men are immediately afflicted by continuous erection, which the mechanics of the phallus could represent grotesquely. Male members of the audience would sympathise with the predicament of Cinesias, who is led on by his wife Myrrhine to believe that she is going to break the strike and grant him his marital rights — right there, on the stage. However, delay follows delay as she dashes off to fetch the props — a mattress, a soft pillow, oils, perfume — until, with everything ready, and Cinesias in obvious agony, she pours cold water on his expectations and rejoins her sisters on the picket line.

In Roman comedy, sexual pursuit and challenge was a common theme. The dirty old man lays plans to spend a night with his wife's maid. Two young bloods conspire to share the favours of the same courtesan and secure a fifty per cent discount. The miser prepares for his wedding, while his wily slave schemes to put a man in drag into the marriage-bed. Father and son compete for the favours of the same girl; but both lose out to their slave. Lust rages night and day. In Plautus' play *Rudens*, Sceparnio says to Ampelisca, 'You can tell just by looking at me, what it is I want . . . .'

Benny Hill: The old knee-trembler

The Bishop of Fools, with his bauble

In fifteenth-century Paris, the Catholic Church sanctioned an annual carnival of rude comedy, known as the 'Feast of Fools'. A document in the University of Paris records that, on New Year's Day,

> Priests and clerks may be seen wearing masks and monstrous visages at the hour of office. They dance in the choirs dressed as women, panders, or minstrels. They sing wanton songs. They eat black puddings at the horn of the altar while the celebrant is saying mass. They play at dice there. They cense with stinking smoke from the soles of old shoes. They drive about the town and its theatres in shabby traps and carts; and rouse the laughter of their fellows and the bystanders in infamous performances, with indecent gestures and verses scurrilous and unchaste.

In Ceylon, nineteenth-century missionaries noted that the dramatic re-enactment of religious myths often degenerated, in performance, into overtly sexual clowning. The threat of castration was a recurring theme, along with the fear of impotence.

The Pueblo Indian tribes of the American south-west also wear false genitalia and simulate all manner of sexual acts as part of their religious ritual. In 1893, the anthropologist Alexander Stephen was horrified by a Hopi burlesque of a wedding, in which the couple wore very exaggerated false genitalia and pantomimed copulation, with the groom eventually collapsing in exhaustion.

In Papua New Guinea, the *gimis* perform a short play, in which a bride and her new husband lie in a garden, sharing intimacies. The groom's younger brother arrives on the scene, hoping to find out how babies are made. He tries to distract his brother by poking him with his bow. Frustrated, he dances round the oblivious pair, demanding to have his turn at this 'game'.

The *Commedia dell' Arte* makes great play of Harlequin's passion for Columbine — or any other pretty lady who happens to be passing.

HARLEQUIN, dying for love, lies in the lap of LICETTA.

HARLEQUIN: Alas, I'm done for: a last word, and I'm dead:
The boatman Charon is coming for me,
Since Columbine, the light of my life,
Rejects my love and treats me cruel.

LICETTA: This poor man — he's only skin and bone,
While Love bruises and torments him:
Harlequin, taste this gruel.
It will restore you and put you on your feet again.

A contemporary cartoon of this tableau shows the startling effect of Licetta's gruel on Harlequin's libido.

A classic scene from the seventeenth-century Comédie Francaise features a grand banquet, hosted by the Comte de Galimafré. The doctor makes a late arrival, with the excuse that he had to perform an emergency operation and amputate a man's penis. 'Did you have to saw through the *bone*?' enquires Madame la Comtesse, whereupon all the guests rise and bow to her husband.

Later variations on the same theme recur, as in the 'patter' of Bozo Snyder, at Minsky's Burlesque, New York, *c.* 1919. Listed in his joke book under 'travelling salesmen':

> This travelling salesman stops at a farm and asks for a bed for the night. The farmer lets him share a bed with his daughter, because the salesman explains that his penis was shot off during the war. In the morning, he is discovered making love to the daughter anyway; but he insists, yes, his penis *was* shot off during the war — but it left a nine-inch stub.

See also Max Miller's *Blue Book*, passim, but note especially the story of the girl who swallowed a pin 'but never felt a prick until she was seventeen'. In films, Mel Brooks explores the same vein. *History of the World — Part One* includes the sad story of the negro, hiding in a crowd of eunuchs, whose erection is his undoing:

'the jig is up' announces the arresting officer. And the saucy British 'Carry On' films celebrate, among others, Henry VIII — 'a great guy with his chopper'; and Dick Turpin — 'known as Big Dick because of the unusual size of his weapon'. From the same source, two wenches admire a passing buck.

WENCH 1:   Hasn't he got a beautiful profile?

WENCH 2:   Don't be silly, — that's only his *keys*.

At the 'hungry i' nightclub in San Francisco, shortly before being arrested, Lenny Bruce pleaded:

(MALE VOICE):   Just touch it once, willya? Please, touch it once.

(IRRITABLE FEMALE):   Look, you want me to touch it when I don't feel like touching it? That's why I don't like to touch it — cause you always tell me to touch it . . . .

(MALE):   I dunno why you don't —

(FEMALE):   Cause I don't *wanna* touch — I gotta headache.

(MALE):   You got more goddam headaches than anyone in the world! [*pretending nonchalance*] O.k., it's up to you. Look: I'll go to sleep, and if you wanna touch it, wake me up.

LENNY: Guys always have that fantasy, right?

(FEMALE VOICE):   I wanna touch it.

(MALE VOICE):   No, no sweetheart, I'm tired. Lemme go to sleep.

Like the sacrilegious celebrant of the 'Feast of Fools', Lenny Bruce assumed the role of the black mass priest, who breaks the taboos and voices the unspeakable. He invites the audience into a conspiracy, with the unspoken bait of 'catharsis', and the hidden promise that they will get magical strength from the taboo-outraging spectacle.

In *The Psychoanalytic Theory of Neurosis*, Dr Otto Fenichel writes:

The motive for the telling of a joke always consists of an attempt to get the approval of the audience for the underlying guilt in the offensive impulses concealed in the joke . . . .

Pantaloon voyeur. From behind the arras, the dirty old man observes the groping Harlequin

Many children feel compelled to play the jester to make other people laugh. Similar disturbances occur in adults. Such behaviour implies that the person fears being punished for his instinctual impulses. By pretending that he is merely jesting, he hopes to avoid punishment. But the jesting also has an *exhibitionist* quality, and is an attempt to get confirmation from the spectators, and to seduce them to participate in the jesting sexual or aggressive acts.

Lenny Bruce always had a kind word for those who refused to participate.

LENNY: One thing I'd like to tell the people who are leaving, is, that you're very genteel. This is the first time I've had an audience that walk out, but *nicely*.

In Milwaukee, *Phew*! They used to walk out and walk *towards* me. Milwaukee, I had such grief — oh, it was really grim. The club was right next to the river, and even *that* started to look good.... Well, no one really enjoys rejection.... But the only thing that confuses me, I used to lie in bed and think 'What do those guys come in for? What kind of humour is *their* humour? Is it the Joe E. Lewis, the Sophie Tucker, the *double-entendre*, the naughty-but-nice, the spicey-haha-you-know-what-that-means wedding-night jokes, motel jokes, Rusty Warren, Johnny got a zero, Dwight Fisk, Mr Yo-yo can't get his yo-yo up, he's got the biggest dingy in the navy?'

Bruce's outspokenness was the death of him. And yet, as Ingmar Bergman wrote, 'his only offence was that he dared to tell people the truth'.

To the pure, all things are pure. In less liberated times, the high priests of naughtiness use a more roundabout route, concealing their salaciousness under a cloak of alternative interpretation. The double entendre flourished under Queen Victoria, who would not have been amused by the items listed in Jack Melville's joke book under 'Saucy'. For example:

JACK: In the middle of July,
         In the hottest of the weather,
         If two can't sleep alone,
         Then one must sleep together.

Underlined in red ink (guarantee of a good laugh) is this remote ancestor of Lenny Bruce's 'touch-it':

JACK [*to LUCY*]:   What are you doing, knitting a doily for your what-not?

LUCY: No — it's a nightie for my p'raps-not.

Another variation:

LUCY [*to JACK*]:   I bet you a pound I can tell what you're thinking.

JACK: Rightho — fire away.

LUCY: You're thinking you'd like to take me to Brighton for the weekend.

JACK [*paying up*]:   It wasn't what I was thinking but it's a great idea!

At the turn of the century, the 'Brighton weekend' had already acquired a suggestive double meaning. The seaside, like the music-hall, had become a form of popular entertainment — a relief from the drudgery and restraints of everyday life, and a huge joke that, seemingly, could never go stale.

In *The Open Air*, Richard Jefferies described Brighton beach as:

An awfully *naughty* place, no sort of idea of rightness here. Humming and strumming and singing and smoking, splashing and sparkling, a buzz of voices and a booming of sea! If only they could be happy like this always.

The liberating effect of the Saturday 'half-holiday', and the Bank Holiday Act of 1871, stimulated the rush to the sea. In the words of the song,

You can do a lot of things at the seaside
That you can't do in town....

A streak of wild vulgarity runs through the history of Britain's seaside resorts, like the pink letters in their rock. A sense of relaxation: loosen the stays, throw off the celluloid collar,

And all, impatient of dry land, agree
With one consent to rush into the sea.

At the age of seven, Charlie Chaplin took the excursion train to Margate, with his mother.

My first sight of the sea was hypnotic. We took off our shoes and paddled. The tepid sea unfurling over my insteps and around my ankles, and the soft sand under my feet were a revelation of delight. What a day that was — the saffron beach, its coloured tents and umbrellas, and sailing boats hurtling gaily over laughing little waves — the memory of it still lingers with enchantment.

The bathing machine, from which the ladies emerged 'dressed in flannel cases, showing

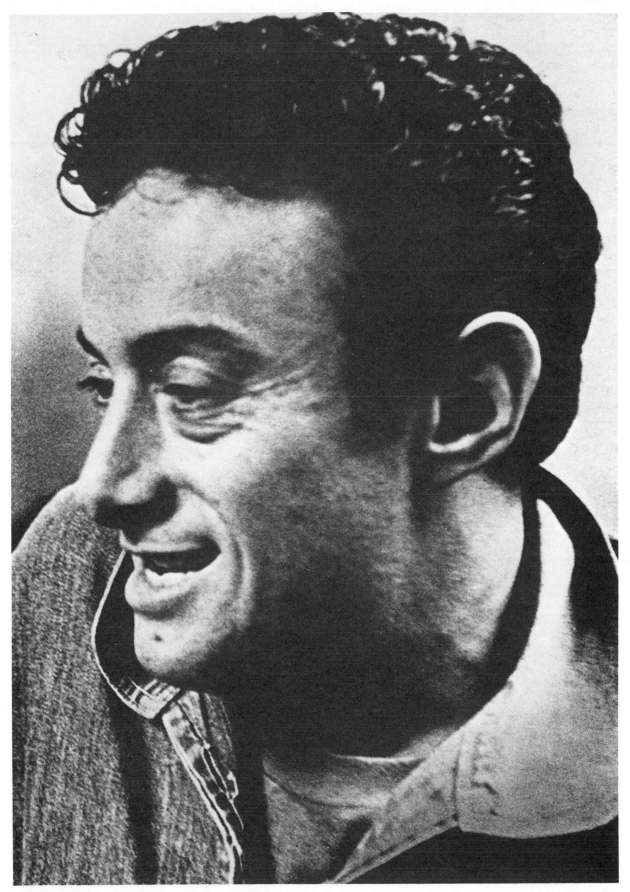

Lenny Bruce: the sharpest denter of taboos. At 41, he died of an overdose

Norman Evans, as Fanny Fairbottom, gossiping 'over the garden wall'

Seaside entertainers, 1905

nothing but their faces', became an inescapable feature of every resort, the subject of innumerable jokes and cartoons, comic symbol of the English seaside until the First World War. And the ice-cold waters of the English Channel and the North Sea were enthusiastically endorsed by politician, physician, and music-hall comedian:

> Bathing strengthens the interlect, braces the body, clears the system, puts new life in the bloods, old heads onto young shoulders, fills the pockets, drives away care, cures corns, warts, bunions, Pilgrim's progresses, water on the brain, *new*-ralgia, *old*-ralgia, and all the Primrose 'ills as flesh is heir to. . . .

Some went so far as to take sea-water internally. Dr Richard Russell wrote in *The Lancet* that 'a pint taken daily is commonly sufficient in grown persons to give three or four sharp stools'.

And to entertain the purged and liberated Victorian holiday-maker, a new breed of entertainer was born on the sands of Brighton, Blackpool and Bridlington. His costume was borrowed from the *Commedia dell' Arte*: the white unisex romper-suit of Pedrolino, or Pierrot —

'pale as the moon'. The Pierrots proliferated and soon every resort had its own troupe, with a title as fancy as any 1980s rock group. 'The Sparklers' at Bognor Regis included a young Tommy Handley in the line-up. On the Madeira Lawns at Brighton, one of 'The Rogues', appropriately enough, was Max Miller. At Hartlepool, 'The Busy Bees'; at Undercliffe, 'Scott Barrie's Chanticleers'; at St Annes, 'Cousin Freddy's Concert Party'; at Whitley Bay, 'The Corruptimists' (with Norman Evans); at Carnoustie, 'The White Coons' (with Arthur Lucan, who became Old Mother Riley); at Cleethorpes, 'The Jovial Jollies; at Maplethorpe, 'The Arcadia Revels'. This last was Jack Melville's company in the years before he enlisted in Fred Karno's Army.

The Pierrots played three shows daily, weather and tides permitting. Songs, dances and sketches — 'A laugh a minute, and never a single blush'. The Pier Theatre was a far cry from the noisy, beery atmosphere of the music-hall. The Pierrots played to a sober audience, of all ages, and comedy material had to be tailored accordingly. No rude songs, or 'blue' jokes, only the occasional suggestive innuendo, a

Pierrots at Scarborough, 1907

conspiratorial dig in dad's ribs that passed over the youngsters' heads.

JACK (to BERT):   How long is it since you left your wife, Bert?

BERT: Eeh, lad, it's just as long as it ever was!

The classic double-meaning jokes of the seaside comic have passed into English folklore, enshrined to this day in the 'twopenny coloured' postcards that carry home the traditional message: 'Having a lovely time — wish you were here'. The cards portray the very ideal of a comic world, where wives are gross and husbands hen-pecked and under-endowed, where skirts ride up, knicker elastic breaks, balls are lost, organs won't play, and wind is more likely to be humanly generated. Master of this mass-distribution art was James Bamforth, from Yorkshire. Bamforth was a Magic Lantern operator and moving picture pioneer, who launched the saucy postcard as an alternative to the 'sea-view' cards. He employed a number of skilled artists, particularly Douglas Tempest and Donald McGill, who later deserted and joined Bamforth's rival, the Pictorial Postcard Company. To the historian, the Bamforth postcards embody a reaction to the

mealy-mouthed puritanism of the age — an earthy response to the yearnings of a buttoned-up society. They lampoon conventional appetites and voice the unspoken desires of the rampant male: 'If I let something slip out, will you hold it against me?'

Bamforth's major contribution to the English language was the deliberate misuse of the pronoun 'it', to give a saucy double meaning to the most innocent-looking sentence. The gossips, observing tiny husband escorting giant wife: 'He used to be ever so shy — I can't imagine who put him up to it!' The passer-by, overhearing a conversation from behind the hedge: 'I beg you, Florence, don't break it off!' The dishevelled couple on the sofa:

HE: If I have another drink I shall feel it in the morning.

SHE: If I have another drink, you can feel it tonight!

In 1942 George Orwell wrote an essay on the art of Donald McGill. He concluded:

It will not do to condemn them on the ground that they are vulgar and ugly. That is exactly

Classics from the Bamforth Collection

what they are meant to be. Their whole meaning and virtue is in their unredeemed lowness, not in the sense of obscenity, but lowness of outlook in every direction whatever. The slightest hint of 'higher' influences would ruin them utterly.

The humour of the cards was recycled in the halls; one feeding off the other. Max Miller told the story of a woman who is washing clothes in the Zambezi and is tapped on the behind by an elephant's trunk. 'Mister,' she says, 'I don't know who you are, but I'm here every Tuesday and

Thursday morning.' Bamforth's version shows a courting couple at the zoo: an elephant's trunk, snaking through the bars, touches the girl on her shoulder. 'Oh, Horace, you are a *dear*!' Also from Max's Blue Book, and the Bamforth archive, is the trusty: 'I think I'll stick it out here for another week . . . .' A close cousin of Ken Dodd's best 'doctor' story:

I went to the doctor last week. He told me to take all my clothes off. Then he said 'You'll have to diet.' I said, 'What colour?'

Or, in the 'optician' version: 'No, no, Mister Dodd! I said "Could I please see your worn old *spectacles*!"'

The Crazy Gang were also keen students of the Bamforth suggestive double entendre. In the frozen wastes of the Yukon, Flanagan complains: 'I've passed nothing but snow and ice since yesterday morning.' To which Jimmy Nervo replies: 'A nice cup of hot coffee'll soon put that right!' And from their earthy version of *Androcles and the Lion* comes the classic: 'Poor chap — he's a eunuch. He's got no scruples.'

In 1962, Dr Jonathan Miller, one of the stars of the new satiric revue *Beyond the Fringe*, paid a house call on the Crazy Gang in their last season at the Victoria Palace. His diagnosis was printed in the magazine *Twentieth Century*:

> Every time I see this smutty rollick I have an uneasy feeling that under the camouflage of outrageous irreverence these ageing gentlemen are bolstering up some of the more unpleasant aspects of our national character. Thinly disguised and often blatantly apparent, the performance deals with sex. I say 'deals' advisedly, since the method involved does exactly this. It deals with sex; disposes of it; and renders it apparently harmless. Though bawdy in the extreme, sex, as such, is actually eliminated as effectively as if it had in fact been bowdlerised from the text.

> The routine consists of a series of sparsely constructed sketches which allow free reign to elaborate jokes in which bottoms, breasts and urinals receive obsessional attention. Also high on the list of topics are trousers, pants, trusses and hernias. Bed-pots, farts and contraceptives are not ignored.... The audience, needless to say, shrieks its delight, indicating by its enthusiasm the power of the psychic tension which these performers seem so kindly to release. I believe that in fact the sense of release is entirely false and that this performance simply discharges neurotic transformations of much deeper tensions which are themselves studiously left untapped. It is a psychological decoy which gives a false impression of relief so that the more dangerous issues can fester undisturbed. For when it comes down to it the items mentioned above — the urinals, the breasts, the brassieres and bed-pots — are no more than the second eleven of sexuality. The first eleven, the central sexual issues, are never allowed to get out to the wicket. The effect, I am sure, is unintentional. Nevertheless it falls in quite happily with the intentions of the Lord Chamberlain, who will blithely license this routine at the same time that he bars an honest treatment of the crucial themes. In this way the Lord Chamberlain is exploiting the immaturity of English humour in order to preserve that very immaturity. The very fact that jokes about farts and bed-pans *can* give a sense of release is a sign of this naïveté. It is a sign of an infantile confusion; one which Freud points out to be a natural phase in normal development — the confusion between excrement and eroticism, the blurred elision between dung and love. It is significant that so much of English humour rests on this confusion: witness *The Miller's Tale* of Chaucer. The Crazy Gang routine only serves to emphasise and confirm this confusion in the public mind. And as long as the confusion exists it will always be possible for Lord Chamberlains to exploit it to obscure the explosive issue of adult sexuality.

The following year Dr Miller was in the welcoming party at London Airport to meet the captain of the American first eleven, Lenny Bruce, booked for a return engagement at the Establishment nightclub. On the orders of the Home Secretary, Bruce was refused permission to enter the country and was put on the next plane back to Los Angeles. Three years later he was dead, and Dr Miller wrote:

> His life and death are significant, and serious attention must be paid. Bruce was a great stage artist.... He had an uncannily accurate eye for the sort of crucial visual detail which could suddenly delight spectators with a shock of recognition.

The second eleven, meanwhile, flourished. With the retirement of the Crazy Gang, the bat was passed to a new ensemble, created by producer Peter Rogers, to make saucy films. The first, made for a modest budget of £75,000, was called *Carry On Sergeant*. Released in 1958, it was phenomenally successful at the box office. In the years that followed thirty-one variations on the same theme have been played, mostly under the 'Carry On' label. Taken as an *oeuvre*, the films fall squarely within the traditions of Dr Miller's second eleven and present the English as appalling sexual hypocrites, somewhat perverted by bad potty training. Actor Jim Dale, who starred in *Carry On Doctor* (1967), explains:

> If on screen you see the front of a house, and someone opens a door and there's a field behind it, that's American humour.
> If, when the door opens, there's a field with a lavatory in it, that's French humour.
> But if there's a field with a lavatory, and someone's sitting on it, using it, that's a 'Carry On' film.

Gerald Thomas, who directs the films, has a clear idea of 'what makes the British laugh':

> Hospital jokes ... bed-pans and ham-handed doctors.... Historical send-ups.... Bare bums ... then boobs.... We've always gone

Carry On Doctor (1967): Kenneth Williams treats a head case, Jim Dale offers a second opinion

Carry On Matron (1972):
Barbara Windsor
and Terry Scott.
The specimen gag

Carry On at Your Convenience (1971):
the bidet is unveiled for
Kenneth Williams *(centre)*
and Charlie Hawtrey *(right)*

Carry On Henry (1970): the power behind the throne. *(From left)* Kenneth Williams, Charles Hawtrey, Sid James, Terry Scott

Carry On Up the Khyber (1968): Charles Hawtrey and Terry Scott on the run

in for a bit of innocent titillation. With the accent on tit.

Producer Peter Rogers concurs:

> If we can get a laugh out of a tit, we will. But we won't show a tit or bum just for the sake of it.... I always try to add a visual laugh to a comic line, so you get a laugh on top of a laugh. And I never worry about a laugh covering the next line. None of our lines is a pearl of wisdom anyway....
>
> Our two worst overseas markets are France and Italy. I think that's because in those countries they want to see the act itself, they don't want to just talk about it.

English or not, the films have penetrated to a number of surprising foreign parts. Sid James, whose battered features and drain-like laugh adorn seventeen of the series, was acclaimed as a superstar in Bangkok (where better?). In Cambodia, he found a cinema dedicated to showing 'Carry On' films twenty-four hours a day (outdoing the record of the Crystal Cinema in New York, which showed Charlie Chaplin films exclusively, but only during waking hours). In Crete, Kenneth Williams, he of the flaring nostrils and rounded vowels, was once accosted by a monk in a remote mountain monastery, with the cry: 'Ahhh! — Carry On!' How do they do it? Peter Rogers pleads:

> Don't try to analyse our success. We just set out to make people laugh. I know what ordinary people like, because I'm common myself. Thank God we don't have to rely on violence and full-frontal nudity to entertain our customers. We talk about sex a lot in our films. But nothing ever happens....

Under the protection of the double entendre, the series has avoided the censor's intervention. Peter Rogers recalls that on one occasion in the 1960s, when doubts were expressed about the propriety of certain lines, he sent the censor a packet of Bamforth postcards — as freely displayed in seaside shop windows from Appledore to Yarmouth. That was the end of the correspondence.

The 'it' factor, as pioneered by Bamforth, is further extended by the 'Carry On' writers. A passing reference to a warming pan: 'Where would you be without me to put it in for you?' At the maternity hospital: 'Are you expecting, or have you had it?' Anywhere and everywhere: 'Did you give it to her?'... 'You've got to get on top of it.'... 'Are you ready for it?'... 'Can you feel it?'... 'Something important's come up.' — 'Won't it keep?' — 'I do hope so.' The permutations are infinite.

In *Carry On Henry*, Sid James plays the lusty monarch.

CARDINAL WOLSEY: Have you seen the wench without?

KING HENRY: Not yet, worse luck...

Barbara Windsor is a pert and busty Anne Boleyn.

CARDINAL WOLSEY: She's a nice little thing, but she hasn't got a lot up here [*taps his head*].

KING HENRY: She makes up for it elsewhere.

In *Carry On Matron*, Hattie Jacques plays the title role, and has most of the punch lines.

ANXIOUS MUM: Matron, will you take a look at his little *thing* — it's all bent to one side?

MATRON [*reassuring*]:   Don't worry, Mrs Pullett — we'll have everything straightened out before you leave us....

Names are all-important, and good for a laugh. Lord Hampton de Wick....Sir Roger de Lodgerly....Mustapha Leke....The Khasi of Kalabar....Mr Boggs....Private Widdle....Bungit Din and his Burpahs.

The plot of *Carry On Up the Khyber* hangs largely upon what the highland regiments don't wear under kilts (another postcard speciality).

SGT. STRAPP: Just wait till you see him rushing at you, his kilt flying in the breeze, flashing his great ... bayonet at you!

Carry On at Your Convenience (1971) epitomises the whole series. It ploughs the same earthy ground as its predecessors, but has the bonus of being set in a lavatory factory (which warrants a unique screen credit to Royal Doulton Sanitary Potteries). Kenneth Williams plays Boggs, the proprietor, and Sid James is his partner, Plummer. Joan Sims is the luckless Miss Wittering, summonsed to the board room to test the new model.

BOGGS: How does it feel, Miss Wittering? Comfy?

MISS WITT.:   Yes, Mister Boggs.

BOGGS: Big in the bowl?

PLUMMER: It's only two centimetres larger than the last, and we shan't fall out about *that*.

BOGGS: It's falling *in* I'm worried about! [*to MISS WITT.*] Thank you, Miss Wittering: you've been most patient, like Job on a monument.

[*Miss Witt. rises from the bowl thankfully. Plummer now tries it, with pipe and* The Sporting Life.]

PLUMMER: I couldn't stand it for more than a half-hour!

Controversy arises over an order for a thousand bidets.

BOGGS: 'Bidet' is not *us*. Grandfather would not have approved.

PLUMMER: You can always wash your feet in the bath!

[*The bidet's use is explained to him, discreetly*]

PLUMMER: Oh, well, if it's for *that*, you can stand on your head in the shower.

There's unrest on the factory floor when management complains about the excessive number of tea-breaks.

BOGGS: On average, each worker takes sixteen trips to the toilet every day — that's seventeen minutes lost each day.

SHOP STEWARD: What is the answer?

PLUMMER: Tie a knot in it!

The works outing to the seaside is flavoured with traditional Bamforth dialogue.

'Let's go for a walk, there's a smashing front here.'
('And there's a lovely one here an' all!')
'Shall we have a go on the mats?'
'What — in front of everyone?'
'No, silly — the helter-skelter!'
'What's that digging in me?'
'It's only my camera!'

The journey home, by charabanc, is punctuated with stops for refreshment, alternating with stops for relief. The Sussex countryside is desecrated and defoliated as the rampaging horde scurries for every convenient bush or tree, and the soundtrack builds to a gushing, splashing climax.

While these urinary adventures are convulsing audiences in South-East Asia, on the other side of the world revolutionary Cuba comes to a standstill when another British second eleven player comes out to bat. On Cuban TV, *The Benny Hill Show* rivals Fidel Castro's three-hour Party Political Broadcasts in the ratings, even without benefit of subtitles.

Hill's comic destiny was determined at the age of ten in the stalls of the King's Theatre, Southsea:

I used to go to all the touring revues, which would have eight, ten or sixteen girls in the chorus, and a comic who was a bit Max Millerish. A bit near the knuckle. And there I'd be, a kid in short pants, thinking of that comic, 'Aren't you lucky up there?'

He had everybody laughing and applauding him, and with him there were always the saucy girls, the glamour pusses, the French maids with black stockings and feather dusters, who would stick their bottoms up. . . . I think my whole life was decided from then on.

Half a century later, the wicked grin of Benny Hill — 'the soiled cherub, the angel with the dirty face' — is a harbinger of visual naughtiness on worldwide television, from Cuba to Czechoslovakia, from Finland to Thailand. In America, his comic-strip comedy was screened five nights a week, coast to coast. Even the *Washington Post* was forced to sit up and take notice. Under the headline 'Delightfully Bad Benny', Tom Shales wrote:

We should not accept the premise that the pun is the lowest form of humor, because if we do, we miss the great pleasure of searching for forms even lower. Benny Hill, from all appearances a fearlessly tasteless explorer in

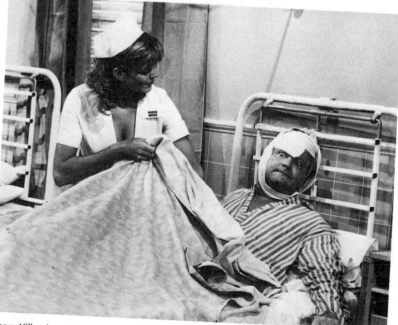

Benny Hill on home ground

this well-trampled realm, makes the quest just short of uproarious in his show to be seen Tuesday through Fridays on Channel 20. 'How potent cheap music is,' Noel Coward wrote. And how funny old jokes are if they are tossed about with the kind of zip that Hill, a veteran British comic, brings to his program. Essentially, Hill's is old-styled burlesque comedy, cranked up to 78 r.p.m. for television, as speedy as it is racy. It is marked by a bawdiness and slap-happy vulgarity unlike anything on American television. The double-entendre flows like Schweppes and is just as curiously refreshing. Hill, who looks like Rod Steiger playing Jonathan Winters, will stoop to anything — we hope. His smorgasbord of the ridiculous is delightfully bereft of redeeming social value. Bad British drama is unbearable; bad British comedy can be sublime.

In Hill's hands, history is reduced to the dirty bits. In 'The Sale of Two Tit . . . no, sorry, the Tale of Two Cities', he plays bewigged aristo, trying to avoid the guillotine by hiding — where else? — under the nearest skirt. In 'The Scarlet Pimple', pretty wenches lock their doors, but dirty old Lords open them from the hinged side. No opportunity is missed to lower a skirt, or whip off a pair of trousers. On a country walk, Benny will help a pretty girl climb over a fence, with a liberal display of suspendered thigh — then open the gate, to walk through himself. He tells the tale of the lady acrobat who could jump five feet straight up in the air — 'six, if you catch her right!' Or, of the naked accordionist who had a nasty accident.

'Did he catch his finger in it?'
'Something like that . . .'

Doctors' surgeries and hospital wards are favourite settings. The nurse bending over the bed shows cleavage to the patient, bottom to the doctor. There's fun to be had from the injudicious placing of the stethoscope, from bedpans, and bottles:

'Can you fill that?'
'Not from where I'm standing!'

A group of male patients emerging from the doctor's office rub their arms after the injection, while the lone female rubs her bottom. A group of nurses perform a sexy Can-can as a treat for a randy ancient — Benny Hill, of course — who in the end expires, with a smile of unalloyed pleasure on his face. What a way to go. . . .
Richard Pryor's father died fucking.

He came and went at the same time. He was fifty-seven, the woman was eighteen. And that woman couldn't *give* away pussy for two years!
She came to see me. She said: 'I'm sorry I killed your father, Rich.'
I said: 'Look, people get killed in plane crashes, cars, all terrible things. My father died in your pussy! That's called re-cycling!'
If you had a choice between dying in a pussy or being hit by a bus, which queue would *you* take? Yeah — me too: I'd be in that *long* mother-fucker!

A black comic for the 1980s, Richard Pryor strides purposefully to the crease, assuming captaincy of Dr Miller's first eleven. No mealy-mouthed shilly-shallying here, no beating about the bush. Pryor matches Lenny Bruce for the four-letter candour of his comedy. His stage show is an intensely dramatic monologue, an exorcising of the fears and anxieties of modern America. Top of the list, of course, is sex.

Did you know that there's a billion people in China? That's a lot of people. Someone in China's doin' some serious fucking. . . . And they fuck *quick*!
Black people, they try to stay in a pussy for three *days*! And they're always trying to find new ways. . . .

I can fuck for three minutes. Three minutes serious fucking and I need eight hours sleep. And a bowl of Wheaties!

Woody Allen uses the distraction method.

SHE: What were you thinking while we were doing it?
HE: Willie Mays.
SHE: Do you always think of baseball players?
HE: It keeps me going.
SHE: I wondered why you kept yelling 'SLIDE!'

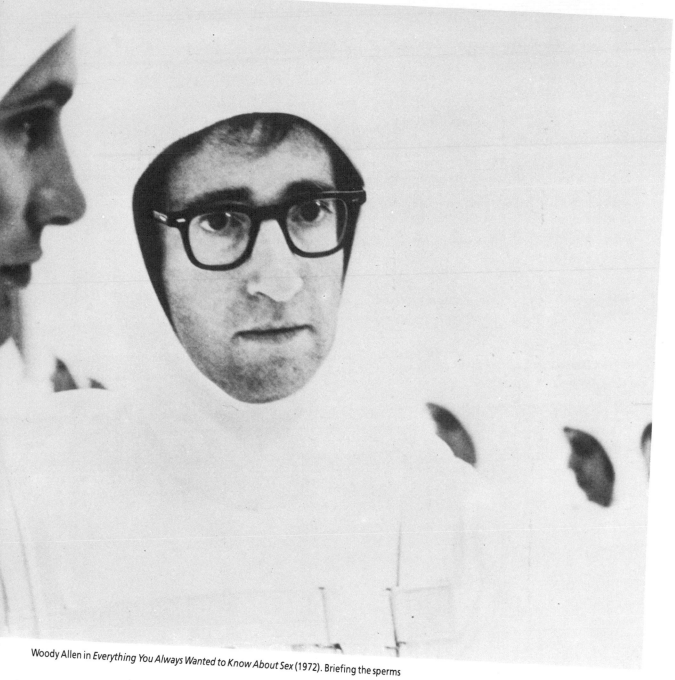

Woody Allen in *Everything You Always Wanted to Know About Sex* (1972). Briefing the sperms

To Woody we are indebted also for the inside story of 'What Happens During Ejaculation', as dramatically reconstructed in his authoritative movie *Everything You Always Wanted to Know About Sex*. The brain is a computerised control room, manned by white-coated boffins. Messages come in, instructions go out.

'Stomach, stand by for food intake.'
'What kind?'
'Fettucini.'
'Jesus Christ, look out — Italian food coming down!'

On the outside, the sexy dinner date is warming up. Ears pass on the message:

'Your place or mine?'

Panic in the control room.

'It looks like they're going to do it. Prepare for launching.'
'Attention, sperms! Standby.'

The sperms line up, ready for the jump.

SPERM ONE: Here we go again!

SPERM TWO [Woody]: D'you think we'll get out this time?

SPERM ONE: I hope it's not another false alarm. They've been having trouble down in engineering.

SPERM TWO: I heard it was all mental....

The control room calls for more adrenalin. The dinner date responds:

'Oh my God, Sidney — can't you *wait*? You wanna do it right here in the parking lot?'

In the engine room, sweating minions are heaving on a winch.

'Brain to sexual organs, can we please have an erection? What the hell's going on down there?'

Shoulders to the wheel, the grinding of cogs ...

'We have an erection of forty-five degrees. Prepare for penetration.'

The sperms shuffle into position.

SPERM ONE: Well, this looks like it.

SPERM TWO: Do you guys know what it's like out there?

SPERM ONE: Like they told us in training school — it's an ovum.

SPERM TWO: I'm scared, I don't want to go. You hear these strange stories about a pill these women take. Or sometimes the guys will slam their heads against a wall of hard rubber....

In the engine room, the gantry's rising.... The sperms struggle for balance.

'We're inside, we're making it! Prepare for the release of sperms.'

The sperms are panicking.

SPERM TWO: I'm not going out there. I'm not going to get shot out of that thing. What if he's masturbating? I'm liable to end up on the ceiling!

Furious activity in the control room. Dials flashing. Full power.

SPERM ONE: See you guys in the ovary.

SPERM TWO: Well — at least he's Jewish...

CHAPTER NINE

VICTIMISATION

Woody Allen coming up for air; *Bananas* (1971)

WOODY ALLEN'S screen persona, except when he's playing a sperm, is himself, taken from life. A small man, bespectacled, sweaty, harassed. Straggly red hair conceals incipient baldness (another cause for anxiety). Usually wearing corduroy trousers, saddle shoes, a hideous green and yellow sports jacket. No dress sense. The hunched look of a small man beset by huge obstacles; a stiff neck from always looking over his shoulder. The sad face of the clown reflects the hell he's going through. Nietzsche explains:

Perhaps I know best why it is man alone who laughs: he alone suffers so deeply that he had to invent laughter. . . .

Marie Lloyd never read Nietzsche, but she did see Dan Leno in performance. She said:

Ever seen his eyes? The saddest eyes in the whole world. That's why we all laughed at Danny. Because if we hadn't laughed we should have cried ourselves sick. I believe that's what real comedy is, y'know. It's almost like crying. . . .

Examine the tragic life of the comic artist. A miserable, deprived childhood (Chaplin, Karno, Norman Wisdom, Lenny Bruce). A violent, drunken or absent father (Leno, Keaton, Richard Pryor). Accidents on-stage and off, split heads, broken bones (Grimaldi, Lupino Lane, Little Tich, Jimmy Jewel, Charlie Drake). Body-blows of misfortune — financial, marital, psychological (Karno, Keaton, Tati, Max Wall, Peter Sellers, Jerry Lewis). Illness, madness, suicide, an untimely end (Leno, Max Linder, Spike Milligan, Tony Hancock, Lenny Bruce, Marty Feldman).

The funny man as Victim — of the bully, of the unexpected, of his own over-reaching, of Fate. He Who Will Be Put Upon, to the audience's delight. A whiff of cruelty here, in the enjoyment of another's misfortune. Which is where we came in.

Woody Allen wonders if beings from another planet would have the answer to our problems.

WOODY: You guys have got to tell me — why is there so much suffering?

ALIEN: This is unanswerable.

WOODY: Is there a God?

ALIEN: These are the wrong questions.

WOODY: Look, here's my point, if nothing lasts, why am I bothering to make films, or do anything, for that matter?

ALIEN: We enjoy your films, especially the early funny ones.

WOODY: But shouldn't I do something useful, like helping blind people, or being a missionary?

ALIEN: You're not the missionary type — if you want to do mankind a real service, tell funnier jokes.

Woody Allen has spent twenty-five years in psychoanalysis, looking for the answers. When John Cleese asked him recently how it was going, Woody replied: 'Slowly'. His experience of victimisation goes back to his childhood days on the streets of Flatbush, New York. He was the only kid on the block who *would* take sweets from a stranger:

> I was kidnapped once. I was standing in front of my school yard and a black sedan pulls up and two guys get out and they say to me, do I want to go away with them to a land where everybody is fairies and elves and I can have all the comic books I want, and chocolate buttons and wax lips, you know. And I said, yes. And they drive me off, and they send a ransom note to my parents. And my father has bad reading habits. So he got into bed that night with the ransom note, read half of it, got drowsy and fell asleep. Meanwhile they take me to New Jersey bound and gagged. And my parents finally realize that I'm kidnapped and they snap into action immediately. They rent out my room. . . .

Physical size is critical to the comedy of victimisation. He Who Gets Put Upon should ideally be dwarfed by his adversaries. The tradition of 'The Little Fellow' runs from the pygmy jesters of the Egyptian Pharaoh, through Pedrolino (piccolo) in the *Commedia dell' Arte*, to the pint-sized prodigies of the music-hall stage: Little Tich, Dan Leno, Buster Keaton, Wee Georgie Wood, Norman Wisdom, Charlie Drake.

Charlie Chaplin measured 5 feet 6 inches. Even in the big black boots and scruffy bowler of the 'Tramp', he is dwarfed by the villains he runs up against: Eric Campbell, Mack Swain and co. Chaplin's 'Tramp' is the very epitome of 'The Little Fellow', disadvantaged in every way — in size, social status, material wealth, opportunity. Victimised by Fate, his very survival, against the odds, will be an achievement. In retrospect, the character might seem to be a conscious working-out of Chaplin's attitude to life and his own early experiences. In fact, its origination was largely accidental. In his third week at the Keystone Studios, Chaplin was summoned by Sennett, told to find himself a comedy make-up — 'anything will do' — and report to a location in downtown Los Angeles where Sennett was filming *Kid Auto Races at Venice*. Chaplin went to the dressing-room he shared with the other actors. From Fatty Arbuckle he borrowed a pair of outsize trousers; from Ford Serling, size fourteen shoes (which he wore on the wrong feet to prevent them from slipping off); from Chester Conklin, a tight-fitting 'cutaway' coat; and from Mack Swain, a bushy 'toothbrush' moustache. His own bamboo cane completed the makeshift outfit in which he presented himself to Sennett. Apparently well satisfied, the director told Chaplin to work himself into the scene they were filming, in which vast crowds of onlookers had been drafted as 'extras' to line the route of a racetrack. Policemen struggled to hold back the crowd, while a newsreel cameraman was preparing to film the arrival of the racing cars. Chaplin's thrown-together character became a general nuisance in the scene, running out onto the track, getting in the way of the cameraman, and brawling with the policemen who try to restrain him. Chaplin used a splayed, shuffling walk and twirled his cane, strutting and preening in front of the spectators.

That first appearance of the embryonic character, soon to become Chaplin's worldwide trademark, goes unrecorded in Chaplin's autobiography, written fifty years later. There's no mention of the film *Kid Auto Races at Venice*; instead, Chaplin pinpoints the invention of the 'Tramp' as taking place during the filming of *Mabel's Strange Predicament* some weeks later. Why he chose to overlook *Kid Auto Races* remains a mystery. Perhaps he hoped to persuade film

Chaplin. The Tramp takes a bow; *Kid Auto Races at Venice* (1914)

historians that his 'Tramp' made his debut in the more polished and inventive performance of his third Keystone film, rather than in the uncertain street-corner posturings of *Kid Auto Races*.

Chester Conklin, one of Chaplin's co-stars at Keystone, makes the same mistake. In an interview recorded in 1963, he said:

> One rainy morning, Roscoe Arbuckle and myself were sitting in the dressing-room playing pinochle. Charlie wandered in and went up to the make-up bench. Now in those days we used crepe hair a lot. Charlie held up various pieces of this crepe hair under his nose. Finally he found a piece he liked, and stuck it on there with spirit gum, went over and got Roscoe's hat and his pants, my coat, and his own cane, and went on the set.
>
> It was a hotel set, for *Mabel's Strange*

Chaplin with Fatty Arbuckle at the Sennett Studios, 1914. Chaplin said of Arbuckle: 'a genial, easy-going type who would not harm a fly'

Predicament, and Charlie went into the lobby and started clowning around doing the drunk act he'd done in vaudeville. He'd get his foot stuck in the cuspidor and couldn't get it out — all that kind of thing. Everyone had gathered around and was laughing. Sennett stood at the back of the crowd and watched. Finally he went over to Charlie and said, 'Listen, do what you've been doing while we shoot this picture with Mabel and Chester.' Well, of course, it wound up that he stole the picture from us!

Chaplin's own account offers further insights into this historic event. He claims that there was nothing haphazard in the choice of elements to make up the costume:

I wanted everything a contradiction: the pants baggy, the coat tight, the hat small and the shoes large. I was undecided whether to look young or old, but remembering that Sennett had expected me to be a much older man, I added a small moustache, which, I reasoned, would add age without hiding my expression. I had no idea of the character. But the moment I was dressed, the clothes and the make-up made me feel the person he was. I began to know him, and by the time I walked on the stage, he was fully born. When I confronted Sennett I assumed the character and strutted about, swinging my cane. Gags and comedy ideas went racing through my mind.

The secret of Sennett's success was his enthusiasm. He was a great audience and laughed genuinely at what he thought was funny. He stood and giggled until his body began to shake. This encouraged me, and I began to explain the character: 'You know, this fellow is many-sided, a tramp, a gentleman, a poet, a dreamer, a lonely fellow, always hopeful of romance and adventure. He would have you believe he is a scientist, a musician, a duke, a polo-player. However he is not above picking up cigarette butts, or robbing a baby of its candy. And of course, if the occasion warrants it, he will kick a lady in the rear — but only in extreme anger!'

By the end of the day, the 'Tramp' was a fully rounded character. There was a stony silence when Chaplin returned to the dressing-room. Serling and Arbuckle were taking off their make-up, and Chaplin detected that his two co-stars were undergoing 'some inner conflict'. A few days later, in the Alexandria bar, he overheard Serling talking about the 'Tramp':

The guy has baggy pants, flat feet, the most miserable, bedraggled-looking bastard you ever saw; makes itchy gestures as though he's got crabs under his arms — but he's funny.

Once adopted, Chaplin refused to let the 'Tramp' go. 'As the clothes had imbued me with the character, I decided I would keep to this costume whatever happened.' Over the months, the costume developed. The trousers became less baggy, the coat a little neater, the moustache trimmer. The splay-footed walk became more exaggerated, and another idiosyncratic mannerism was acquired — the sad little shrug of hopelessness whenever cruel Fate deals him another body-blow. When the first 'Tramp' films were shown in England — *The Champion*, *In the Park*, *The Tramp*, *The Vagabond*, *Easy Street* — Jack Melville was one of the first to spot the similarities between Charlie's screen persona and the character created on stage (and on a larger scale) by Fred Kitchen, the Karno comedian from whom Chaplin had learned his knockabout basics. The Kitchen gait — 'a curious shambling walk, a cross between a shuffle and a hop' — was identified in the 'Tramp's' bowlegged swagger, while a trick of throwing a cigarette butt into the air and kicking it away with the heel, was invented by Kitchen in 'Jail Birds'. And from the French comedian, Max Linder, Chaplin appears to have adopted the shoulder-wrenching shrug of resignation.

In later years Chaplin contributed to the speculation about the 'Tramp's' antecedents. In 1952 he revealed that his own father had been his model for the character, when once he had to stand in for a sick music-hall comedian and assume a costume that was far too big for him — the costume of a tramp.

With the ill-fitting costume, came the tramp personality. It wasn't a studied character. It was just released whole from somewhere deep in my father. It was really my father's *alter ego*, the little boy who never grew up: ragged, cold, hungry, but still thumbing his nose at the world.

This must be taken with a pinch of salt. It's quite improbable that his father, Charles Chaplin — a mediocre ballad singer who drank himself to death at the age of thirty-seven — could have stood in for a comedian, inventing a comic character in the process. 'The little boy who never grew up' is surely Chaplin himself, projecting onto his father his *own* childhood experience in the Hanwell Institution, a workhouse orphanage for destitute children.

Another possible antecedent for Chaplin's 'Tramp' is the traditional clown character in circus, known as the 'Auguste' (the word is

The Fratellini: *(from left)* Paul (born Sicily, 1877), François (born Paris, 1879), Albert (born Moscow, 1886)

German slang for 'silly'). Unlike his white-faced, spangled partner, the 'Auguste' wears tatty street clothes — black coat with over-long tails, a roomy white waistcoat, tight black pants, a squashed opera hat and quilted white gaiters. He plays the role of the victim (Chocolat), He Who Must Be Slapped (by Footit). In the Paris Circus of the 1920s, Albert Fratellini played the 'Auguste' and was bullied by his two brothers, Paul and Francois. J. B. Priestley, who saw them in action, said:

> Unlike ordinary clowns, they represented a social structure, as if visiting us from some clowndom that had its own division into classes. (But were they mocking us? It is just possible.) All three were clowns of course but at the same time they were each quite different. Their whole appearance indicated the class to which they belonged in clowndom.

Number One was beautifully dressed; handsome, confident, full of authority and privilege; he was the only aristocratic clown I have ever seen. Number Two, sombrely if still clownishly dressed, obviously came from the professional middle classes of the distant realm. He took orders from Number One, but soon passed them on, if any labour was involved, to Number Three. This last, an Auguste always nearly coming to pieces, had been imported from the most depressed and forlorn class in Clowndom, a dazed and hopeless proletarian if ever I saw one. And whatever work had to be done, muttering and stumbling, he did it.

I seem to remember quite clearly one of their acts. Number One arrived in the ring, fresh as a daisy, looking about him as if wondering where to settle. Number Two, anxious and conscientious, a good professional

Dick Emery as College, one of his gallery of eccentric comic types

type, came in a moment later, to confer and accept any orders coming down from the upper class. Then he turned about to make an abrupt authoritative gesture, to bring on Number Three, not only about to fall to pieces, but also weighed down with a monstrous amount of luggage. Number One, without deigning to speak, pointed to another part of the ring, and delicately began to move there, ignoring the lower classes behind him. Number Two gave an order, perhaps couched in legal form, to Number Three, who by this time, poor fellow, had divested himself of all that baggage, and was trying to enjoy a rest while still falling to pieces. Muttering and grumbling, he took up his load again, to stumble after his betters. But no sooner had Number Three arrived with his burden of baggage than Number One, nothing if not arbitrary and capricious, had changed his mind and decided on another part of the ring. So it went on, though I believe at some point poor Number Three threw down all his trunks and cases and refused to move, whereupon Numbers One and Two, outraged, turned on him and probably reminded him of the iron laws of Clowndom, under which he served.

I realise that all this sounds sad rather than funny. But it was very funny and sad at the same time. Great clowns are able to mix our feelings in this way . . . .

The comic tramp flourished in the early music-hall. Victor Liston sang:

I'm too proud to beg, too honest to steal;
I know what it is to be wanting a meal.
My tatters and rags I try to conceal —
I'm one of the shabby genteel.

George Carney, from Bristol, was another tramp. His theme song, 'I Live in Leicester Square', extolled the merits of a park bench under two layers of newspaper. And from Yorkshire came Jack Pleasants, 'Feeding the Ducks in the Park'. In the television age, Arthur Haynes played a monstrous sympathy-seeking old soldier, while Dick Emery created the bowler-hatted 'College' — a gentleman with cultural pretensions, struggling to retain his dignity on the breadline. *The Young Ones* are the punk derelicts of the 1980s, and the cult comedians of BBC Television. There's Rick, a martyr to acne; Vyvyan, ringed by the nose; smelly Neil; and almost normal Mike. They live in hand-to-mouth squalor, scavenging in garbage cans, dining on rat, shunning the laundrette.

NEIL: Let's never wash our clothes again.

MIKE: What d'you mean 'again'?

Wreaking self-inflicted damage, living in vacuous lunacy, the quartet fly the flag for 'alternative' situation comedy: the reverse side to the well-ordered, mild-mannered G-Planned staple.

Along with the underprivileged classes, the persecuted minorities all have their parts to play in the comedy of victimisation. Lenny Bruce was Jewish.

A Jew, in the dictionary, is one who is descended from the ancient tribes of Judea. That's what it says; but you and I know what a Jew is — *One Who Killed Our Lord*. I don't know if we got much press on that in Illinois — we did this about two thousand years ago — two thousand years of Polack kids whacking the shit out of us coming home from school.

Dear, dear. And although there should be a statute of limitations for that crime, it seems that those who have neither the actions nor the gait of Christians, pagan or not, will bust us out, unrelenting dues, for another deuce.

And I really searched it out, why we pay

the dues. Why do you keep breaking our balls for this crime?

'Why, Jew, because you skirt the issue. You blame it on Roman soldiers.'

Alright, I'll clear the air once and for all, and confess. Yes, we did it, I did it, my family. I found a note in my basement. It said:

'We killed him.
                    signed,
                            Morty.'

And a lot of people say to me, 'Why did you kill Christ?'

'I dunno . . . it was one of those parties, got out of hand, you know.'

We killed him because he didn't want to become a doctor, that's why we killed him.

From Kafka through Bruce, to Woody Allen

and Mel Brooks, the Jewish comic figure is helpless before hostile man as well as before nature and God. All the varieties of vulnerability are concentrated in the character created by Brooks on radio and record — the two-thousand-year-old man. He is the universal Jewish parent, loving and abandoned melodramatically: 'I have over forty-two thousand children and not one comes to visit me. How dey forget a father?' He's become so accustomed to an antagonistic society that he has always considered Paul Revere 'an anti-Semite bastard' for yelling 'The Yiddish are coming! The Yiddish are coming!' Corrected, he is

A rare sighting of The Young Ones in a laundrette: *(from left)* Vyvyan (Ade Edmonson), Neil (Nigel Planer), Rick (Rik Mayall), Mike (Christopher Ryan)

full of remorse:'Oy, my God! I'm going to have to send his wife a note.' He observes that hospitals haven't changed since the caveman days; the same medical principles are practised — 'the principle of people walking past you when you're screaming and not caring . . . the same wonderful indifference to the sick and the dying'. He ascribes his own longevity to never touching fried food and never running for a bus ('there'll always be another'). He has lived at a slow pace of development, which had its own rewards: 'I breast-fed for two hundred years . . . I used to con a lot of ladies into doing it. They took pity on me.' His advice for mankind's survival: 'If every human being in the world played a violin, we'd be bigger and better than Mantovani.' The Jewishness in this unique characterisation was extremely personal to Brooks: 'I really wailed. I could hear my antecedents. I could hear five thousand years of Jews pouring through me.' There was a serious purpose too, a desire to preserve a fading culture:

> Within a couple of decades, there won't be any more accents like that. They're being ironed out by history, because there are no more Jewish immigrants. It's the sound I was brought up on, and it's dying.

Mel Brooks first discovered the saving power of comedy at the Sussex Camp for Underprivileged Jewish children. 'I always felt that it was my job to amuse those around me. Don't ask me why.' His wit and intelligence gave him an in with the older boys: 'Why should they let this puny kid hang out with them? I gave them a reason. I became their jester . . . I found a way of getting even in an oblique way through comedy, instead of just yelling insults and taunts and getting my head smashed in.'

The joker in the playground — a part played for real by Chaplin, Laurel, Tati, Jimmy Jewel, Jerry Lewis, Graham Chapman, Tim Brooke-Taylor and many others for whom schooldays were an endurance course. Some took their revenge in adult life by creating monstrously comic schoolmasters, victimised by their pupils. In music-hall and films of the 1930s, Will Hay created 'Dr Muffin' at Narkover School. Inadequate and shiftless, he was beset by pupils both bright and cunning. His trademark was his pince-nez, over which Hay's acrobatic eyes performed a trapeze act of the emotions — dismay, greed, irascibility and, above all, suspicion of his small charges who ranged against him threateningly, ready at any moment to

Will Hay as Dr Muffin: 'Thank you, d'Arcy'; *Good Morning Boys* (1937)

sabotage his ineffectual authoritarianism.

MUFFIN: Pay attention. For the first lesson we'll take algebra. Now, who knows what it is?

BECKETT: Please, sir — I've seen one.

MUFFIN: *Seen* one?

BECKETT: Yes, sir.

MUFFIN: I've heard of people seeing pink elephants, but I've never — what do these look like?

BECKETT: Please, sir, it had stripes.

MUFFIN: Stripes? You're not thinking of a sergeant, are you?

BECKETT: No, sir, this had more than three stripes, and long ears like a donkey.

SMART: He means a zebra, sir.

BECKETT: Yes, sir; isn't that what you said, sir?

MUFFIN: No, no, no, no, no. That's a different thing altogether. Algebra is – er – er – well – anybody like to tell Beckett what algebra is?

Jimmy Edwards inherited the cane and mortar-board for a series of television comedies in

John Cleese as the headmaster: 'Sex. Sex. Sex. Sex. Sex. Where were we?' *The Meaning of Life* (1983)

the 1950s. As disreputable and unacademic as Hay's 'Dr Muffin', Professor Edwards was an inveterate skiver, resenting his pupils for keeping him from more pleasurable pursuits in bar-room and brothel. A stern disciplinarian, though — with cane and gun.

PROF. EDWARDS [*standing at open window with smoking revolver*]: He'll never be able to make that sign at me with *one* finger!

Rowan Atkinson achieved distinction at the Edinburgh Festival of 1978 with a monologue, 'Schoolmaster', written by Richard Sparks. The simple device of the reading of the morning roll-call, embellished by Atkinson's finely tuned sneer, becomes a masterpiece of victimisation:

Right, quiet . . . Ainsley . . . Babcock . . . Bland . . . Dint . . . Ellsworth-Beast Major . . . Ellsworth-Beast Minor . . . Fiat . . . Haemoglobin . . . Kosygin . . . Loudhailer . . . Nibble . . . Orifice . . . Plectrum . . . (Come on, settle down) . . . Poins . . . Sediment . . . Soda . . . Ta . . . Ta? . . . Undermanager . . . Zob. Put

it *away*, Plectrum. If I see it once more this period, Plectrum, I shall have to tweak you. Do you have a solicitor? Don't sulk, boy, for God's sake — has Matron seen those *boils*? NIBBLE! LEAVE ORIFICE ALONE!

Right, for the rest of this period you will write about Enobarbus. Undermanager — just try and write Enobarbus. Either way up, boy. Use ink only — via a nib if possible. You may use dividers, but not on each other.

Kosygin — you're in charge.

John Cleese exorcised some Clifton College ghosts with an early television caricature of the Headmaster on Speech Day berating pupils and parents alike in a hysterical tirade:

You, boy — where's your pullover? Well, go and *get* it. We'll all just wait here, all the boys and all the parents, while you fetch it. Stop *snivelling*, boy!

Where's the chaplain?
Chaplain, why isn't the marquee up?
Why have you got no clothes on?
TEA, EVERYONE, TEA!

Three faces of Fawlty. John Cleese as the hypomanic hotelier. *Fawlty Towers* (1979)

Mack Sennett defined comedy as 'contrast and catastrophe involving the unseating of dignity'. The emergence of the authority figure — He Who Must Be Taken Down a Peg — represents a subtle variation in the comedy of victimisation. It requires a player who does not immediately engage the audience's sympathy. Far from it. Instead of being small, sweet-natured and vulnerable, he is gross, overbearing and obnoxious. The audience can't wait for him to get his come-uppance. They cheer when he does.

John Cleese is a master of this comic art, which derives from the comic villains of Greek and Roman pantomime — the braggart, the miser, the bullying soldier, the stern father. Shakespeare's pompous and self-deluded Malvolio also fits the bill. But Cleese has gone even further out on this fragile limb to create a character who evokes laughter because of his complete lack of kindness, compassion, and understanding; because of his inability to appreciate these and similar virtues in others; and because of his impressive list of shortcomings. Insensitivity apart, he is deceitful, lying, vain, toadying, smarmy, mean, bullying, snobbish, prudish and thick. He is a human where the genetic code was cracked halfway to the foetal cipher office and the message got through only in corrupt groups. He is, of course, Basil Fawlty, ungenial host of *Fawlty Towers* — 'Have you booked? HAVE YOU BOOKED?'

In *The Listener*, Jack Waterman suggests that Fawlty represents the missing bit of Aristotle:

the mirror image in farce of the tragic hero who, through inborn faults, encompasses ruin and disaster for all. Our emotions are then purged, not with pity, but with laughter by the device of come-uppance which always overtakes this manic, envenomed, juggernaut version of Mr Pooter just as surely as the original Mr Pooter was able to write in his diary: 'Made exit with dignity, but tripped over mat.'

Although Fawlty contains in his dreadful characteristics the clockwork mechanism of comedy, it is others who put the tension on the spring. Sometimes it is his bossy, blathering wife; sometimes the hapless Spanish waiter ('He's from Barcelona'); sometimes inanimate objects (a moose's head, for example, that Fawlty plans to hang on the lobby wall for 'ambience and tone'); and, most often, the guests with whom he comes into collision: 'Have they no consideration? Don't they realise I'm trying to run a HOTEL?'

W. C. Fields. 'Never give a sucker an even break, or smarten up a chump'

Robin Skynner, who was John Cleese's psychotherapist for some years, is very worried about Fawlty:

Of course he's paranoid. He blames everyone else — indeed he finds it hard to credit how stupid and inconsiderate other people are, while preserving an image of himself as morally perfect.

People like this need to use their opponents as dustbins, somewhere they can dump all the bits of themselves they can't accept. So, they need to hate their opponents, to keep themselves sane.

And he's depressed, too, though he couldn't admit it. He spends his life sending out signals to everyone else that it's their fault for making his life so miserable.

Tarred with the same misanthropic brush is W. C. Fields, born William Claude Dukinfield, alias Figley B. Whitesides, Doctor Opis Guelpe, and Felton J. Satchelstern. Like Fawlty, Fields creates comedy out of self-induced harassment — by family, neighbours, tradespeople, insurance salesmen, loose molasses, disintegrating automobiles, collapsing homesteads. The face of Fields, with its aggressive bulb of a nose and small, wary eyes, identifies the unlovely victim — in life as much as in art. In his thirties, Fields toured the United States with flea-bitten vaudeville companies, working as a juggler and comedian. He was always either broke, stranded, starving or freezing, usually all of them together. This left its mark. When he achieved success in Hollywood, he suffered constantly from irrational fears. He feared being kidnapped and believed his servants were plotting to poison him. He feared the popularity of rival comedians. Of Chaplin, he said, 'He's the best ballet dancer that ever lived, and if I get a chance I'll kill him with my bare hands.'

Fields's friends were driven to the brink by his eccentric, often maddening behaviour. But, for Fields, conflict was all that seemed real. The battling and the liquor took their toll. In 1946, when he was mortally ill, a friend visited his sickbed and was surprised to find him reading the Bible. 'Just looking for loopholes', cracked Fields. Three weeks later he muttered something about 'the fellow in the bright nightgown', winked, and died.

The Grim Reaper has the last laugh, although

Woody Allen insists that there are worse things in life than death.

> If you've ever spent an evening with an insurance salesman you'll know what I mean. The key is not to think of death as an end, but more as a very effective way of cutting down on your expenses.

Professor Otto Fenichel puts it another way: 'The secret source of humour is not joy, but sorrow; there is no humour in heaven.' How does *he* know? As Woody is quick to point out: 'There is the fear that there is an after-life but no one will know where it is being held'. He admits his preoccupation with death. To him it is an irrational, hostile act on the part of the universe. He cites Tolstoy when he says that 'any man over thirty-five with whom death is not the main consideration is a fool'. To those who ask whether his films are an attempt to build something permanent, he replies: 'I don't want to achieve immortality through my work. I want to achieve it through not dying.'

The death of the clown is an occasion for national mourning. In *The Tatler*, Leigh Hunt wrote an obituary for Dan Leno:

> The death of a comic artist is felt much more than that of a tragedian. He has sympathised more with us in our everyday feelings, and has given us more amusement . . . It seems a hard thing upon the comic actor to quench his airiness and vivacity — to make us think of him on the sudden with solemnity — and to miss him for ever.

Sometimes the Grim Reaper is hovering in the wings, waiting to strike. At Drury Lane Theatre, in 1725, a performance of *Harlequin Dr Faustus* ground to a halt when 'one James Field who represented the Miller's Man fell from the upper stage in a flying machine by the breaking of the wires: he fractured his skull and died miserably: three others were much hurt. Some of the audience swooned, and the whole was in great confusion upon the sad accident'.

In 1954, at the Tivoli Theatre, Hull, Arthur Lucan collapsed shortly after the curtain had gone up on *Old Mother Riley in Paris*. He died in the wings, and Frank Seton had the thankless task of stepping into Lucan's costume and playing the part. The show must go on.

Sid Field was only forty-nine when he died of a heart attack, on 3 February 1950. His last words, apocryphally, were 'what a performance' — his own well-worn catchphrase from a series of comically camp character studies, in the Leno tradition, including the golfing rabbit, the cinema organist, the society photographer. Ken Tynan wrote: 'alcohol and self-criticism were his pall-bearers'.

In April 1984, Tommy Cooper suffered a massive heart attack on the stage of Her Majesty's Theatre, London, watched by millions of television viewers. A pretty blonde showgirl had just come on with his cloak. She tied it round his neck — and he crumpled to the floor. His head went back and the audience heard a snoring noise. Bob Monkhouse said:

> Knowing Tommy, I'm sure he couldn't have wanted a better exit. When he went down, everyone thought it was part of the act, and that's the way Tommy went out . . . making us laugh.

The following month another much-loved English comic collapsed in the wings of the Roses Theatre in Tewkesbury. Eric Morecambe, for once working without his partner Ernie Wise, had done his turn and taken six curtain calls when he collapsed in the wings. There *was* a doctor in the house and he tried to revive poor Eric, but he died shortly after arriving in hospital. Ironically, his 'patter' that night had included jocular references to his previous heart attacks.

At Southport, in January 1986, impressionist Dustin Gee collapsed with a heart attack during a performance of *Cinderella*. He died in hospital. Jim Bowen took over.

Peter Sellers experienced his own death and lived to tell the tale. In April 1964 his heart stopped beating for one and a half minutes. Later, he told Shirley MacLaine that he distinctly felt his soul leave his body . . .

> He felt a white light enveloping him. He saw a circle — with a welcoming hand come through it. He didn't want to die, but he felt a strong, friendly attraction to the other side. Then he felt his consciousness dissolving back into his body . . . and he knew that Dr Kennamer had succeeded in re-starting his heart, and he would have to stay alive.

Sellers had a second coronary in 1977 and a pacemaker was fitted to his heart. In July 1980, aged fifty-four, his third attack was fatal. At his cremation, Glenn Miller's 'In the Mood' was played as the coffin trundled out. This was done to

Woody Allen with a friend; *Love and Death* (1975)

the dead man's specific instructions. It was one of his most unfavourite records. A few days later, Sellers purportedly manifested himself to his widow, Lynne, in Michael Bentine's sitting-room, via the medium of Doris Collins. What he had to say remains a secret.

For some comedians, the end of life is not the worst death they will experience. To 'die' on stage has another meaning for those who live on laughter: that awful moment, as Fred Karno described it, 'when everything goes quiet and cold, and there are bloody big holes where the laughs ought to be'.

The Glasgow Empire is traditionally known as the 'comedian's graveyard', and many budding reputations are buried there. In 1918, the comic singer Mark 'I Do Like to Be Beside the Seaside' Sheridan was given a rough ride by the Glasgow galleryites. After the show he walked to Kelvin Grove Park and shot himself. The eccentric T. E. Dunville, who sang nonsense songs like 'Bunk-a-doodle-I-do', overheard someone say, in the bar at the Clapham Grand Theatre, 'that fellow's through'. He drowned himself in the Thames at Reading. The French clown Marceline, who played in pantomime with Chaplin, fell from grace and became one of the anonymous clowns in Ringling Brothers' three-ring circus. In 1919 he committed suicide in New York. A neighbour found him lying on the floor. He had a smoking pistol in his hand, and 'Moonlight and Roses' was playing on the gramophone. The dapper French comedian Max Linder, who followed Chaplin to Hollywood, was only forty-two when he entered a suicide pact with his young wife.

In a Sydney basement flat, in 1968, Tony Hancock put the finishing touches to a career of self-destruction when he took an overdose of amylo-barbitone, washed down with vodka. A note, scribbled on the back of a script, read: 'This is quite rational . . . but there was nothing left to do. Things seemed to go wrong too many times.'

Only a few months earlier, Kenneth Williams had visited Hancock in hospital and found the bed covered with books by Leibnitz, Nietzsche and Bertrand Russell. 'I'm trying to discover the purpose of it all,' explained Hancock. 'What if there's no one up there? Sometimes I think it's all a joke.' 'Well, in that case,' advised Williams, 'you must try and make it a good one.'

In the early days of 'The Goons', Sellers, Milligan and Secombe made personal appearances in variety. At the Coventry Hippodrome they appeared as 'Les Trois Charleys'. They wore white tights, leopard-skin drawers and gold headbands. Each played a solo turn, and Milligan's trumpet-playing drew some catcalls from the audience. Incensed, Milligan advanced to the footlights and shouted to the audience: 'You hate me, don't you?' With one voice the audience answered: 'Yes!' Milligan fled to his dressing-room, locked himself in, and was in the process of hanging himself from the light-fitting when his fellow-Goons broke down the door.

After one of his many encounters with plate-glass windows, Charlie Drake was rushed to the London Clinic for repairs. Later he recalled:

I was getting better, and receiving lots of nice letters from viewers, and one from Lord Lonsdale inviting me to shoot vermin on his estate. So I thought I'd better get a gun, and a book on how to shoot vermin. And I had them brought to the Clinic. Now, I read in the book 'Twelve-bore shot-gun: put it to your shoulder: black out the target: pull the trigger.' So, I'm rehearsing this, in my room, in the London clinic, all alone. 'Put it to the shoulder: black out the target: pull the trigger' over and over. And after about twenty minutes of this, I fainted.

Now, the nurse comes in to give me my pills, sees me lying on the floor with a shot-gun beside me. And before I know where I am,

Richard Pryor in *Brewster's Millions* (1985)

they've got me in intensive care, pipes up my nose, wired up, the works. Until one of the more observant doctors noticed that there was *no blood*. So they pulled out all the pipes and put me back to bed. The nurse said: 'D'you know, Mr Drake, we thought you'd killed yourself.' And the night porter said 'Oh, no, sister — he only does that on television!'

The comedy of mortality remains the last taboo. Richard Pryor is one of the first to brave it, and extract a good laugh from his own brush with death.

I was walking in my front yard, and somebody said
    'DON'T BREATHE.'
'O.k., I won't breathe.'
    'AND SHUT THE FUCK UP.'
'O.k., o.k. — don't kill me.'
    'GET ON ONE KNEE AND PROVE IT.'
'O.k., o.k...'
    'THINKING ABOUT DYING NOW, AREN'T YOU?'

Opposite: They all came to an untimely end: *(clockwise, from top)* Tony Hancock in *The Rebel* (1961); Old Mother Riley (Arthur Lucan); Sid Field: 'Keep your eye on the ball'; T. E. Dunville

'Yeah, yeah.'

'DIDN'T THINK ABOUT IT WHEN YOU WERE EATING ALL THAT PORK, DID YOU?'

(Now I'm flat on my back. Those mother-fuckers *hurt*.)

'Don't kill me, don't kill me.'

(When you think you're dying, you put in an emergency call to God — but some angel says 'I'll have to put you on *hold*'. And then your heart gets mad, 'cos it's found out you're going behind its back to God!)

I woke up in an ambulance — and there were *white* people staring at me. I thought 'Ain't this the catch? Here I've gone and died, and wound up in the wrong fucking heaven!'

Pryor's coronary experience hasn't turned him into a Good Samaritan.

They say we civilians can save lives, but I don't know much about that. I mean if you're walking down the street, and you see some feller laid out there — and slobber and stuff hanging out of his mouth: he ain't gonna make it! 'Cos you could give somebody mouth-to-mouth resuscitation, and they die — and death ease down *your* lungs! 'Cos death don't give a fuck where he go. And if death gets two for one — that's a good day for death!

To prove that man *can* survive, however terrified and anxious he may be, Mel Brooks created his two-thousand-year-old man, whose long life has been dedicated to the postponement of the inevitable. He worries about his appearance and health: 'I don't look more than sixteen or seventeen hundred, right?' He prays fiercely for twenty-two minutes daily 'that a ceiling shouldn't fall on me and my heart shouldn't attack me'. He recommends garlic for longevity, on the principle that the Angel of Death can be driven away by a garlic-breathed 'Wwwhhooooo is it?'

This vulnerable, wise and unconventional spirit was inspired by Brooks's own antic attitude to life and death:

If you're alive, you've got to flap your arms and legs, you've got to jump around a lot, you've got to make a lot of noise, because life is the very opposite of death. And therefore, as I see it, if you're quiet, you're not living. I mean you're just slowly drifting into death. So you've got to be noisy, or at least your *thoughts* should be noisy and colourful and lively. My liveliness is based on an incredible fear of death . . . Most people are afraid of death, but I really *hate* it! My humour is a scream and a protest against goodbye.

Woody Allen is a paid-up member of the same club: 'It's not that I'm afraid to die. I just don't want to be there when it happens.' In *Love and Death*, Woody plays the hero, Boris, who shuffles off the mortal coil in the last reel. As Death leads him away, his wife asks him what it's like to be dead:

'It's bad.'

'How bad?'

'You know the chicken at Treskey's Restaurant? It's worse.'

In *The Meaning of Life*, the Grim Reaper (John Cleese) drops in on a Home Counties dinner party. He is accorded a tradesman's welcome by the snooty diners ('Are you sure you won't have some sherry?'), before he carts them all off with salmonella poisoning.

Gallows humour, Python-style, pulls no punches. In their first film, John Cleese and Eric Idle played a suicide sketch with a competitive edge.

Two dark-suited chartered accountants share a desk. Behind them, a plate-glass window, looking out over the London skyline. They are on the twentieth floor.

A body falls past the window. ERIC looks up.

ERIC: Somebody just went past the window. Downwards.

[*JOHN looks disbelieving. Another body falls.*]

ERIC: Another one!

JOHN: Must be a board meeting.

[*Another body*]

ERIC: That was Wilkins of finance.

JOHN: No, it was Robinson.

ERIC: *Wilkins*.

JOHN: *Robinson*.

[*Another body*]

ERIC [*smugly*]: *That* was Robinson.

[*A pause*]

ERIC: Bet you it's Parkinson next.

JOHN: Alright, I bet you it isn't.

[*Another pause. ERIC goes to the window.*]

ERIC [*shouting upwards*]: Come on, Parkie!

Mel Brooks in *History of the World — Part One* (1980)

The funny side of suicide. Compare with 'The Despair Scene' from the *Commedia dell' Arte*. Harlequin, spurned by Columbine, is on the brink.

HARLEQUIN: Ah! How unhappy I am! Let me hasten towards death. I shall go to my room, I shall fix a rope to the ceiling, I shall climb onto a chair, I shall put the rope around the chair, I shall kick away the chair, and there I am — hung. (*He assumes the posture of a hanged man.*) No. To hang is an ordinary death, an everyday sort of affair. I'll get no honour from it. Let's find some extraordinary death, heroic death, Harlequinian death. (*He ponders*) I've got it. I shall stop up my mouth and my nose, my breath won't be able to escape, and so I shall die. It's as good as done. (*He covers his mouth and nose. After some time:*) No, that's no good either, it just comes out elsewhere.

[*to the audience*]   Gentlemen, if anyone would be good enough to die, just to show me how it's done, I would be very much obliged to him. . .Ah! I've had an idea. If I could die *laughing*, that

would be a risible death. . .I'm wonderfully ticklish — I shall tickle myself to death.

[*He tickles himself, laughs, and falls to the ground. PASQUARIEL arrives and, seeing him in this state, believes him to be drunk, lifts him up, consoles him and leads him off.*]

A last connecting thread links this antique scenario with events that took place, for real, in a Lincolnshire council house in 1977. Alex Mitchell, a bricklayer, was watching *The Goodies* on BBC Television and enjoying it hugely. The comic trio of Tim Brooke-Taylor, Graeme Garden and Bill Oddie had invented a Lancashire equivalent of kung-fu, the school of 'Ecky Thump', where Bill Oddie, in a ten-gallon cloth cap, was learning to dispose of his opponents with a lethal length of black pudding. His adversaries included the Australian boomerang champion and an expert in the martial arts of the bagpipes. Mrs Mitchell recalls:

Alex just couldn't stop laughing. He was a

The Goodies: Bill Oddie, Graeme Garden, and Tim Brooke-Taylor floored by the bagpipes

Scot, you see, and so he was especially tickled to see a Scotsman wrestling with his bagpipes! And he kept laughing, right through the programme. Well I think he just laughed too heartily and too long, because just before the closing titles he gave a tremendous belly-laugh, slumped on the sofa, and died.

The BBC said they were very sorry for what had happened.

Mrs Mitchell wrote a letter to *The Goodies* thanking them for making the last moments of her husband's life so happy. And in Fleet Street, editors made the most of the news that, in spite of industrial stagnation, galloping inflation, and the threat of the nuclear holocaust, at least one man had got his priorities right. The headline became the most appropriate of epitaphs: 'MAN OF FUN DIES LAUGHING'.

What a way to go.

TOP OF THE BILL
A · PERSONAL · SELECTION

ABBOTT AND COSTELLO Archetypal double-act, bully and victim. Bud Abbott, born William Abbott in New Jersey, 1895. His parents worked in Barnum and Bailey's Circus and then in burlesque theatres. Lou Costello, born Louis Francis Cristillo, also in New Jersey, 1906. His father was an Italian immigrant. Lou wanted to be a basketball player but he was too short (5′ 4″) so he became a stuntman in the movies, doubling for Joan Crawford and Dolores Del Rio. Then he was a burlesque comic. In 1936, Bud and Lou were on the same bill in New York, and decided to pair up. They toured with *Life Begins at Minsky's*, broadcast on NBC radio in *The Kate Smith Hour* and starred on Broadway in *The Streets of Paris*. Broadway success took them to Hollywood. Their first joint appearance in films was in *One Night in the Tropics* (1939). Thereafter they made thirty-three features for Universal Studios. Best of the bunch are their encounters with *Frankenstein* (1948), *The Invisible Man* (1951), *Captain Kidd* (1952), and *The Keystone Kops* (1955). They recycled their vaudeville routines for a television series in the 1950s. The partnership was dissolved in 1957. Costello made one film on his own, *The Thirty-Foot Bride of Candy Rock* (1959), and died of a heart attack later the same year. Abbott put the voices to a series of cartoons for television. He survived epilepsy and two strokes; died of cancer in 1974.

WOODY ALLEN Cabaret comic, scriptwriter, director, hypochondriac. Born Allen Stewart Konigsberg in Brooklyn, New York, 1935. Wrote television scripts for Sid Caesar (*Your Show of Shows*) and Mort Sahl. Made his film debut in *What's New Pussycat?* (1965). Went on to create a series of idiosyncratic film comedies, including *Take the Money and Run* (1969), *Bananas* (1971), *Everything You Always Wanted to Know About Sex* (1972), *Sleeper* (1973), *Love And Death* (1976), *Annie Hall* (1977), *Manhattan* (1979), *Zelig* (1983), *Broadway*

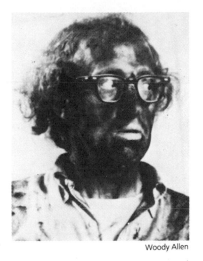
Woody Allen

Danny Rose (1984), and *The Purple Rose of Cairo* (1985). The later films show Allen more preoccupied with the comedy of failing relationships than falling bodies. Won an Oscar for Best Director in 1978, which he failed to collect.

FATTY ARBUCKLE Pioneer 'fat man' of the silent cinema. Born Roscoe Arbuckle in Cleveland, Ohio, 1887. Played an overweight Keystone Kop in *The Clutches of the Gang* (1913). Partnered Mabel Normand in a string of 'Mabel and Fatty' two-reel comedies: *Mabel's New Hero*, *Mabel's Dramatic Debut*, *For the Love of Mabel* (1913), *Mabel and Fatty's Wash Day*, *Mabel and Fatty Viewing the World's Fair at San Francisco* (1915). His first feature, *The Life of the Party* (1920), was also his last starring role. The following year, with horrible irony, a wild and boozy party in a San Francisco hotel left a small-time actress dead, and Fatty indicted for rape and murder. Acquitted after three messy trials, he never worked again under his own name, but directed five short films under the pseudonym of William Goodrich. Died of a heart attack, 1933.

ARTHUR ASKEY Perky, bespectacled comic all-rounder. Born Liverpool, 1900. Worked as a clerk with the Liverpool

Corporation. Joined the Song Salad concert party, as a comic vocalist, in 1924. Starred in *Sunshine* at the Summer Theatre, Shanklin, Isle of Wight. Became a national celebrity in 1938 through BBC Radio's first weekly comedy series, *Band Wagon*. Also a pioneer of television: his *Bee Song* was included in one of the first broadcasts. Thereafter, much in demand for variety shows, pantomime (a devastating Widow Twankey) and films: *Calling All Stars* (1937), *Band Wagon* (1939), *I Thank You* (1941), *Bees in Paradise* (1944), *Ramsbottom Rides Again* (1956), *Make Mine a Million* (1958). Television series included: *Before Your Very Eyes*, *The AA Show*, *Comedy Bandbox*, *Jokers Wild*. Appeared in twelve Royal Variety Performances between 1946 and 1968. OBE awarded 1969. Died 1982.

MICHAEL BENTINE Peruvian eccentric. Born Watford, 1922. Educated at Eton. Became a Shakespearean actor in Robert Atkins's company. Joined RAF during World War Two. Worked at the Windmill Theatre after the war. Formed a double-act for radio with Tony Sherwood. They billed themselves as Sherwood and Forrest. Founder-member of *The Goon Show* with Spike Milligan, Peter Sellers and Harry Secombe. Branched out on his own in television: *It's a Square World* (1960–1965), *Potty Time*. Occasional films: *The Sandwich Man* (1966), *Bachelor of Arts* (1969). Author of *The Door Marked Summer* (1981), *The Long Banana Skin* (1982), *The Doors of the Mind* (1984).

MEL BROOKS Broad Jewish writer–performer, loud and lively. Born Melvin Kaminsky in Brooklyn, New York, 1927. Early success as a bantamweight boxer. He called himself 'Kid Smutsch'. Made his stage debut at the Sussex Camp for Underprivileged Jewish Children. Wrote comedy sketches for Sid Caesar's television series, *Your Show of Shows* (1950–1954). Scriptwriter on spoof spy series *Get Smart*. Wrote, produced and directed *The Producers* (1967), *Blazing Saddles* (1974), *Young Frankenstein* (1975), *Silent Movie* (1976), *High Anxiety* (1977), *History of the World — Part One* (1980), *To Be or Not To Be* (1984). Won two Oscars: Best Short Film for *The Critic* (1963), and Best Screenplay for *The Producers* (1967). In search of immortality, he created, on radio and record, his Jewish alter ego, the 2000-year-old man.

LENNY BRUCE Forthright nightclub comic. Born New York, 1927. Educated, in his own words, 'from the sounds that wafted from the alley of Angelo's Bar and Grille, Ladies Invited, Free Lunch'. In 1942 he ran away from home to join the navy. Made his showbiz debut as master of ceremonies at the Victory Club on Ocean Parkway, Brooklyn. Won 1st prize on Arthur Godfrey's *Talent Scouts Show* (1951). Married Honey Harlowe, a stripper. Worked burlesque clubs, nightclubs: the Duane Hotel, New York; The Gate of Horn, Chicago; the hungry i, San Francisco. 1962, arrested for obscenity in San Francisco. Also 1962, played The Establishment nightclub in London. December that year, arrested for obscenity, Chicago. 1963, refused entry to Britain by the Home Secretary. 1964, arrested for obscenity, New York. A public protest on his behalf was signed by Woody Allen, Richard Burton, Bob Dylan, Rudy Vallee, Paul Newman, Saul Bellow, Arthur Miller, Lillian Helman, Susan Sontag, John Updike, Jules Feiffer and Jonathan Miller. Died in Hollywood of an apparent drug overdose in 1966.

CAMBRIDGE CIRCUS The launch pad for much of the best comedy of the 1960s. The Cambridge Footlights revue of 1963 played the West End of London, Broadway, Australia and New Zealand, with sketches written and performed by Tim Brooke-Taylor (born Buxton, 1940), John Cleese (born Weston-super-Mare, 1939), and Bill Oddie (born Rochdale, 1941). The revue spawned a radio comedy series, *I'm Sorry I'll Read That Again*, which brought in two more Cambridge graduates, Graham Chapman (born Leicester, 1941) and Graeme Garden (born Aberdeen, 1942). From radio, the group moved to television and, in different permutations, created *At Last the 1948 Show*, *Broaden Your Mind*, *The Goodies*, and *Monty Python's Flying Circus*. Late starter Eric Idle (born South Shields, 1943) joined the troupe for this last, in which rival Oxford also had a stake through Michael Palin (born Sheffield, 1943) and Terry Jones (born Colwyn Bay, 1942).

Cannon and Ball

CANNON AND BALL Double-act in the best tradition. Tommy Cannon, short victim, born Oldham, 1938; Bobby Ball, tall bully, born Oldham, 1944. Both worked in a Lancashire engineering works during the day, and sang together as the Harper Brothers at night. Shifted the balance of the act from music to comedy, and became Cannon and Ball in 1973. Voted clubland's top comedy duo in 1975. Established themselves through regular ITV series, summer shows and pantomime (*Babes in the Wood*, Bristol, 1985). Have made one foray into film: *The Boys in Blue* (1983). Cannon is a working director of Rochdale Football Club. Ball runs his own nightclub, Braces, in Rochdale.

GEORGE CARL Silent clown/mime. Born Zurich, 1922. Trained as an acrobat and juggler. Accident-prone, so decided to turn his skills to comedy in the Circus Knie. Honoured with the 'Golden Clown' award at the Monte Carlo Circus. Booked for a season at the Crazy Horse Saloon in Paris; stayed for seven years. In the USA played the Tropicana, New Frontier, Sands and Riviera Hotels in Las Vegas; the Coconut Grove in New York. On television in *The Smothers Brothers Show*, *Kraft Music Theatre* and the *Ed Sullivan Show* (twelve appearances). *Royal Variety Performance*, 1984.

CARRY ON The label for a long series of saucy film comedies, investigating every aspect of British life 'below the belt'. *Carry on Sergeant* was the first (1958). Later editions have cocked a snook at *Nurse*, *Teacher*, *Constable*, *Cowboy*, *Cleo*, *Henry*, *Dick*, *Doctor*, *Matron*, *England* and *Emmanuelle*. A repertory of fine comic talents has kept the fruity flag flying, especially Kenneth Williams (born North London, 1926),

Charlie Chaplin

Charles Hawtrey (born Hounslow, 1914), Kenneth Connor (born London, 1918), Bernard Bresslaw (born London, 1933), Sid James (born Johannesburg, 1913; died 1976), Joan Sims (born Laindon, Essex, 1930), Barbara Windsor (born Whitechapel, 1937) and Hattie Jacques (born Sandgate, Kent, 1924; died 1980).

CHARLIE CHAPLIN The master of silent film comedy. Born Walworth, London, 1889. Son of Charles Chaplin, Irish ballad singer. At the age of eight, he became one of the Eight Lancashire Lads. 1900 played the Kitchen Cat in *Cinderella*, at the London Coliseum. 1906 was in *Casey's Court*, later *Casey's Circus*. 1907 joined Fred Karno's Speechless Comedians. Played in Karno sketches: *London Suburbia*, *The Football Match*, *Mumming Birds*. 1910 went with a Karno troupe to the USA. Played Hammerstein's Music-hall, New York. 1912 toured the USA with a second Karno company. At the Empress Theatre, Chicago, played the Drunken Swell in *A Night in an English Music-hall*. Film director Mack Sennett was in the audience; he invited Chaplin to California. With Sennett's Keystone company, Chaplin made two-reel comedy films: *Making a Living* (1914), *Kid Auto Races at Venice* (1914), in which the 'Tramp' character first appeared, *A Film Johnnie* (1914), *Dough and Dynamite* (1914), *His Prehistoric Past* (1914). Later worked for Essanay and Mutual. First feature-length films were *Carmen* (1915), *The Kid* (1920), *The Gold Rush* (1925). Persevered with silent comedy for some years after the invention of synchronised sound: *The Circus* (1927), *City Lights* (1931), *Modern Times* (1936), *The Great Dictator* (1940). His last film was *A Countess from Hong Kong* (1966). Awarded two special Oscars, in 1928 and 1972. Married four times. Knighted in 1975. Died in 1977.

JOHN CLEESE Angular eccentric. Born Weston-super-Mare, 1939. Educated at Clifton College, Bristol, and then Cambridge. His tall, frenzied figure is identified with some of the most memorable images of contemporary comedy: the prosecuting attorney (*Cambridge Circus*), the harassed headmaster (*At Last the 1948 Show* and later *Clockwise*), the Minister of Funny Walks and the disgruntled purchaser of a lifeless parrot (*Monty Python's Flying Circus*). The characterisation that best epitomises the Cleese style is the luckless Basil Fawlty, high-handed host of *Fawlty Towers* (BBC TV, Best Situation Comedy, 1975 still repeating). Film appearances have included *Interlude* (1968), *The Rise and Rise of Michael Rimmer* (1970), *And Now for Something Completely Different* (1971), *Monty Python and the Holy Grail* (1974), *The Life of Brian* (1979), *The Meaning of Life* (1983), *Silverado* (1985), *Clockwise* (1986). In a political hat, Cleese fronts party-political broadcasts for the Social Democratic Party.

PETER COOK Writer, performer, lampooner. Born Torquay, 1937. Son of a diplomat. Educated at Radley and Cambridge. President of the Footlights Club, 1959. Wrote sketches for West End revues *Pieces of Eight* (1959) and *One Over the Eight* (1961). With Dudley Moore, Alan Bennett and Jonathan Miller, created the milestone revue *Beyond the Fringe* for the Edinburgh Festival (1960). Then they moved on to London (1961) and Broadway (1962). Cook founded the satirical nightclub The Establishment in Soho, and launched its companion magazine *Private Eye*. He partnered Dudley Moore in several television series under the title *Not only . . . But Also*. The duo toured Australia and the USA in *Behind the Fridge* (1972).

Tommy Cooper

The Crazy Gang in *Jokers Wild* (1954)

As Derek and Clive, they recorded rude records and videos. Cook's film appearances have included *The Wrong Box* (1966), *Bedazzled* (1968), *Monte Carlo or Bust* (1969), *The Bed Sitting Room* (1969), *The Rise and Rise of Michael Rimmer* (1970), *The Adventures of Barry Mackenzie* (1972), *The Hound of the Baskervilles* (1977), *Yellowbeard* (1983). Played the English butler in American

television sitcom *The Two of Us* (1982–1983).

TOMMY COOPER Gigantic bungling conjurer. Born Caerphilly, 1922. Spent his childhood in Exeter and Southampton. He joined the army and spent seven years in the Horse Guards. After World War Two, became an entertainer in cabaret and variety. Made his television debut in *Christmas Party* (1947). In 1952 had his own series, *It's Magic*, on BBC TV. Moved to ITV and starred in successive series (ITV Personality of the Year 1969) until his death, on stage, in 1984.

THE CRAZY GANG Theatrical anarchists. The magnificent seven were: Chesney Allen (born Brighton, 1894), Bud Flanagan (born Spitalfields, London, 1896), Jimmy Gold (born Glasgow, 1896), Eddie Gray (born Pimlico, London, 1898), Teddy Knox (born London, 1896), Charlie Naughton (born Glasgow, 1897), and Jimmy Nervo (born London, 1897). The gang was assembled by Fred Karno in 1932 for a show called *Laffs* at the London Palladium. Later that year *Crazy Week* was a sell-out: in 1933 *Crazy Month* was a riot. The Crazy Gang became a national institution, encamped at the London Palladium (1935–1940), and the Victoria Palace (1947–1960). They made some films: *OK for Sound* (1937), *Alf's Button Afloat* (1938), *The Frozen Limits* (1939), *Gasbags* (1940), *Life is a Circus* (1954). In 1945 Chesney Allen retired because of ill-health; he had the last laugh by outliving the rest of the gang. Official retirement for the Crazy Gang was recorded in 1962. Gold died in 1967, Flanagan 1968, Gray 1969, Knox 1974, Nervo 1975, Naughton 1976, and Allen 1983.

Ken Dodd

KEN DODD Toothy scouse jester. Born Liverpool, 1929. Made his stage debut as one of Cinderella's coachmen, Liverpool Pavilion, 1938. First professional appearance at the Empire Theatre, Nottingham, 1954. Armed with his feathery 'tickling stick', 'Doddy' has undertaken serious research into the roots of comedy, and produced a 'Giggle Map of Britain', charting the regional variations of the English Sense of Humour (no sex in Wigan, bags of sentiment in the Midlands, keep the zany stuff for the Welsh . . .). London debut at the Palladium, 1965: *Doddy's Here*. Invented the Diddy Men. Topped the UK hit parade with soppy songs: 'Happiness' (1964), 'Tears' (1965), 'Promises' (1966). Sell-out seasons at the Golden Garter in Wythenshawe (1965 and 1967). Frequent series on television (*The Ken Dodd Show*) and radio (*Ken Dodd's World of Laughter*). Equally at home as Professor Yaffle Chuckabutty or Malvolio in Shakespeare's *Twelfth Night*, he's the only comic to have addressed a symposium on humour at Cardiff University College and lived to tell the tale.

CHARLIE DRAKE Much-battered small comedian. Born Elephant and Castle, London, 1925. Made his first stage appearance at the age of seven. Evacuated to a Dorset village in 1939, where he became a cowman. Then joined the RAF. Made his mark as a human missile in early television comedies, including *Fast and Loose* (1955). Frequently concussed and hospitalised. Films: *The Golden Link* (1954), *Sands of the Desert* (1960), *Petticoat Pirates* (1961), *The Cracksman* (1963), *Mister Ten Per Cent* (1967). Less violently put-upon in *The Worker* (ITV from 1965). Branched out into Shakespeare (Touchstone in *As You Like It*, 1981), Brecht, and television adaptations of Charles Dickens (*Bleak House*, 1984).

JIMMY EDWARDS Whiskered buffoon. Born Barnes, 1920. Educated at St Paul's Cathedral School and Cambridge. Played the trombone in the university dance band, and played the fool in the *Footlights Revue*. Flew with the RAF during the war (won the DFC). Appeared at the Windmill Theatre in 1946. During 1947 took part in the radio series *Navy Mixture* and, later, *Take It From Here*. In West End revues: *Sky High* (1949), and *London Laughs* (1952–1954). Played the monstrous headmaster of Chiselbury school, in the television situation comedy *Whack-O!* (six series from 1956). Occasional film appearances: *Treasure Hunt* (1948), *Murder at the Windmill* (1948), *Three Men in a Boat* (1955), *Bottoms Up* (1960), *Nearly a Nasty Accident* (1962), *Rhubarb* (1970). Stood as Conservative candidate for North Paddington in the 1964 election.

NORMAN EVANS Gravel-voiced north-country comic. Born Rochdale, 1901. Worked as a travelling salesman, with a fund of good stories. Gracie Fields heard him give a speech at a dinner in Leeds, and booked him for her shows. Made his first London appearance at the Alhambra, in 1934. Best known for his gummy characterisation of Fanny Fairbottom, gossiping 'over the garden wall', in which guise he appeared at the Palladium, the Coliseum, in pantomime, and *Royal Variety Performances* (1937, 1947, 1951). The routine was also the basis for a radio series (1948). Toured with his own road show *Good Evans*. In 1950 toured the USA, including Hollywood where he played the El Capitan Theatre. Film appearances: *Demobbed* (1945), *Under New Management* (1946), *Over the Garden Wall* (1950). Died 1962.

DAME EDNA EVERAGE First lady of Australian showbiz. Protégée of satirist Barry Humphries. Born Wagga Wagga, date unknown. Educated at Moonee Ponds Ladies College. First stage appearance as Mary Magdalen in Moonee Ponds *Passion Play*, 1950. Starred in Melbourne revues: *A Nice Night's Entertainment* (1962), *A Load of Olde Stuffe* (1971). Then to London, where she became *Housewife Superstar* (1976); this was followed by *A Night With Dame Edna* (1978), *The Last Night of the Poms* (1981) and *An Evening's Intercourse* (1982). Author of Dame Edna's *Coffee Table Book* (1977), *Dame Edna's Bedside Book* (1982). Awarded a Damehood for her services to Australian culture. In 1985 there were rumours of impending retirement.

Marty Feldman in *Yellowbeard* (1982)

MARTY FELDMAN Manic imp. Born Canning Town, London, 1933. Street trader and jazz trumpeter. Wrote scripts for radio with Barry Took: *Round the Horn*, *Beyond Our Ken*. Made his television debut in *At Last the 1948 Show* (ITV). Went over to BBC for his own series *Marty* (with Tim Brooke-Taylor). In British films: *The Bed Sitting Room* (1969), *Every Home Should Have One* (1970). Appeared in Mel Brooks' films: *Young Frankenstein* (1974), *The Adventures of Sherlock Holmes' Smarter Brother* (1975), *Silent Movie* (1976). Also directed: *The Last Remake of Beau Geste* (1977), *In God We Trust* (1979). Died in Mexico while filming *Yellowbeard*, 1982.

SID FIELD Wide-eyed wide boy. Born Edgbaston, Birmingham, 1904. At twelve, joined 'Fourteen Royal Kino Juveniles'. In the 1920s, was a comic 'feed' in variety and revue. Worked his way to the top and in 1943 starred in George Black's revue *Strike a New Note*. Specialised in slightly camp character studies: the Golfing Rabbit, the Cinema Organist, the Society Photographer. *Royal Variety Performances*, 1945 and 1946. Topped the bill at the London Palladium in 1948, standing in for Mickey Rooney. Films: *That's the Ticket* (1940), *London Town* (1946), *Cardboard Cavalier* (1949). Died in 1950.

THE FRATELLINI A trio of circus clowns. Three brothers, sons of an itinerant circus performer, born on the road: Paul (Sicily, 1877), François (Paris, 1879), Albert (Moscow, 1886). Trained as acrobats, musicians, tumblers. Decided to combine their talents, in order to support the huge family of elder brother, Louis, who died in 1909. Extended the traditional clown 'entrée' to an elaborate routine, based on a clownish triumvirate. François was the elegant, unflappable 'whiteface'. Paul was the 'auguste', the pedantic petty bourgeois, bossy and indignant. Albert was the 'grotesque', down at heel, much put upon. The brothers' appearance at the Cirque Medrano in Paris, after World War One, sparked a resurgence of interest in the circus. In 1923 they were invited to play on the stage of the Comédie Française. Jean Cocteau wrote them into his farce *Le boeuf sur le toit*. Samuel Beckett used some of their 'business' in *Waiting for Godot*. Equally at home on stage and in the ring, they toured Europe until the outbreak of World War Two. A biography, *Nous — les Fratellini*, written by Albert, was published in 1955. Paul's grand-daughter, Annie Fratellini, is now the director of the Ecole Nationale du Cirque in Paris. With her husband, Pierre Etaix, she works the family routines as a double act.

W. C. FIELDS Child-baiting, wife-hating eccentric. Born William Claude Dukinfield, in Philadelphia, 1879. Formal education ended in the third grade, when he was eight. Aged fifteen, learned to juggle. In 1895 joined Jim Fulton's road show company. Played in London before King Edward VII and the crowned heads of Europe. 1915 booked for a season with Ziegfield's Follies. Took to films, was contracted by Paramount, made two-reel shorts: *Sharks, His Lordship's Dilemma*. The coming of sound gave another dimension to his grumbling, muttering, beleaguered misogynist, and the films he made in the 1930s are hard-edged gems: *The Golf Specialist* (1930), *If I Had a Million* (1932), *Tillie and Gus* (1933), *It's a Gift* (1934), *The Man on the Flying Trapeze* (1935), *You Can't Cheat an Honest Man*

(1938), *The Bank Dick* (1939). Wrote screenplays under bizarre pseudonyms — Mahatma Kane Jeeves, Otis Criblecoblis. On radio in the *Lucky Strike Hour*. In 1940 published *Fields for President*. Died on Christmas Day, 1946.

GRIMALDI Roguish clown. Born London, 1778, the bastard son of a syphilitic Italian ballet-master and a cockney girl who was 40 years his junior. Danced at Sadler's Wells Theatre at the age of two. Graduated to playing dwarfs and bent old hags in pantomimes at Drury Lane Theatre. In 1806, played the part of Clown in *Harlequin and Mother Goose*, or *The Golden Egg*. Devised a new costume and make-up for the part, and gave himself a role for life: a guzzling, thieving, inventive comic villain who ruled the roost at Drury Lane and Sadler's Wells until Grimaldi retired in 1823. He died in 1837. His stage name Joey, is still identified with clowning (except in Australia, where a joey is a baby kangaroo).

GROCK Pear-shaped musical clown. Born Adrien Wellach in Switzerland, 1880. His father was a watchmaker. Toured with his mother and sisters in a troupe of Tyrolean singers. Trained as wire-walker, juggler and contortionist. In 1903, teamed up with a clown called Brick, and became Grock. When Brick married, Grock partnered Antonnet to play in circus and music-hall. On his own, played the Palace Theatre in London, 1911. Although he was expert on eight musical instruments, his act was built around his inability to get a note out of any of them. His basic routine became a one-man show, which could

last an hour or more. When theatres were closing, in the 1920s, Grock was one of the few bankable music-hall stars. He retired in 1954, died in 1959. A film *Au Revoir Mr Grock* records his routine with violin for posterity.

TONY HANCOCK The comic role model for the 1950s. Born Small Heath, Birmingham, 1924. Appeared as 'Anthony Hancock, the Confidential Comic', at the Theatre Royal, Bournemouth, 1940. Failed an audition for ENSA. Joined the RAF. After the war, became a stand-up comic in Ralph Reader's ex-RAF show *Wings*. In 1948 played the Windmill Theatre. On radio, from 1950: *Variety Bandbox, Educating Archie*. In West End revues: *Peep Show* (1951), *London Laughs* (1952). Came into his own in 1954 with *Hancock's Half-Hour*, which was transferred to television in 1956. Playing a slightly more vain, pretentious, opinionated and gullible version of himself, in scripts by Ray Galton and Alan Simpson, Hancock was voted Comedian of the Year in 1957 and 1959. Film appearances included *The Rebel* (1961), *The Punch and Judy Man* (1962), *Those Magnificent Men in Their Flying Machines* (1965), *The Wrong Box* (1966). Series for ITV in 1963 and 1967 fell flat. In 1968 Hancock went to Australia to make programmes for Sydney's Channel Seven. He committed suicide there, 24 June 1968.

THE HANLON-LEES Kamikaze acrobats. Originally, six sons of actor Thomas Hanlon. Worked as tumblers with the foot juggler 'Professor' John Lees. Made their debut at the Theatre Royal Adelphi, London, in 1846. Toured the world in 1848. When Lees died of yellow fever, the brothers reworked the act, billing themselves as 'The Hanlon-Lees, Entortillationists'. Played Niblo's Gardens, New York, 1858. In 1865 one of the brothers, Thomas, suffered severe head injuries in a fall in Cincinnati. He killed himself three years later. The surviving brothers persevered. In 1879 they unveiled their most ambitious show, *Voyage en Suisse*, which incorporated a storm at sea, an exploding train, a bus crash, and a juggling banquet. In 1883, three of the brothers put on a show in New York called *Fantasma*. In 1945, George's two sons were working as clowns in Ringling-Barnum's circus.

WILL HAY Character comedian. Born Stockton-on-Tees, 1888. Appeared in his family's concert party from the age of eight. Music-hall debut at the Empire Theatre, Hull, in 1908. Worked with Fred

W. C. Fields

Karno's Speechless Comedians in the 1920s; then developed his own act, as 'The Schoolmaster Comedian'. The mortarboard and pince-nez served him for the rest of his working life. *Royal Variety Performances*, 1925, 1928, 1930, 1945. A series of films for Gainsborough Studios: *Those Were the Days* (1934), *Boys Will Be Boys* (1936), *Good Morning, Boys* (1937), *The Ghost of St Michaels* (1941). After the war, his son, Will Hay Junior, took over the headmaster role. Will Hay Senior became a Fellow of the Royal Astronomical Society in recognition of his discovery of a white spot on Saturn. He died in 1949.

BENNY HILL Cherubic salty comic. Born Southampton, 1925. Father was a circus roustabout who became a surgical appliance outfitter. Benny made his first stage appearance as a rabbit in a school production of *Alice in Wonderland*. At fourteen, he auditioned for *Bobbie's Concert Party* and was taken on as second comic. Then he became a milkman and part-time drummer. During the war, he was in REME (driver/mechanic) and *Stars in Battledress* (stand-up comic). Rejected by the Windmill Theatre, he turned to television in 1951, and has been faithful to the medium ever since. Elected to the Television Hall of Fame, 1978. Voted Funniest Man on Television, 1981. Film appearances have included *Who Done It?* (1956), *Light Up the Sky* (1959), *Those Magnificent Men in Their Flying Machines* (1965), *Chitty Chitty Bang Bang* (1968), *The Italian Job* (1969).

JIMMY JAMES The classic inebriate. Born James Casey in Stockton-on-Tees, 1892. As 'Terry the Blue-Eyed Irish Boy', did a song-and-dance act in north-country music-halls from 1904. Then joined a juvenile troupe, 'Jockeys', and later Phil Rees's 'Stable Lads'. In 1921 played the character of a drunken bridegroom in a sketch called 'The Spare Room'. It went so well that he kept the character for the rest of his working life (offstage he was teetotal). Played the London Palladium in 1929. Toured variety theatres with two stooges and three sketches: 'Drunk', 'Chipster', and 'Shoebox'. *Royal Variety Performance* in 1953. Struggling with ill-health and insolvency, he died in 1965.

JEWEL AND WARRISS Cousins in comedy. Jimmy Jewel, born Sheffield, 1912; Ben Warriss, born Sheffield, 1909. Ben's father, a bookmaker, married Jimmy's aunt. Jimmy's father was a scenic artist and showman. Jimmy did Jack Buchanan impersonations and played the saxophone, Ben did a 'black-face' routine. At the Palace Theatre,

Benny Hill

Newcastle, in 1934, a Jewish double-act, Murray and Cohen, failed to show up, so the cousins took their place. They stayed together for the next thirty-two years. Toured Australia and New Zealand, 1937. A radio series, *Up the Pole*, made them household names (1946–1951). Briefly visited the USA in 1952. Television from 1948: *Turn It Up*, *The Jewel and Warriss Show*, *It's a Living*. Films include: *Starlight Serenade* (1942), *What a Carry On*, *Let's Have a Murder*. Partnership dissolved in 1966, when Ben retired from show business. Jimmy Jewel has since found a new career as an actor in television situation comedies like *Nearest and Dearest* (from 1968), *Spring and Autumn* (1973), and the theatre: *The Sunshine Boys* (1975), *The Comedians* (1976). His own story was the basis for a television drama series, *Funny Man* (1980).

FRED KARNO Master showman. Born Fred Westcott in Exeter, 1866. His father was a cabinet-maker. Young Fred was a lather-boy to a barber, and part-time gymnast. Ran away from home to become a circus acrobat, as part of Alvene and Leonaro, then the Four Aubreys, and finally the Karno Trio. Adapted slapstick sketches for the music-hall: 'Jail Birds', 'Early Birds', 'His Majesty's Guests', 'The Football Match', 'The Yap Yaps', 'Mumming Birds'. Created his own comic repertory company, billed as 'Fred Karno's Speechless Comedians'. Built a 'Fun Factory' in Camberwell, combining scenic workshops, property store, costumiers. By 1901 he had five companies on the road, led by Fred Kitchen, Sydney Chaplin, Syd Walker, Billy Bennett, Harry Weldon and Fred Evans. Later recruits included Charlie

Fred Karno

Chaplin, Stan Laurel, Will Hay, Sandy Powell, Bud Flanagan, Fred Emney. In 1910, a Karno company played Hammerstein's Music-hall, New York. Booked originally for eight weeks, the show, which was called *A Night in an English Music-hall*, played on and off for eight years. In 1913, Karno built his Karsino on an island in the Thames. Gave his name to the shambolic recruits of the British Expeditionary Forces, 1914. After World War One produced revues, revivals of *Mumming Birds*. Declared bankrupt 1926. 1932 assembled the nucleus of the Crazy Gang, for *Laffs* at the London Palladium. In 1935 produced his only feature film, *Don't Rush Me*, starring Robb Wilton. Retired to Lilliput in Dorset in 1937. Died 1941.

DANNY KAYE Sprightly fast-talking entertainer. Born David Kaminsky in Brooklyn, 1913. His father had been a horse-dealer in Russia. Danny wanted to be a boxer, a chef, or a surgeon. Became a 'toomler' in Jewish holiday hotels. Worked as stooge for comedian Nick Long. Toured with Abe Lyman's band. Made his Broadway debut in *The Straw Hat Revue* (1939). Also in cabaret (*La Martinique*) and films: *Dime a Dance* (1937), *Cupid Takes a Holiday* (1938), *Money or Your Life* (1938). Given the star treatment by Sam Goldwyn, for whom he made *Up in Arms* (1944), *The Kid from Brooklyn* (1946), *The Secret Life of Walter Mitty* (1947), *The Inspector General* (1949), *Knock on Wood* (1953), *The Court Jester* (1956), *Merry Andrew* (1958). In 1948 played the London Palladium, where the Royal Family and Winston Churchill came to see him. 1954 awarded a special Oscar 'for his unique talents, his service to the industry and the American people'. In recent years, has preferred to perform under the auspices of UNICEF, for whom he has raised nearly five million dollars. 1973 hosted *Opera Laugh-In* at the Metropolitan Opera House, New York. 1975 conducted the London Symphony Orchestra at the Festival Hall, London.

BUSTER KEATON The Great Stone Face. Born Pickway, Kansas, 1895. One of the 'Three Keatons' from the age of five. Father Joe did comic dancing, mother Myra played the saxophone, Buster was 'The Human Mop'. When he grew too big to be thrown around (5' 4", 160 pounds), the act split up and Buster went to California. Worked with Fatty Arbuckle on two-reel short comedies: *The Butcher Boy*, *The Rough House*, *His Wedding Night*, *Coney Island*, *Oh Doctor!* (1917), *Out West*, *The Bell Boy*, *Moonshine*, *Good Night Nurse*, *The Cook* (1918), *A Desert Hero*, *A Country Hero*, *Back Stage*, *The Garage* (1919). After Fatty's fall from grace, Buster found his metier in high-speed visual comedies, with his own expressionless screen persona as the hub of the action: *The Boat* (1922), *Our Hospitality* (1923), *Sherlock Junior* (1924), *The Navigator* (1924), *The General* (1927), *Doughboys* (1930). Then there were money problems. Marriage problems. Booze problems. MGM terminated his contract in 1932. He made guest appearances in *Sunset Boulevard* (1950), Chaplin's *Limelight* (1952), *Around the World in Eighty Days* (1952), *It's a Mad Mad Mad Mad World* (1963), *How to Stuff a Wild Bikini* (1965). In 1954 he appeared out of the blue in the sawdust ring of the Cirque Medrano, Paris. In 1959 Buster was awarded a special Oscar 'for his unique talent which brought immortal comedies to the screen'. Died of lung cancer in 1966.

FRED KITCHEN Splay-footed giant. Born Southampton 1872, son of a Shakespearean actor. Joined Fred Karno's troupe in 1901. Played Sergeant Lightning in *His Majesty's Guests*, then Perkins in *Moses and Son* and Simpkins in *The Bailiffs*. 1918 appeared at the Folies Bergère in Paris, paid £450 per week. After Karno, played variety theatres as Private Potts. With ENSA during World War Two, lecturing on 'How to Cook a Sausage'. Retired 1945. Died 1951.

LUPINO LANE Acrobatic tumbler. Born Henry George Lupino (London, 1892) into a family of acrobats, pantomimists and actors, all descended from an Italian puppet master who came to England in the reign of James I. Adopted the name of Lupino Lane. Trained in ballet, tap, folk dances, fencing, boxing, gymnastics, juggling, building and painting scenery, Shakespearean acting, composing music, mime, costume design, elocution, production. Devised pantomime sketches with intricate stage machinery and trick scenery. Took some of his best stunts to Hollywood, where he made some action-packed two-reelers: *The Reporter* (1922), *Isn't Life Wonderful?* (1924), *Bride of the Regiment* (1930), *The Golden Mask* (1930). Starred in the long-running musical comedy *Me and My Girl* (London 1938–1944; also filmed 1939). Published *How to Become a Comedian*, 1945. Died 1959.

LAUREL AND HARDY The top-flight twosome. Stan Laurel, born Arthur Stanley Jefferson in Ulverston, Lancashire, 1890. Oliver Hardy, born Harlem, Georgia, 1892. Stanley became an eccentric dancer. Joined Fred Karno's troupe in 1907. Appeared at the Hackney Empire in 1908 in the title role of 'Jimmy the Fearless'. In 1910, he was a lowly member of the Karno company that played Hammerstein's Music-hall, New York. His duties included understudying Chaplin. In 1912 he visited the USA again, and stayed. Teamed up with an Australian singer, Mae Dahlburg, in a vaudeville act. They called themselves Stan and Mae Dahlberg. Oliver Norvell Hardy, known to his friends as 'Babe', was educated at a military academy. He dropped out of the University of Georgia to join a travelling minstrel show. In 1913 he auditioned for the Lubin Studios in Florida and was cast as a comic heavy in *Outwitting Dad*. Three years of film work followed, paying five dollars a day, guaranteed three days a week. He also doubled as a crooner in nightclubs. In 1917, Laurel and Hardy came together in a two-reel comedy for MGM, called *Lucky Dog*. But it was nine years later that Hal Roach saw the comic potential in the partnership, and over the next twenty-five years they appeared together in 104 films: 75 shorts, 23 features, 6 'guest' spots. Their first sound film was *Unaccustomed as We Are* (1929). They won an Oscar for *The Music Box* (1932). Their last film was *Atoll K* (1951). In 1952 they made a nine-month tour of variety theatres in England which was so successful that they repeated it in 1953. Their fans included Churchill, Stalin, Dylan Thomas and John Grierson, who

Lupino Lane as Pekoe in *Aladdin* (1930)

dubbed them 'the Civil Servants of Comedy'. Hardy died of a stroke in 1957. Laurel was given a special Oscar in 1960 'for his creative pioneering in the field of cinema comedy'. He died of a heart attack in 1965.

DAN LENO Capering pantomimist. Born George Galvin in London, 1860. Champion clog-dancer and singer, billed as 'Dan Patrick Leno, Descriptive and Irish Character Vocalist'. Played Dame in *Jack and the Beanstalk* at the Surrey Theatre in 1886. Booked for the Christmas Pantomime at Drury Lane Theatre in 1888, and returned for fifteen consecutive years, usually in skirts. In 1897 he appeared at Hammerstein's Music-hall, New York. In 1901 he was commanded to entertain King Edward VII at Sandringham. Played his last pantomime, as the Queen in *Humpty Dumpty*, in 1903. Died of a brain haemorrhage in 1904.

JERRY LEWIS Gawky loon. Born Joseph Levitch in Newark, New Jersey, 1926. His parents were a musical act in vaudeville. Joseph dropped out of school, worked as an usher at a New York theatre, then as a hotel waiter in the Catskill Mountains. Developed a comedy act as a clumsy waiter. In 1946 he teamed up with Dean Martin, a crooner, at a nightclub in Atlantic City. Hollywood producer, Hal Wallis, saw the act, and gave the duo a five-year contract to make seven films for Paramount. The first was *My Friend Irma* (1949). They also signed with NBC, to appear on television in the *Colgate Comedy Hour*. Their third film, *At War with the Army*, established their winning formula: 'the playboy and the monkey'. They made a

guest appearance with Hope and Crosby in *The Road to Bali* (1952). They experimented with 3-D comedy in *Money From Home* (1954). They topped the box-office ratings from 1953 to 1956, when they made their last film together, *Hollywood or Bust*. Jerry Lewis persevered on his own, and created some genuinely original and often hilarious film comedies, including *The Bellboy* (1960), *Cinderfella* (1960), *The Nutty Professor* (1963), *The Patsy* (1964). Then he slightly ran out of steam. In 1971 he went to Sweden to make a film about a clown in a concentration camp, *The Day the Clown Cried*. It remains unfinished. In recent years he has played a season at the Olympia in Paris, and hosted several charitable telethons on television. In 1981, he starred with Robert De Niro in *The King of Comedy*.

MAX LINDER Eagle-eyed elegant comedian. Born Gabriel Levielle in St Loubes, Bordeaux, 1885. His father owned a vineyard. Max went to the Paris Conservatoire, where he won first prize for comedy. Made his film debut in 1905. Charles Pathé saw him on stage at the Paris Varieties, put him under contract and made him one of the first international film stars. *The Collegian's First Outing* (1905), *An Unexpected Meeting* (1906), *The Skater's Debut* (1906), *A Rustic Idyll* (1907) were distributed in Europe and America, and widely admired. Chaplin sent him a portrait inscribed 'To the one and only Max, "the Professor", from his disciple, Charles Chaplin'. Called up in 1914, Linder was gassed and suffered a nervous breakdown. He went to Switzerland, where he made two films, *Max and the Clutching Hand*, and *Max Between Two Fires*. In 1916 he moved to Los Angeles. His last films included *Seven Years Bad Luck* (1921) and *Help!* (1923). He shot himself in 1925.

THE MARX BROTHERS Maestri of mayhem. At first there were five. Chico (Leonard, born 1891), Harpo (born Adolph, 1893, became Arthur), Groucho (Julius, born 1895), Gummo (Milton, born 1897), Zeppo (Herbert, born 1901). Mother was Minnie Marx, sister of comedian Al Sheen. She put her four eldest on stage as 'The Four Nightingales'. Then they went into an act called 'Fun in Hi Skule'. They changed their stage name to the Marx Brothers and Co. Gummo withdrew from the act to became their business manager. The quartet appeared on Broadway in musical comedies, *I'll Say She Is*, *The Cocoanuts* and *Animal*

Crackers. Their first films were recreations of their stage successes: *The Coconuts* (1929) and *Animal Crackers* (1930), filmed on Long Island. Wooed to Hollywood, they made three films for Paramount: *Monkey Business* (1931), *Horse Feathers* (1932), *Duck Soup* (1933). In 1935, Zeppo dropped out to become an agent. The surviving trio went to MGM, where they made eight films, including *A Night at the Opera* (1935), *A Day at the Races* (1937), *Room Service* (1938) and *The Marx Brothers Go West* (1940). Their last film together was *Love Happy* (1950), with Marilyn Monroe. Groucho launched a quiz show on radio, *You Bet Your Life* (later transferred to television). Harpo became a devoted family man. Chico gambled, and died of a heart attack in 1961. Harpo never recovered from heart surgery in 1964. Groucho was awarded a special Oscar in 1973; died from pneumonia, 1977.

SPIKE MILLIGAN Pioneering Goon. Born Ahmaddnagar, India, 1918. Educated by the Christian Brothers, Rangoon, and at the London Polytechnic. Jazz trumpeter and singer. Gunner during the war. Made his radio debut in 1949, on *Opportunity Knocks*. Was then type-cast for *Crazy People*, which became *The Goon Show* (mostly written by Spike). Also in films: *Penny Points to Paradise* (1951), *Let's Go Crazy* (1951), *The Case of the Mukkinese Battlehorn* (1956), *The Running Jumping and Standing Still Film* (1960), *Postman's Knock* (1966), *The Bed Sitting Room* (1969), *Adolf Hitler — My Part in His Downfall* (1972), *The Great McGonagall* (1974), *The Last Remake of Beau Geste* (1977), *The Life of Brian* (1979). Television series have included: *Idiot*

Jerry Lewis

Spike Milligan

Morecambe and Wise

Sandy Powell

Weekly Price 2d, A Show Called Fred, Son of Fred, Milligan's Wake, Q5, Q6, Q7, Q8 etc. Prolific author and poet. Why no knighthood?

MORECAMBE AND WISE Two of a kind. Eric Morecambe, born Eric Bartholomew in Morecambe, Lancashire, 1926. Appeared as a 'gormless' comic at the Empire Theatre, Nottingham, 1939. Ernie Wise, born Ernest Wiseman in Leeds, 1925. Made his stage debut with his father, as 'Carson and Kid'. Eric met Ernie in Bryan Michie's talent show *Youth Takes a Bow* (1940). Then Eric became a 'Bevin Boy' down the mines, while Ernie joined the Merchant Navy. After the war, the duo played in Lord John Sanger's Variety Circus. They were heard on radio, in *Workers' Playtime* and *You're Only Young Once*. Television debut, best forgotten, in 1954. Came back in 1960 on *Sunday Night at the London Palladium*, thereafter regular television series of their own, BBC and ITV. They made three films for the cinema: *The Intelligence Men* (1964), *That Riviera Touch* (1966), *The Magnificent Two* (1967). In 1976 both were awarded OBEs and became Freemen of the City of London. Eric died of a heart attack in 1984.

OLSEN AND JOHNSON Doyens of disorder. Ole Olsen, born John Olsen in Indiana, 1892. Piano-player in vaudeville from 1914. Chic Johnson, born Harold Johnson in Chicago, 1891. Trained as a violinist. They got together in 1915 and devised a routine of crazy comedy which served them for the next thirty years. In 1922 they starred in the Ziegfeld Follies. Toured Australia and England. On

Broadway in *Monkey Business of 1926* and *Atrocities of 1932*. Made three two-reel comedies for Warner Brothers. Things came to a head in 1938, when they launched their free-for-all revue *Hellzapoppin* at the 46th Street Theatre, New York. It ran for 1404 performances, and was followed in 1941 by *Sons of Fun*, at the Winter Gardens, produced in London in 1948. The partners also played havoc with some films: *Oh Sailor Behave!* (1930), *Gold Dust Gertie* (1931), *Hollywood on Parade* (1932 and 1934), *All Over Town* (1937), *The Country Gentleman* (1937), *Hellzapoppin* (1942), *Crazy House* (1944), *Ghost Catchers* (1944), *See My Lawyer* (1945). In the 1950s, they got further mileage from *Hellzapoppin*, in a scaled-down nightclub version. Chic died in 1962, Ole in 1963.

POPOV Classic clown to the ring. Born in Vyrobova, outside Moscow, 1930. Learned gymnastics from Vladimir Leonov at the Krylia Sovietov sports club. Made his circus debut in Tiflis, Georgia, as a juggling wire-walker. Graduated from the Moscow State Circus School in 1949. Worked as assistant to Karandash, and in the 1950s with Konstantin Berman. Since 1955 has toured Europe and North America as the star clown of the Moscow State Circus. In 1962 he played to his largest audience — 14,000 — in Havana, Cuba.

SANDY POWELL Ventriloquial vandalism. Born Albert Powell in Rotherham, Yorkshire, 1900. His mother ran a touring puppet show and Sandy helped out. Made his debut as a boy soprano in 1907. Played the London Hippodrome in 1915 as one of Harry Tate's stooges. Worked a double-act with

his mother, as 'Lillie and Sandy', until 1918, when he went solo. 'Can you hear me, Mother?' remained his catchphrase. On radio and records from 1928. Touring with The Sandy Powell Road Show from 1932. *Royal Variety Performance* in 1935. Also remarkably successful in films: *The Third String* (1932), *Can You Hear Me, Mother?* (1934), *Leave It To Me* (1936), *I've Got a Horse* (1938), *All At Sea* (1939), *Home From Home* (1939), *Cup Tie Honeymoon* (1948). Ran his own variety theatre at Eastbourne for many years. Awarded an MBE in 1975. Died 1982.

RICHARD PRYOR Street-wise screamer. Born Peoria, Illinois, 1940. His granny was the madam of a whorehouse. In 1963 he was a nightclub comic in Greenwich village. Nothing special, until one night, at the Aladdin Hotel in Las Vegas, 'something snapped', and the slick tuxedoed patter was replaced by an acid cry from the gut. His savage tirades against liberal hypocrisy, police brutality, sexual rivalry, untimely mortality, and other subjects traditionally off-limits to the comedian, became big box-office. He made records, two of which have won Grammy awards: 'Bicentennial Nigger', and 'That Nigger's Crazy'. His films have included: *The Busy Body* (1966), *Wild in the Streets* (1968), *Dynamite Chicken* (1971), *Wattstax* (1973), *Car Wash* (1976), *Silver Streak* (1976), *Greased Lightning* (1977), *The Wiz* (1978), *Richard Pryor Live in Concert* (1979), *Stir Crazy* (1980), *The Toy* (1982), *Brewster's Millions* (1985). In 1980 he accidentally set fire to himself when a lighter exploded. Third degree burns over half of his body. Skin grafts still proceeding.

The Three Stooges

PETER SELLERS Master mimic. Born Southsea, 1925. His parents ran a seaside theatre. Mother Peg was an actress, who also did 'speciality poses'. Father Bill was a pianist. Peter swept the floors and did impressions. Played in his father's ENSA concert party as a drummer, doubling on ukelele. Joined the RAF, aged eighteen. Toured India and Burma in Ralph Reader's *Gang Show No. 10*. After the war, played the Windmill Theatre. In 1951 he made his film debut in *Penny Points to Paradise*. Teamed up with Milligan, Secombe and Bentine, to launch *Crazy People* on BBC Radio. It became *The Goon Show*, cult comedy for the 1950s, still revered. Sellers went on to become a bankable international film star. Outstanding in: *The Ladykillers* (1955), *The Smallest Show on Earth* (1957), *Carlton-Browne of the F.O.* (1958), *I'm All Right, Jack* (1959), *The Running Jumping and Standing Still Film* (1960), *Only Two Can Play* (1961), *Lolita* (1962), *Dr Strangelove* (1963). *The Pink Panther* (1963) was the first and funniest of a series of film comedies featuring the ham-fisted Inspector Clouseau, Sellers' best-loved comic creation. Later film performances were variable. *The Bobo* (1967), *The Magic Christian* (1969), *Ghost in the Noonday Sun* (1974), *The Prisoner of Zenda* (1978), *The Fiendish Plot of Dr Fu Manchu* (1980) are best forgotten, while *The Optimists of Nine Elms* (1972) and *The Great McGonagall* (1974) are worth hunting out. In 1979, Sellers starred in *Being There*, playing an entirely empty character, upon whom the media men and politicians visit their own wish fulfilments. Died of heart failure, 1980.

THE THREE STOOGES Punch-drunk primitives. Larry Fine, born Philadelphia, 1902. Became a violinist. The three Horowitz brothers: Samuel (later Shemp), born Brooklyn, 1891; Moses (Moe), born Brooklyn, 1895; Jerry (Curly), born Brooklyn, 1906. In the 1920s, Moe and Shemp joined Ted Healey's troupe, as his 'stooges'. In 1930, Larry Fine joined the company, and they made a film in Hollywood called *Soup to Nuts*. When they discovered that Healy had cheated them on their pay cheques, the trio created their own act for vaudeville: 'Fine and Howard — Three Lost Souls'. In 1932, Shemp went solo, and Curly came into the act. Making peace with Healy, they made some feature films: *Meet the Baron* (1933), with Jimmy Durante, *Turn Back the Clock* (1933), *Dancing Lady* (1933). Then the trio ditched Healy for good, and signed with Columbia to make two-reel comedies. They stayed there for thirty years, and made some crackers, including *Men in Black* (1934, nominated for an Oscar), *Hoi Polloi* (1935), *Hold That Lion* (1937), *Half-Wits Holiday* (1947). When Curly had a stroke, Shemp came back to replace him. Curly died in 1952. Shemp died in 1955, and Joe Besser took his place. In 1958 the Three Stooges announced their retirement. However, television re-runs of their shorts created a new audience for their antics, and the trio went back to work at Columbia (where else?), with Joe de Rita replacing Joe Besser. Now they made feature-length comedies: *Have Rocket, Will Travel* (1960), *Stop Look and Laugh* (1961), *Snow White and the Three Stooges* (1961), *The Three Stooges Meet Hercules*

(1963), *The Outlaws Is Coming* (1964), *The Three Stooges Go Around the World in a Daze* (1965). Then they called it a day, except for a new series of cartoon versions of their routines, onto which they dubbed the voices. Larry was rehearsing for yet another comeback when he suffered a stroke in 1971. The trio was contracted to appear in *Blazing Stewardesses* in 1975, but Larry died before the start of filming. Moe died four months later. The Ritz Brothers got the job.

ERIC SYKES Baffled bewilderment. Born Oldham, 1923. Educated at Ward Street Central School, Oldham. Worked at a mill for fifteen shillings a week. Sang like Bing Crosby. Forces entertainer during the war. Then wrote scripts for radio: *Educating Archie*, *Variety Bandbox*, *A Hatful of Sykes*. Effective in British film comedies: *Orders Are Orders* (1954), *Charley Moon* (1954), *Watch Your Stern* (1960), *Very Important Person* (1961), *Heavens Above* (1963), *One-Way Pendulum* (1964), *The Sky With the Cold Nose* (1966). Created his own series of nearly silent films: *The Plank* (1967), *Rhubarb* (1970), *It's Your Move* (1978). Also on television in his own sit-com series, in partnership with Hattie Jacques.

HARRY TATE The Sporting Gent. Born Ronald MacDonald Hutchinson, in 1872. Worked in Harry Tate and Sons' sugar refinery. Borrowed the name when he became a concert-party singer. Made his London debut at the Oxford Music-hall in 1895, doing impersonations of Dan Leno and Eugene Stratton. Built elaborate comedy sketches around sporting hazards: 'Golfing', 'Motoring', 'Fishing', 'Billiards'. *Royal Variety Performances* in 1912 and 1919. In revue at the London Hippodrome, 1935. Occasional films: *Motoring* (1927), *Her First Affair* (1932), *Happy* (1934), *Hyde Park Corner* (1935), *Keep Your Seats Please* (1936), *Wings of the Morning* (1937). Made his last stage appearance in *All Clear*, at the Theatre Royal, Brighton in 1939. Died in 1940 from injuries received during an air raid on Dundee.

JACQUES TATI Inclining towards the ridiculous. Born Jacques Tatischeff in Le Pecq, a suburb of Paris, 1908. One grandfather was an attaché at the Russian Embassy, the other a Dutch art dealer. Jacques came to England to be apprenticed to a picture framer. Became an enthusiast of Rugby football and the music-hall. Devised comic mimes caricaturing sporting types which became the basis for a successful music-

Jacques Tati

Max Wall

NORMAN WISDOM Appealing agility. Born Paddington, 1920. Fostered several times. Grew to just over 5', despite desperate attempts to stretch himself (sleeping with feet tied to bedpost). Left school at fourteen, and lived rough. Walked from London to Cardiff to find a ship and adventure. Joined the 10th Hussars, as a bandboy. Sent to India where he learned how to play the xylophone and raise a laugh. Made his professional debut as a comic and singer, at Collins Music-hall in 1945. From a gents outfitters in Scarborough, he bought, for thirty shillings, a tight-fitting 'gump' suit with cap to match, which became the uniform for his best-loved 'gormless' characterisation. Worked a double-act with Jerry Desmonde, in variety and pantomime. Also hugely successful in films, at a time when British cinema was in decline: *Trouble in Store* (1953), *One Good Turn* (1954), *Man of the Moment* (1955), *Up in the World* (1956), *Just My Luck* (1958), *Follow a Star* (1959), *The Bulldog Breed* (1961), *On the Beat* (1962), *A Stitch in Time* (1963), *Press for Time* (1966), *The Night They Raided Minsky's* (1968), *What's Good for the Goose* (1969). On Broadway, 1966, in *Walking Happy*, which won two Broadway Awards. More recently, working as an actor in straight-faced television plays. His theme song could be the comedian's epitaph:

'Don't laugh at me
'Cos I'm a fool . . .'

hall act, and some short films: *Oscar, Champion de Tennis* (1932), *On Demande une Brute* (1934), *Gai Dimanche* (1935), *Soigne Ton Gauche* (1936), *Retour à la Terre* (1938). Also directed: *Jour de Fête* (1947) and *Les Vacances de Monsieur Hulot* (1951), which won the Critics Prize at the Cannes Film Festival. M. Hulot became one of the best-loved comic characters in the history of film, although it took Tati twenty years to make just four more films: *Mon Oncle* (1958), *Playtime* (1968), *Traffic* (1970), *Parade* (1974). He died in 1982.

LITTLE TICH Small is beautiful. Born Harry Relph in Cudham, Kent, 1867; sixteenth child of the 77-year-old landlord of the Blacksmith's Arms. Born with ten fingers and two thumbs, he stopped growing at the age of ten, by which time he had reached 4' 6". Worked as a lather-boy in a barber-shop. Played the tin whistle, and did funny dances on the cellar-flaps of public houses in Gravesend. In 1884, he became a black-face clog-dancer in music-hall, billed as 'Little Tich'. Toured America in 1887 (he was advised to drop the burnt cork). Invented a 'Big Boot Dance', which became his speciality and took him to the top of the bill in London, Paris and New York. Starred in pantomime as Humpty Dumpty, Hop o' My Thumb, Man Friday. He was also a skilled juggler and character actor. Painted by Toulouse-Lautrec. Revered by Sir Ralph Richardson ('Little Tich was enormous!'). Died 1928 after an accident with a mop.

MAX WALL Lugubriously laughable. Born Brixton, 1908. His father was Jack

Lorimer 'the Hielan' Laddie', a kilted eccentric dancer. His mother was Stella Stahl, a singer. Young Max made his stage debut as a child dancer in variety: 'The Boy with the Obedient Feet'. Grown up, he became 'Max Wall and His Independent Legs'. In 1926 he worked a double dancing act with Mary Lawson. Toured Europe and the USA (1932). Joined the RAF as a WOP/AG. Invalided out in 1943. In 1946, he starred in the revue *Make It a Date* at the Duchess Theatre; as a replacement for the piano duet of Rawicz and Landauer, Max created the outrageous Professor Wallofski, who has dogged his footsteps ever since. In the 1960s, he became an actor (Malvolio, Père Ubu, Archie Rice). In 1975 he revived his old variety act for *Aspects of Max Wall*, at the Greenwich Theatre, in the West End, and on television. Given a Variety Club special award, in 1975.

HARRY WELDON Tough nut. Born Liverpool, 1881. Worked as a florist's assistant. Made his stage debut at the Tivoli Theatre, Barrow, 1900. Joined Fred Karno's company in 1905, to play Stiffy the Goalkeeper in 'The Football Match'. Toured music-halls with Karno's Speechless Comedians. Played the Olympia Music-hall in Paris, 1908. Leaving Karno, he used the character of Stiffy as the basis for his own music-hall routine.
Later characterisations included 'Joe, the Crossing Sweeper', 'The White Hope', and 'The Matador'. Made two Command Appearances at Buckingham Palace, also in the *Royal Variety Show*, 1922. Taken ill with dropsy in 1923. Died 1930.

Harry Weldon

SELECT BIBLIOGRAPHY

A number of books on comedy, for stage and screen, are indispensable to archivists. I have used, and am indebted to:

Beaumont, Cyril. *The History of Harlequin*, Beaumont, 1926

Beerbohm, Max. *Around Theatres*, Rupert Hart-Davis, 1930

Busby, Roy. *British Music Hall*, Paul Elek, 1976

Chaplin, Charles. *My Autobiography*, Bodley Head, 1964

Disher, M. Wilson. *Clowns and Pantomimes*, Constable, 1925

Findlater, Richard. *Grimaldi, King of Clowns*, MacGibbon & Kee, 1955

Fisher, John. *A Funny Way to be a Hero*, Frederick Muller, 1973

Halliwell, Leslie. *Halliwell's Filmgoer's Companion*, Granada, 1980

Jewel, Jimmy. *Three Times Lucky*, Enigma, 1982

Kerr, Walter. *The Silent Clowns*, Knopf, 1975

Montgomery, John. *Comedy Films*, George, Allen & Unwin, 1968

Nicoll, Allardyce. *Masks, Mimes and Miracles*, Harrap, 1931

Priestley, J. B. *Particular Pleasures*, Heinemann, 1975

Quinlan, David. *The Illustrated Directory of Film Stars*, B. T. Batsford, 1981

Speaight, George. *A History of the Circus*, The Tantivy Press, 1980

Towsen, John H. *Clowns*, Hawthorn Books, 1979

Wilmut, Roger. *From Fringe to Flying Circus*, Eyre Methuen, 1980

For wider reading, I recommend:

Armin, Robert. *Fools and Jesters*, Shakespeare Society, 1842

Asplund, Uno. *Chaplin's Films*, David and Charles, 1974

Bentine, Michael. *The Long Banana Skin*, Granada, 1982

Boz. *The Memoirs of Joseph Grimaldi*, London, 1860

Bruce, Lenny. *How to Talk Dirty and Influence People*, Peter Owen, 1973

Cahn, William. *Harold Lloyd's World of Comedy*, George, Allen and Unwin, 1966

Cohen, John. ed. *The Essential Lenny Bruce*, Peter Owen, 1966

Cook, Gladys. *Circus Clowns on Parade*, Franklin Watts, 1956

Cotes, Peter, and Nichlaus, Thelma. *The Little Fellow*, Bodley Head, 1951

Dmitriev, Yuri. *The Russian Circus*, Iskusstvo, 1953

Ducharte, Pierre-Louis. *The Italian Comedy*, MacGibbon & Kee, 1955

Fields, W. C. *Fields for President*, Peter Owen, 1972

Flanagan, Bud. *My Crazy Life*, Muller, 1961

Gifford, Denis. *The Movie Makers*, Macmillan, 1974

Gilliatt, Penelope. *Unholy Fools*, Secker and Warburg, 1973

Hotson, Leslie. *Shakespeare's Motley*, O.U.P., 1952

Hovey, Burgess. *Circus Techniques*, Drama Book Specialists, 1976

Hoyt, Edwin P. *Sir Charlie*, Robert Hale, 1977

Mariel, Pierre. *Les Fratellini*, Soc. Anon. d'Editions, 1923

Mander, Raymond, and Mitchenson, Joe. *British Music Hall*, Gentry Books, 1973

Mander, Raymond, and Mitchenson, Joe. *Pantomime*, Peter Davies, 1973

Mic, Constant. *La Commedia dell' Arte*, Editions de la Pléiade, 1927

Midwinter, Eric. *Make 'em Laugh*, George, Allen & Unwin, 1979

Milligan, Spike. *The Goon Show Scripts*, Woburn Press, 1972

Nicklaus, Thelma. *Harlequin, or the Rise and Fall of a Bergamask Rogue*, Bodley Head, 1956

Nohain, Franc. *Les Mémoires de Footit et Chocolat*, Pierre Lafitte, 1910

Nuttall, Jeff. *King Twist*, Routledge & Kegan Paul, 1978

Oxford Companion to the Theatre, The, O.U.P., 1957

Priestley, J. B. *English Humour*, Heinemann, 1976

Radin, Paul. *The Trickster: A Study in American Indian Mythology*, Schocken Books, 1972

Rhode, Eric. *A History of the Cinema*, Allen Lane, 1976

Rivels, Charlie. *Poor Clown*, Michael Joseph, 1972

Robinson, David. *Chaplin, His Life and Art*, Collins, 1985

Robinson, Jeffrey. *Teamwork*, Proteus, 1982

Sobel, Raoul, and Francis, David. *Chaplin — Genesis of a Clown*, Quartet, 1977

Tich, Mary, and Findlater, Richard. *Little Tich*, Elm Tree, 1979

Walker, Whimsical. *From Sawdust to Windsor Castle*, Stanley Paul, 1922

Wettach, Adrian. *Grock: King of Clowns*, Methuen, 1957

INDEX